The Hospitality of God

The Hospitality of God

A Reading
of Luke's Gospel

Revised Edition

Brendan Byrne, SJ

LITURGICAL PRESS
Collegeville, Minnesota

www.litpress.org

Cover design by Ann Blattner. Icon: *The Road to Emmaus* by Sister Marie Paul, OSB, Jerusalem. © Editions Choisir and courtesy of The Printery House.

Scripture texts in this work are both the author's own translation and taken from the *New Revised Standard Version Bible: Catholic Edition* © 1989, 1993, Division of Christian Education of the National Council of the Churches of Christ in the United States of America. Used by permission. All rights reserved.

Library of Congress Cataloging-in-Publication Data

Byrne, Brendan (Brendan J.)
   The hospitality of God : a reading of Luke's gospel / Brendan Byrne, SJ — Revised Edition.
      pages   cm
   Includes bibliographical references and index.
   ISBN 978-0-8146-4950-3 — ISBN 978-0-8146-4975-6 (ebook)
   1. Bible. Luke—Commentaries.   2. Hospitality—Biblical teaching.
   I. Title.

BS2595.3.B87   2015
226.4'07—dc23   2015012003

Contents

Preface to the Revised Edition

It is now a decade and a half since the publication of *The Hospitality of God*. While the book has done well in terms of popularity and sales, one's understanding necessarily moves on—as does also, of course, scholarship on the Gospel of Luke. The time is ripe, therefore, to bring out a new edition incorporating fresh insights, attending to areas of neglect, and taking note of some developments in scholarly study of the gospel.

The principal new element that has been introduced is a separate introductory chapter entitled "Features of Luke's Gospel." Here I have incorporated material on the theme of "hospitality" that appeared in the introduction in the original edition, followed by a series of paragraphs devoted to themes and features that are particularly characteristic of Luke. Locating these together at the start should enrich the reading of the commentary to follow. Despite this addition and perhaps at the risk of some duplication, I have retained, in somewhat expanded form, the thesis-type conclusion from the original edition, which students and many readers in general have found helpful.

Areas where the actual commentary has been more notably expanded or altered include treatment of Mary's *Magnificat*, the Beatitudes, the parable of the Good Samaritan, and the figure of Peter at the Last Supper. Apart from these sections, quite a number of the smaller episodes (or pericopes) of the gospel that were barely touched upon in the first edition have now received comment. Not a few of these represent more "difficult" sayings of Jesus that it was not helpful to pass over.

Though this new edition is somewhat expanded and a little more acknowledging of debt to scholarly literature, I hope it will retain the approachability of the original for the student, the teacher, and the general reader.

Brendan Byrne, SJ
Parkville, Australia
January 3, 2015

Introduction

This book has its origins in a series of workshops on Luke's gospel given to various audiences over a number of years. Approaching Luke under the rubric of "the hospitality of God" has proved helpful and congenial for people. It is also, as I hope will appear, faithful to the design and purpose of the gospel.

In the workshop situation, constraints of time normally meant treating in detail only those scenes in the gospel where the idea of "hospitality" seemed particularly prominent. So, after some remarks upon the story of Jesus' infancy (Luke 1–2), I would deal with the inauguration of Jesus' mission at Nazareth (4:16-30), the episode in the house of Simon where an unnamed woman anoints Jesus' feet (7:36-50), Jesus' visit to the tax collector Zacchaeus (19:1-10), the institution of the Eucharist (22:14-20), and the appearance of Jesus to the disciples on the way to Emmaus (24:13-35).

When, at the urging of many who took part in these workshops, I set about putting the material in written form, my first intention was to adhere basically to this scheme. However, the closer attention to the gospel that writing required soon made me realize that something more was needed. In the first place, the gospel appeared to contain many other episodes featuring "hospitality" in one form or another. Secondly, it seemed one-sided to pick out all the "nice" passages of Luke and leave readers (and preachers) to deal with the more difficult areas as best they could. The poet Dante famously gave Luke the title *scriba mansuetudinis Christi*—not an easy phrase to translate but perhaps "narrator of the winning gentleness of Christ" might catch the sense. However, there are several passages in the gospel (notably around chapters 12–14) where neither Jesus nor his message is mild. To bypass the challenge posed by these areas seemed unfaithful to the gospel and unhelpful to readers, who would of course inevitably stumble upon them and wonder what to make of them.

So I found myself writing a longer book—one that takes account of the whole gospel and provides a total interpretation. The original plan remains in the sense that I have tended to linger over scenes like those listed above where "hospitality" seems particularly prominent. But I

1

have commented, at least briefly, on every episode and tried to set everything within a total, unified interpretation.

Unlike standard commentaries, this work does not present and assess a wide range of scholarly viewpoints on particular points or upon the gospel as a whole. I write from a personal point of view—one I find to be attractive and helpful for making the gospel speak to people today. A biblical text is open to interpretation in various ways and on several levels.[1] I am not proposing this reading of Luke as the only reading possible, nor even as the most obvious. I do believe it to be a valid interpretation, well-founded in the text of the gospel. However, I do not constantly seek to argue for it, trusting that a developing inner logic of its own will do most to commend it. The notes discuss technical details and disputed points that require further comment.

To keep the book within reasonable size and expense, I have not, save in very few places, set out the text of the gospel in English translation. The translation to which I adhere most closely is that of the New Revised Standard Version. I urge readers to have this by them as they consult or work their way through the book. Of great assistance to more serious students will be a synopsis of the three Synoptic Gospels, such as Burton H. Throckmorton's *Gospel Parallels*, the most recent edition of which uses the NRSV.[2] But, of course, the first and most essential resource is the Old or First Testament, the body of literature that Luke saw simply as "the Scriptures," containing the promise and models for all he described.

I hope that the book will be accessible for the general reader as well as useful for the student. While the tone is not overtly devotional, this interpretation of Luke stems from a commitment to the Christian faith and a conviction that the gospel's essential purpose is to bring home to people a sense of the extravagance of God's love in their regard. There are so many passages in Luke where that message is abundantly clear. There are others, as I noted above, where Jesus seems to speak in less encouraging, more threatening tones. Without watering down the challenge of the gospel, I have tried to integrate these into what I believe to be Luke's total perspective, one where acceptance and salvation prevail over judgment and sin.

---

[1] This is accepted and well explained in the well-received document of the Pontifical Biblical Commission (Rome), *The Interpretation of the Bible in the Church* (Rome: Libreria Editrice Vaticana; Boston, MA: St. Paul Books and Media, 1993); see esp. pp. 83–84.

[2] *Gospel Parallels: A Comparison of the Synoptic Gospels*, 5th ed. (Nashville: Nelson, 1992).

In the same connection, let me be frank concerning the perspective from which I write. I am a white male citizen of a first-world country, a Roman Catholic priest principally involved in academic teaching, though not without pastoral involvement. I comment upon Luke with, I hope, sensitivity to feminist concerns, though this is in no sense a feminist commentary and women readers may find it disappointing in places. While female characters are more prominent in Luke's gospel than in any of the other three, the attitude of the evangelist to women is ambiguous and very controversial. Is Luke the great champion of women, or does he patronize them and subtly but firmly put them in what he believed ought to be their place? The very prominence of women in some episodes of the gospel makes their absence in others all the more glaring. Resolving this issue is not a major concern of this commentary.[3] At times it can distract from the central point being made. But I do hope that my interpretation will further rather than inhibit the liberation of women from oppressive and disadvantaging structures in church and society.

In recent years many have also looked to Luke as a powerful champion of liberation from oppressive economic and social structures. A fresh appreciation of the radicalism of Mary's *Magnificat* canticle (1:46-55), the Beatitudes and Woes (6:20-26), and Luke's general privileging of the poor and marginalized at the expense of the wealthy and secure has led to liberatory readings of this particular gospel—and of the life and message of Jesus himself "through" the lens it provides. Again, I have to admit that I am not writing out of the socially and economically disadvantaged condition that is the lot of two-thirds of the people on this planet. I would hope, however, that the interpretation given does display some sensitivity to the situation in which the majority of the global community finds itself at the start of the new millennium. Some exposure to poverty, displacement of peoples, and ecological breakdown during stays in Africa and Asia have sharpened my perspective on "salvation" in Luke and made it a little more realistic. In some of the workshops that gave rise to this book, there were present as copresenters leading figures from Koori (Australian indigenous) communities. Their responses to what I was presenting were a challenge and stimulus to think more concretely and contextually about the liberation promised in the gospel.

---

[3] For a balanced and comprehensive survey of this topic in Luke, see Barbara E. Reid, *Choosing the Better Part? Women in the Gospel of Luke* (Collegeville, MN: Liturgical Press, 1996).

No interpreter of the New Testament can ignore the extent to which the Christian gospels are open to anti-Jewish or even anti-Semitic readings. The appalling sufferings inflicted upon Jewish people in the last century have finally brought home how dangerous the gospels can be when the tensions they appear to portray between Jesus and Jewish groups of his time are seen as offering paradigms for Christian attitudes to Jews and Judaism through the ages. Friendship with people of Jewish faith and frequent participation in more formal sessions of dialogue, such as those set up by the Council of Christians and Jews, have led me to be ever more sensitive in this area. I do not believe any other issue presses so urgently upon interpretation of the Christian gospels, and I would, again, hope that the reading of Luke offered here serves in many respects to address it.

Some Presuppositions

In developing this approach to Luke's gospel, I would like to make clear certain things I am presupposing without further justification.

First, I take the gospel in its final canonical form, paying little attention to issues concerning its likely sources or what might have been the process of its composition. Along with most scholars, I take it to be written by a third-generation Christian in the closing decades of the first century CE, sometime after the fall of Jerusalem to the Roman armies in the year 70. In line with tradition, I shall refer to its author as "Luke" without intending to foreclose one way or the other the issue as to whether the "Luke" in question was the companion of Paul mentioned in several letters (Phlm 24; Col 4:14; 2 Tim 4:11).

Again, along with the majority of scholars, I accept the "Two-Source" theory of the relationship between the Synoptic Gospels. According to this theory both Luke and Matthew, in addition to private sources of their own, drew independently upon Mark's gospel and also upon a Sayings Source that scholars reconstruct and call "Q." It seems necessary to postulate such a Sayings Source in order to account for the large amount of material Luke and Matthew have in common but that is not represented in Mark (though occasionally there are Markan parallels in rather different form[4]). At times, though chiefly in the notes, in the light

---

[4] This gives rise to what scholars call "doublets," that is, traditions that appear in the Synoptic tradition in two forms, one from Mark and one, apparently, from "Q." Examples are the parable of the Mustard Seed (Matt 13:31-32;

of this theory I shall point out places where Luke, for his own purposes, has notably embellished his Markan source or departed from its order.

The author of the Gospel of Luke is almost certainly the author of the sequel traditionally known as the Acts of the Apostles. In many respects the project of Luke is essentially incomplete at the close of the gospel, and to some extent I am doing the evangelist a disservice by not carrying this commentary on into his second volume. Desirable as that may be, it is not feasible to do so within the limits of this present project. I shall nonetheless from time to time point out episodes in Acts that carry forward and reinforce significant themes of the gospel.

The place of composition of the gospel and the situation of its original intended readers are matters that are hard to determine and, in any case, seem to be secondary to interpretation of the text itself. Students who may wish to pursue these and other issues at greater depth may do so in the more standard commentaries. My principal concern is with the text of the gospel as an independent narrative whole. Clearly, the more informed we are about the history, language, and customs of the world from which it sprang, the better will be our interpretation. Such knowledge often sheds light on details and allusions that would otherwise remain obscure or open to misinterpretation. In this area I am greatly indebted to major commentaries such as that of Joseph Fitzmyer.[5] However, unlike that classic commentary of the historical-critical tradition, my approach is primarily literary rather than historical. In this respect, too, I have debts to acknowledge: principally to Luke Timothy Johnson, Robert Tannehill, and my colleague and friend Mark Coleridge.[6]

Mark 4:30-32; Luke 13:18-19), the Beelzebul controversy (Matt 12:25-32; Mark 3:23-30; Luke 11:17-23; 12:10), and the saying about divorce (Matt 5:31-32; 19:9; Mark 10:11-12; Luke 16:18).

[5] Joseph A. Fitzmyer, *The Gospel according to Luke I-IX*, AB 28 (Garden City, NY: Doubleday, 1981); *The Gospel according to Luke X-XXIV*, AB 28A (Garden City, NY: Doubleday, 1985). In this revised edition I include debt to I. Howard Marshall, *The Gospel of Luke: A Commentary on the Greek Text*, NIGTC (Grand Rapids, MI: Eerdmans, 1978, repr. 1987); François Bovon, *A Commentary on the Gospel of Luke*, Hermeneia, 3 vols. (Minneapolis: Fortress, 2002–13).

[6] Luke Timothy Johnson, *The Gospel of Luke*, Sacra Pagina 3 (Collegeville, MN: Liturgical Press, 1991); Robert C. Tannehill, *The Narrative Unity of Luke-Acts: A Literary Interpretation: Volume One: The Gospel according to Luke* (Philadelphia: Fortress, 1986); Mark Coleridge, *The Birth of the Lukan Narrative: Narrative as Christology in Luke 1-2.* (Sheffield, UK: JSOT Press, 1993).

Encounter with the Living Lord

Last but by no means least, readers have to be aware that the interpretation offered here proceeds entirely from a distinct view of what
the gospels are and what they are not. First, what they are not. Though
cast in the form that follows the pattern of Jesus' life, they are in no
way biographies in the modern sense. They certainly record memories
about Jesus and give us a fair indication of the basic pattern and shape
of his life. But their primary purpose is not to pass on accurate historical information concerning things Jesus of Nazareth said and did in his
historical life. As the next section of this work will show, this is true just
as much of Luke's gospel as of the other three, even if at first sight the
prologue to the gospel (1:1-4) might seem to suggest otherwise. Luke
wishes to set his account of Jesus within the context of world history,
but that does not mean that everything in it is "history" in the modern
understanding of that term.

Luke's account of Jesus, no less than those of Mark, Matthew, and
John, is shot through with a vision of faith. The essential core of what
Christians believe about Jesus—that his death upon the cross under
Pontius Pilate was followed by his resurrection and exaltation to the
right hand of God—colors the entire account from beginning to end. It
forms a thick "lens" through which any details of his historical life have
to be discerned. It determined what details were remembered and how
such memories were embellished and extended as they were passed on
through the decades in a context of faith and worship. Very influential
in this process, as we shall see, was the understanding of Jesus as the
fulfillment of hopes and promises embedded in the Scriptures of Israel
(for Christians the Old Testament). A scriptural aura in this sense hovers
around the stories about Jesus, contributing color, detail, and language. In
Luke's gospel traditions about the prophet Elijah have been particularly
influential in this way.

Thus the Jesus portrayed in the gospels is the risen Lord active in
the community today. The whole aim of the narrative is to engage the
reader in the drama in such a way as to effectively communicate the
sense of being a participant, not a spectator, in what is going on. *I* am
Peter overcome with confusion in the boat (Luke 5:1-11); *I* am the widow
whose son Jesus raised (Luke 7:11-17); *I* am the woman who touched the
fringe of his cloak (8:43-48); *I* am the leper who returned to say thanks
(17:11-19). This is not make-believe. Behind it lies the reality for the believer, that Jesus really is alive and that those whom his Spirit touches
undergo an experience of salvation that is just as immediate and real for

them as it was for those who saw him, heard him, and felt his touch in Galilee and Judea.

So the gospel may appear to be a story about "back there." But it is not really about "back there" at all. I shall on occasion comment upon the extent to which a particular tradition in the Gospel of Luke may or may not reflect what Jesus said or did in his historical life. But my concern is not to take the reader "back" to this Jesus—something not really possible save in a very speculative and limited degree. Some readers may find this lack of concern for history disappointing or even disturbing. I can only ask them to enter upon the journey for a while. What they have lost of "history" will, I hope, be more than compensated for by the sense of being grasped by the power of the risen Lord that the Lukan narrative with great artistry conveys.

We would not read the Gospel of Luke at all if we did not recognize that it is in some sense "our story" too. The hopes and longings for liberation voiced by characters in the gospel remain our hopes today. Like them, we stand between promise and fulfillment. The "day" of salvation is "far spent," but it is by no means fully achieved. My hope for this book is that it might help present-day readers discover what "salvation" might mean for themselves, for the communities in which they live, and perhaps even for our world as a whole in these early decades of a new millennium. My aim is to help people read and hear the gospel as "our story" today—to help them become the "Theophilus" for whom Luke says he is writing (1:3).

Features of Luke's Gospel

Before we begin our journey through Luke's gospel in detail, it will help to take note of some of the features that make it stand out from its fellow gospels—not only John, but Mark and Matthew as well. Taking note of such features beforehand will help the reader to recognize them as they occur and so enrich the reading. Let me begin by explaining why "hospitality" is a particularly fruitful way to approach the Gospel of Luke.

The Hospitality of God

"Hospitality" conjures up the context of guests, visitors, putting on meals for them, providing board and lodging, making the stranger feel "at home" in our home—enlarging our home to make that wider "at homeness" possible. Even a casual reading of Luke makes clear how often in this gospel significant events and exchanges take place in the context of meals and the offering (or non-offering) of hospitality in general. Hospitality, in a variety of expressions, forms a notable frame of reference for the ministry of Jesus.

But there is more to it than that. Luke sees the whole life and ministry of Jesus as a *visitation* on God's part to Israel and the world. From the start this raises the question, how will this guest, this visitor, be *received*? The crucial point is that those who do receive him find that he brings them into a much wider sphere of hospitality: the "hospitality of God." The One who comes as visitor and guest in fact becomes *host* and offers a hospitality in which human beings and, potentially, the entire world can become truly human, be at home, *know* salvation in the depths of their hearts.

There is one episode in Luke's gospel that provides a paradigm of all this in a notably clear way. Toward the end of his long journey to Jerusalem, Jesus passes through the city of Jericho and finds lodging at the house of a tax collector named Zacchaeus (19:1-10). Ostracized from the community because of his trade, Zacchaeus, to his surprise and delight, finds himself giving hospitality to Jesus. When people mutter and complain because he has gone in to be the guest of a sinner (v. 7), Jesus speaks up in defense of Zacchaeus (v. 9): "Today salvation has come to this house, because he too is a son of Abraham" (that is, a full member of the community). The marginalized one who has given hospitality to Jesus finds himself drawn into a much wider hospitality, the hospitality of God.

Human Response: The Lukan "Triangle"

It is easy in scenes like this to focus simply upon the interaction between Jesus and the character (here Zacchaeus) who is the principal object of his concern. But, again and again in Luke, we have what I would call a "triangular" situation. Alongside Jesus and the other principal character, there is a third party: a "they" who observe and comment. This third group invariably has difficulty with what is going on. They reject the exchange of hospitality, they mutter and murmur. The resistance of such people to what Jesus is offering highlights, by way of contrast, the joy and transformation of those who, like Zacchaeus, respond positively. We can set out the pattern in diagram form as follows:

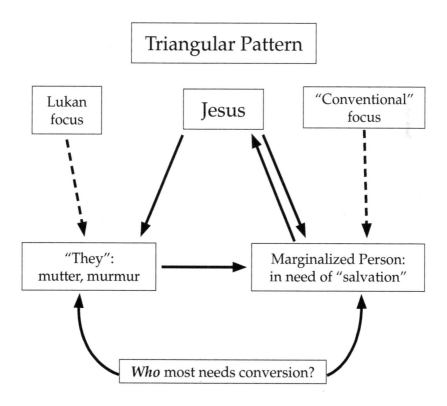

Triangular Pattern

Lukan focus — Jesus — "Conventional" focus

"They": mutter, murmur → Marginalized Person: in need of "salvation"

Who most needs conversion?

Luke is thus very interested in human response. It is not enough to describe the coming of salvation in an objective way. Again and again the gospel grapples with the problem of why some people and groups respond positively to Jesus and why others do not, why some enjoy the fruits of salvation while others bar themselves against it. Acceptance and rejection—human and divine—is, then, a key trajectory running through the narrative.

Human Transformation: Removing the "Label"

One particular aspect of human response that evidently interests Luke concerns what I would dub "the label" that human beings are so prone to impose upon others whom they regard as disturbing, alien, or threatening. Again the Zacchaeus episode mentioned above provides a classic example. The murmuring, muttering crowd impose upon the tax collector the label "sinner": "He has gone to be the guest of one who is a sinner" (19:7). Precisely the same label is imposed by Simon the Pharisee upon the woman who gate-crashes his dinner and anoints Jesus in extravagant mode (7:39; see also v. 37). A key aspect of the salvation that Jesus brings in such episodes concerns the removal of the label: compelling the judgmental "they" to see the person in a new light, removing the social stigma of the label from the person in question. The same procedure is integral to the parable of the Good Samaritan (10:25-37), as I will show.

Luke, then, is very interested in human transformation. The gospel shows how people appropriate salvation, how they resist it, and the effects that reception or rejection, as the case may be, has in human lives. "Salvation" is not some kind of religious "goodie" that drops down from heaven to be appropriated along with other advantages in life. Nor—though Luke retains the transcendent dimension—is it simply a state or destiny awaiting individuals when they die. "Salvation" concerns the whole of life and begins here and now. When Jesus says with respect to Zacchaeus, "Today salvation has come to this house," he indicates that what has happened to Zacchaeus—and to the community to which he has been restored—is a model or paradigm of what his whole mission is about ("For the Son of Man came to seek out and to save the lost" [19:10]). The episode "defines" in action what Luke means by salvation.

The "Great Story" of Salvation

Luke is by general agreement the paramount storyteller among the gospel writers. This is true not only on the level of particular episodes—

for example, the Emmaus story—but in the scope and conception of the Luke–Acts project as a whole. Luke draws us into one "great story" of salvation that has its beginnings in the story of Israel told in the Old Testament, especially the promises of salvation contained therein. For Luke this biblical story comes to a climax in the mission, death, resurrection, and ascension of Jesus, and then continues to find fulfillment in the life and Spirit-empowered mission of the church. Knowing where one sits within the "story" of one's family or community is, by general agreement, a key forger and preserver of human identity. With believers from the extra-Jewish "Gentile" world primarily in view, Luke writes to communicate to them where they fit within the great story that hitherto seemed focused upon Israel alone.

A Story in Three Stages: The Time Frame of Salvation

The Gospel of Luke, which is our primary concern, is actually the central act of the three-stage drama that makes up Luke's project as a whole. At first glance the gospel seems to begin with events immediately prior to the birth of Jesus (the annunciations to Zechariah and Mary) and then carry on to tell the story of his life, up to the climax of his death, resurrection, and ascension. This may be so if we attend simply to the run of the story. However, the drama of the gospel presupposes a far earlier beginning: way back with promises of salvation made by God to Israel. As soon as, following the prologue (1:1-4), we enter upon the story of Jesus' infancy (1:5–2:52), we are not entering among characters simply going about their daily business. Particularly in the infancy story, though in fact extending throughout the gospel, we are entering into an aura of expectation—expectation that God who has promised salvation to Israel will very soon make good on that promise by setting Israel free. An essential feature of the infancy stories in Luke is the acknowledgment on the part of leading characters in the drama (Mary, Elizabeth, Zechariah, Simeon, Anna) that in the births of John and Jesus the long-awaited salvation has dawned. Put more literally—by Zechariah in his canticle (*Benedictus*)—"God has visited his people" (1:68).

This sense of promise being fulfilled continues as the gospel moves into the adult life and ministry of Jesus. The issue comes to a climax in the events of his death and resurrection. As the two disciples on the way to Emmaus lament to each other (24:19-21), what happened to Jesus on Good Friday ran absolutely counter to the hopes for salvation that they and others had cherished. Luke tells the story of Jesus' risen life in a way that depicts people gradually coming to see that this is not in fact the case: that God has fulfilled the promise, but done so in a way that quite blows apart conventional expectation of how that promised salvation was to occur. The same sense of promise fulfilled continues in Acts as Peter, in his first speech to the people of Jerusalem (2:14-36), points out that the disciples' experience of the Spirit at Pentecost is the fulfillment of what God had promised for the messianic era through the mouth of the prophet Joel. So the first act of the drama or, more precisely, the first epoch presupposed in the drama is the long period of promise recorded in the Scriptures of Israel.

The infancy story (Luke 1:5–2:52) acts as a kind of bridge between the era of promise and the time of fulfillment. The narrative of fulfillment, beginning with the preaching of the Baptist (3:1-6) and extending to the end of Acts (28:31), presupposes a further demarcation of epochs. There is the "day" ("Today") of Jesus, the time of his public ministry, when, empowered by the Spirit, he makes available to people the free acceptance of God (Luke 4:21). This "day" lasts from the beginning of his public ministry right up to the moment of his death on the cross when he asks forgiveness for those who are effecting his crucifixion (Luke 23:34). But this apparent defeat does not bring the "day" of salvation to an end. The narrative of Acts makes clear from the start that the Spirit that rested upon Jesus is still available in the ministry of the disciples, empowered at Pentecost by the same divine power. Beyond the "day" of Jesus extends the "day" of the church, and this "day" will continue right up to the return of Jesus in glory at the end of time.

Luke hardly envisaged that this latter "day" would last as long as it has. But that is not the main point. His schema of salvation is open-ended and flexible, and that is one reason why it is so attractive. The image of God that emerges from this gospel is a God of the "second chance." Those who fail to respond the first time around (during Jesus' own life) get a second chance in the time of the church. The speeches in the early chapters of Acts (2:14-41; 3:12-26) underline this expressly. To put it more colloquially, the God of Luke is a God who, in the game of salvation, is always moving the goalposts—but doing so to the advantage, not the disadvantage, of weak, laboring humankind.

We can set out the "program" of salvation according to Luke more schematically as follows:

Luke-Acts: Schema of Salvation History

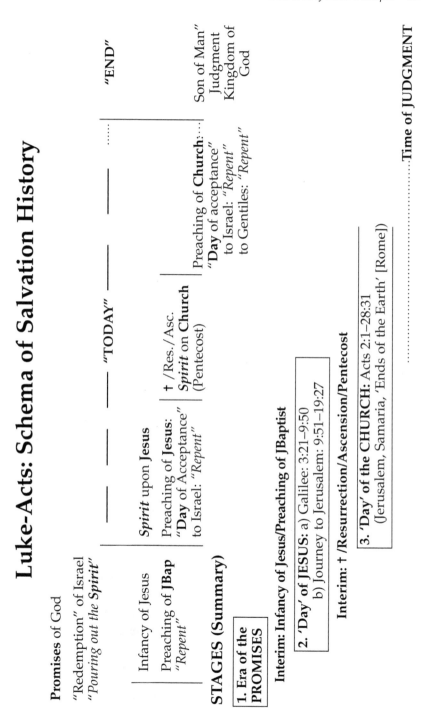

Promises of God

"Redemption" of Israel
"Pouring out the Spirit"

Infancy of Jesus

Preaching of **JBap**
"Repent"

Spirit upon **Jesus**

Preaching of **Jesus:**
"Day of Acceptance"
to Israel: *"Repent"*

— "TODAY" —

† /Res./Asc.
Spirit on **Church**
(Pentecost)

Preaching of **Church:**
"Day of acceptance"
to Israel: *"Repent"*
to Gentiles: *"Repent"*

"END"

Son of Man"
Judgment
Kingdom of
God

STAGES (Summary)

1. Era of the
PROMISES

Interim: Infancy of Jesus/Preaching of JBaptist

2. **'Day' of JESUS:** a) Galilee: 3:21–9:50
b) Journey to Jerusalem: 9:51–19:27

Interim: † /Resurrection/Ascension/Pentecost

3. **'Day' of the CHURCH:** Acts 2:1–28:31
(Jerusalem, Samaria, 'Ends of the Earth' [Rome])

················Time of JUDGMENT

You will note that in this schema, while the whole dramatic action begins "way back" in the epoch of the promises enshrined in Scripture, it concludes in the indefinite future, the time of Jesus' return as Son of Man to usher in the judgment. This motif of final judgment appears in virtually all the writings of the New Testament. It was part of the worldview that early Christianity inherited from the Jewish matrix in which it was formed. In some New Testament writings the expectation of the "end" or judgment is very intense (Gospel of Mark, 1 Thessalonians, Revelation). In others (Ephesians, Gospel of John), while not abandoned altogether, it has ceased to be a primary focus. The time "in between," the present time between the resurrection of Jesus and his coming in glory, has taken on new significance. This is the case with Luke. The chief focus is firmly upon the "today" of salvation, offered in the ministry of Jesus and continued (to this day) in the ministry of the church. The primary task of the church, according to Luke, is not so much to proclaim judgment as the great "today" of salvation—a "day" that, as Luke's open-ended schema allows, has become a very long "day" indeed.

Continuity and Rupture

As will be clear from the schema just outlined, the Spirit is the vehicle of continuity across the three stages—from promise to fulfillment. This sense of continuity is important for Luke. The acknowledgment in the infancy story that God has begun to fulfill ties the gospel very closely to the era of promise stretching behind it. The early episodes of the gospel present both Jesus and the members of his family as devout and observant Jews. Likewise, just as the narrative of the gospel begins in Jerusalem, so Jerusalem will be the starting point for the mission of the disciples recorded in Acts: the Spirit that empowered Jesus for mission (3:21-22; 4:14) comes down upon the fearful disciples at Pentecost (Acts 2:1-4), empowering them to carry that same mission "to the ends of the earth" (Acts 1:8).

Along with this strong measure of continuity, however, there is also surprise and rupture. The scope of the salvation brought by Jesus will burst conventional categories of expectation and put on edge the guardians of tradition, especially the scribes, the lawyers, and the Pharisees. At the same time, it will delight those on the margins of the community who never expected that forgiveness, grace, and healing would reach out to them in such unconditional measure (7:29-30). The sense of rupture, along with continuity, will carry on right through Acts as, again and again, the gospel as proclaimed by the apostles, most notably Paul, finds at best a mixed and limited response amongst Jews but a ready welcome among well-disposed Gentiles ("God-fearers") on the fringe of the synagogue (13:46; 14:27; 18:5-6; 28:28). The interplay and tension between continuity and rupture will be a thread running right through the gospel.

Reversal

Closely connected with this interplay between continuity and rupture in Luke's gospel is the motif of reversal. Reversal can be seen already in Mary's *Magnificat*, where the onset of salvation, which the canticle (in the mode of liturgical texts) sees as already "realized," means that the powerful have been brought down from their thrones and the lowly uplifted, the hungry fed with good things and the rich sent away empty (1:52-53; see also the second oracle of Simeon: 2:34-35). Cast now in the future, the same sense of reversal is central to the Beatitudes and Woes proclaimed by Jesus at the beginning of his great sermon (6:20-26). It features, too, in several of the parables: Choosing Places at Table (14:7-14); the Rogue Manager (16:1-13); the Rich Man and Lazarus (16:19-31); the Pharisee and the Tax Collector (18:9-14). In general, reversal is a motif to be on the lookout for throughout the gospel. It is all part of the shake-up of established patterns and expectations brought by God's "visitation" of the world in the person of Jesus.

Poverty and Riches

As the Beatitudes in particular indicate, those in whose favor the reversal will work are particularly the poor and dispossessed. In this sense the Beatitudes simply continue the theme of divine predilection for the poor and vulnerable in society that is prominent in the Old Testament, expressed particularly in legislation to protect "the widow, the orphan, and the stranger in the land" (Deut 10:18; 24:19, 21; 27:19), a triad whose claim to protection is insisted upon in prophetic books as well (Jer 7:6; 22:3; Ezek 22:7; Zech 7:10; see Ps 94:6; 146:9). The same theme of divine favor for the poor and associated warnings about the dangers of wealth are prominent in the Synoptic tradition in general, and clearly go back to the practice and preaching of Jesus. In Luke, however, these twin themes receive an accentuation far beyond what we find in Mark and Matthew. This accentuation is clear both in the quantity of material devoted to these concerns and the radicalism of what the Lukan Jesus asks of his followers (see especially 14:33!). In particular, Luke seems to have a special sensitivity to the human propensity to be "enslaved" by attachment to wealth and the (false) security that wealth purports to provide. Such attachment not only results in indifference to the plight of the poor but blights a person's readiness to follow Jesus and so obtain the true riches, which are those of the kingdom. We shall encounter both aspects as we move through the gospel.

Inclusive Scope of Salvation

Another theme that goes back to the practice of Jesus himself but is notably accentuated by Luke is the inclusive scope of the salvation brought by Jesus. We have already noted in connection with hospitality that it is chiefly those on the margins of respectable society who give a welcome to Jesus while those in the center tend to be resistant. Very frequently, it is his unconditional reaching out to those deemed to be beyond the pale of acceptance that provokes the resistance. The pattern for this is set very early: in fact, from Jesus' proclamation of the inclusive scope of his mission in the synagogue at Nazareth and the (ultimately violent) resistance he experiences from his townsfolk (4:16-30). Jesus' reaching out to the marginalized in society described in the gospel foreshadows the reaching out on a far wider scale when Acts tells how, impelled by the same Spirit, the apostles spread his message beyond Israel, Judea, Samaria, Asia Minor, and Greece, ultimately to "the ends of the earth" (Rome [see 1:8]).

Jesus: The Rejected Prophet

Along with the other evangelists, Luke presents Jesus as Messiah (Christ) and Son of God—with the more transcendent understanding of those titles that specifically Christian faith requires. Distinctive of the Christology of Luke is the presentation of Jesus as a prophet and particularly, in line with a long-standing biblical tradition, as a prophet destined to suffer rejection from his people. The portrayal of Jesus in these terms is foreshadowed already in the infancy story when the elderly Simeon, in his second oracle addressed to Mary, the mother of Jesus, speaks of her child as "destined for the falling and the rising of many in Israel, and to be a sign of contradiction" (2:34). It has a more formal beginning in the scene just mentioned where Jesus inaugurates his public ministry in the synagogue of his hometown Nazareth (4:16-30). Citing Isaiah 61:1-2, Jesus identifies himself with the prophet anointed by the Spirit to preach a message of good news for the poor and liberation of captives. Though initially the response of his townsfolk is positive, the incident turns ugly when he begins to speak of the wider scope of his mission: beyond Nazareth and indeed beyond the confines of Israel itself. The violent rejection he suffers on this occasion foreshadows the rejection on a far more significant scale that he will later suffer from the leaders of his own people in Jerusalem. Unlike the episode at Nazareth, where he "passes through" the crowd and goes on his way (4:30), rejection in Jerusalem will prove fatal for Jesus. However, in resurrection and ascension Jesus will "pass through" the bonds of death and his mission will expand, on an ever wider scale from Jerusalem "to the ends of the earth" (Acts 1:8). This pattern, whereby rejection, far from checking the spread of the Gospel, leads in fact to its more widespread propagation, is repeated over and over again in the Acts of the Apostles. It is a key aspect of Lukan Christology playing itself out in the experience of the emissaries of the early church.

The Lost Family of God

Behind the outreaching scope of the gospel lies a particular view of humanity presupposed by Luke: humanity as the "lost family" of God. The paradigm for this understanding of the plight of humanity is the great parable of the Lost Son (the Prodigal Son) in Luke 15. While the older son in the parable would represent Israel, the Jewish people, who have not strayed from the Father's home and, through practice of the law, have kept all the Father's commands, the younger son would represent the remaining nations of the world, who have abandoned the Father's house and are sunk in the kind of debased humanity represented by the plight of the young man when all his inheritance has run out. It is signifi- cant in this connection that when Luke gives a list of the ancestry of Jesus (3:23-38), in contrast to Matthew who "descends" from Abraham, Luke, going in the opposite direction, takes the list past Abraham right back to the origins of the human race in Adam, who is called "son of God" (3:38). Adam thus founds a line originally destined to have a filial relationship with God. In the face of human squandering of this relationship in the ensuing generations and the resulting loss of true humanity, Jesus comes to summon human beings back to the hospitality of the Father's home, where alone true humanity can be attained. Like the older brother in the parable, however, the Jewish leadership, conscious of having never left the Father's house and, unlike the nations of the world, having remained obedient to the Father's will (expressed in the law), resent the "welcome home" offered by Jesus and especially the unconditional generosity of the terms on which it is made.

Eating and Drinking: The Significance of Meals

Luke presents Jesus at meals, celebrating—usually in "bad company" (tax collectors and "sinners")—the acceptance and mercy of God, to a degree well beyond what is the case in the other gospels. Luke amply illustrates the charge thrown against Jesus that he is "a glutton and a drunkard, a friend of tax collectors and sinners" (7:34; also Matt 11:19). Again and again, we find that meals are the settings for significant activity or teaching of Jesus—including the Lukan presentation of his risen life. Although not confined to Luke, the tradition of the miraculous feeding of the multitude (9:10-17) anticipates the divine hospitality of the fully arrived kingdom, while the Eucharist is the mode in which the church will celebrate this divine hospitality in the time "between" the departure of Jesus and the definitive celebration of the kingdom. As the invitations to celebratory meals in the three paradigm parables of the Lost (Sheep, Coin, Son) in Luke 15 show, the meals that Jesus celebrates in "bad company" are simply reflections on earth of the celebration going on in heaven over the return of the lost children to the home of the Father.

Joy in the Spirit

As noted above, the Spirit is the chief vehicle of continuity across the three stages of the Lukan narrative drama. It is not surprising, then, that the Spirit features more prominently in Luke than in the remaining gospels. The gift of the Spirit is, of course, especially prominent in the infancy story, where it is closely associated with the joy that attends the experience of the onset of salvation. Following his baptism at the hands of John, the Spirit descends upon Jesus as a token of the Father's love. Luke reminds us that it is as empowered in this way by the Spirit that Jesus begins his mission in the synagogue in Nazareth (4:14) and applies to himself the prophetic text from Isaiah 61:1: "The Spirit of the Lord is upon me" (4:17-21). Later, in the moment of communion with the Father that both Luke and Matthew allow us to overhear (Matt 11:25-27; Luke 10:21-22), it is Luke who introduces this moment with the words, "At that same hour Jesus rejoiced in the Holy Spirit and said, 'I thank you, Father . . . '." While not always explicitly associated with the Spirit, the motif of "joy" rings throughout the gospel—and continues in Acts—as a sure token of the onset of the salvation brought by Jesus and a foretaste of the ultimate joy to be experienced in the home of the Father.

The Extravagance of Grace

Not unconnected with the motif of joy in Luke's gospel is the palpable extravagance that is so often a feature of the human response to the experience of grace. At the visitation, Mary does not simply journey to see her cousin Elizabeth: she goes "with haste" to the hill country of Judea (1:39). Extravagance marks the account of the calling of the first disciples (5:1-11), not only in the size of the miraculous draught of fish but also in the response of Simon (Peter) to the catch (vv. 8-10). Those who are forgiving and generous will have poured into their lap (from God) "a good measure, pressed down, shaken together, running over" (6:38). The extravagant gestures of the woman who anoints Jesus in the house of Simon the Pharisee (7:36-50)—washing his feet with her tears, wiping them dry with her hair, anointing them with costly ointment she has brought (7:38)—stand in sharp contrast to the cold failure of Simon in the duties of hospitality to his guest. The Good Samaritan not only provides first aid in good measure to the wounded traveler he comes upon on the road; he takes great pains to ensure that nothing will be wanting in ongoing care (10:33-35). The three parables of the Lost in Luke 15 all feature extravagant celebration of when the lost item (Sheep, Coin, Son) is found; it is in fact the extravagance of the father's response in the latter that so provokes the anger and resentment of the older brother (15:20, 22-24, 28-30). The Samaritan cured of his leprosy by Jesus, when he saw that he was healed, praising God with a loud voice, prostrated himself at Jesus' feet and thanked him (17:15-16). Finally, Zacchaeus, who has made the over-the-top gesture of climbing a tree in his eagerness to see Jesus, descends from it in haste and welcomes him into his house with joy (19:3-7). As will be clear from the foregoing survey, the motif of extravagance in Luke can take widely different forms. There is, though, a clear underlying pattern: those who are notably touched by the extravagance of God's grace coming to them in Jesus tend to respond with a matching extravagance in response.

A Gospel of Prayer

Just as Jesus is frequently depicted at meals and banquets in Luke's gospel, so too important things happen when he is at prayer. It was "while he was praying" immediately after his baptism by John that the heavens were opened and the Spirit came down upon him (3:21-22). It was his custom, we are told (5:16), to withdraw to desert places to pray. The night before he chose twelve disciples to be his apostles, he spent the night on a mountain in prayer to God (6:12). In the account of the transfiguration only Luke tells us that Jesus "went up on the mountain to pray" (9:28). It was while he was praying that the disciples came and asked that he teach them how to pray—following which Jesus teaches them the Lukan version of the Lord's Prayer (11:1-4). Only in Luke do we read Jesus' injunction about the "need to pray always and not to lose heart," a teaching that he illustrates with the parable of the Widow and the Unjust Judge (18:1-8). Immediately afterwards he gives instruction about the right disposition for prayer by telling the parable about the Pharisee and the Tax Collector, both of whom went up to the temple to pray (18:9-14). Luke notably accentuates the aspect of prayer in his account of Jesus' agony on the Mount of Olives prior to his arrest and eventual execution (22:40-46). In all of this Luke seems to be making the point that prayer is the channel between the human and the heavenly world. It is in and through prayer, on the model provided by Jesus, that human beings align themselves most intentionally in relationship with God and find guidance and strength to live out the requirements of that relationship in love and trust.

Journey to Jerusalem

Luke picks up the Markan motif of Jesus being constantly on the move, "on the way." For Luke, however, what is significant is not so much that Jesus is on a journey but that he is on a journey to Jerusalem. The entire second half of the ministry of Jesus is enclosed within the framework of his deliberately "setting his face" to go to Jerusalem (9:51) and his entry into the city as its messianic king (19:28-44). Again and again, in the course of this journey, we are reminded that he is on his way to Jerusalem (13:22, 33; 17:11; 18:31; 19:11, 28). Only in Luke does Jesus "weep" over Jerusalem at the thought of the destruction destined to come upon it because it did not recognize the time of its "visitation" by God (19:41-44). Jerusalem is the location not only of the passion and death of Jesus but also of his resurrection and ascension, since Luke restricts the appearances of the risen Lord either to the city itself or to a village (Emmaus) less than a day's journey from it. The gospel begins with the annunciation to Zechariah, which takes place while he is performing his priestly duty in the temple in Jerusalem (1:5-25); it concludes with the disciples, after the ascension of Jesus, "continually in the temple praising God" (24:53). As told in Acts, it is while remaining in Jerusalem that the disciples will be empowered by the Spirit at Pentecost for their worldwide mission (2:1-4). Beginning with the preaching of the leading apostles in Jerusalem (2:14–7:60), the mission gradually fans out in clearly defined geographical stages to arrive eventually at Rome (28:16-31; see 1:8). Jerusalem, then, is both the climactic goal of the personal mission of Jesus and the essential starting point for carrying the fruits of his mission to the world.

Located in and Faced toward the World

Luke is sometimes referred to as the theologian of the "history of salvation."[1] This is an apt description but it should be understood along with the fact that, of all the gospel writers, Luke is the one most concerned to set the story of the salvation brought by Christ firmly within the context of ordinary human history and in close relationship to it. So, Luke is careful to set the story of Jesus' birth in the context of the decree that went out from the Roman emperor Augustus that all should be registered, adding that this was the first registration that was taken when Quirinius was governor of Syria (2:1-2). As the immediate prelude to the adult ministry of Jesus, Luke, at even greater length, sets the proclamation of John the Baptist within the time period of all the relevant rulers of the time (3:1-2). Though the relationship and interaction with the Roman imperium and cultural milieu understandably becomes more prominent in Acts, concern to get this right can already be seen in the way in which in the passion story Luke stresses over and over again recognition of the innocence of Jesus, especially on the part of Pilate the Roman governor. While Rome is not portrayed as overly benign in the Lukan project, there is a sense in which Luke is saying to his audience, "Look, it's not all bad out there. We are going to be around in the world for some indefinite time. We have to relate to that world, find the good in it, while offering it the word of life in view of the coming divine judgment." Of all the New Testament writers, then, Luke is the one who has the most positive attitude to the world. Without Luke the Christian movement may well have become just another unworldly sect in some sort of detachment from Judaism. The evangelist in his two-volume work projected a unified vision that set Christianity on the path to become a worldwide religion.

---

[1] So especially, Hans Conzelmann, *The Theology of St. Luke* (New York: Harper and Row, 1960).

Luke's Gospel Today

As readers of the gospel today we are inheritors of that unified vision of a community within the world on a journey to salvation. As the "day" of acceptance continues, we remain in the tension between promise and final fulfillment. We can identify with the characters in the infancy story—recognizing the dawn of salvation and joining them in their canticles of praise. At the same time, in our world and in ourselves we find so much "unfinished business." We are "Advent people," still waiting upon the coming of the Lord.

We are conscious, too, of painful gaps between expectations we had cherished and how things have actually turned out. So often in our inmost thoughts we hear echoes of the wistful "we were hoping" of the Emmaus disciples (24:21) or we minister to those for whom life experience has meant a bitter loss of hope. In our own time we look for the "assurance" that Luke wished readers to derive from his gospel as they came to see painful and conflicting realities held together within a wider purpose of God.

The Prologue

1:1-4

Alone among the four evangelists, Luke begins his work with a formal literary introduction:

> Since many have undertaken to compose an account of the events that have been fulfilled among us, just as they were handed on to us by those who from the beginning were eyewitnesses and ministers of the word, I too decided, after investigating everything carefully from the very first, to write an orderly account for you, most excellent Theophilus, so that, in regard to the things about which you have been instructed, you may indeed have firm assurance. (1:1-4)

This long, balanced sentence, dense in content and high-flown in language, adheres closely to prologues found in the works of cultured Greek writers of the time such as the Jewish historian Josephus and the Alexandrian Jewish philosopher Philo Judaeus. The fact that Luke has chosen to begin in this way signals that he wants his work to be seen on a par with theirs. The Christian movement, whose origins he is about to describe, is not a sect or something to hide away in a ghetto. It is an honorable association of human beings that he wishes to commend to all people of goodwill in the wider Greco-Roman world. The high point of this sense that Christianity must engage the world comes when Paul stands boldly before the Areopagus in Athens, refuting idolatry not from Scripture but from the best of Greek philosophy and wisdom (Acts 17). The need to engage and dialogue with the world is one of Luke's signal contributions to Christianity.

The prologue also tells us much about Luke's understanding of himself and about the methods and aims of his project. First, he "locates" himself in the sweep of the tradition. At the beginning stand those who were "eyewitnesses and ministers of the word" (v. 2). The reference is presumably to the original disciples of Jesus ("eyewitnesses"), who after Pentecost were empowered by the Spirit to proclaim what they had seen and experienced ("ministers of the word"). Later there were others ("many"[1]) who "set their hands" to composing narratives of the "events that have been fulfilled among us." While Luke draws upon the work of these predecessors, there is a distinct sense that he wants to improve upon their efforts or at least move the process in a new direction.

First, Luke has "investigat[ed] everything carefully from the very first." While drawing upon previous material, he has conducted his own careful and independent inquiry.

Secondly, Luke's aim has been to produce—in contrast, it would seem, to his predecessors—an "orderly account," designed to produce in the reader (Theophilus) "firm assurance" in regard to the things in which he has been instructed. What these high-sounding phrases are meant to convey is a matter of considerable discussion. At first sight, we might think that historical accuracy—"telling it how it is" (or "was")—is the main concern. There is no doubt that Luke wished to project himself as a careful historian in the mold of fellow historians of his age. But this does not mean that he always gets things right.[2] Nor would it prevent him from taking liberties in the construction of his account, which a modern historian would feel obliged to avoid.

Of crucial importance here is the phrase "write an orderly account." "Orderly" (*kathexēs*) does not necessarily mean an account that narrates things in strict chronological order. The sense is rather that of setting the various episodes in a sequence that best allows the truth of the whole story to emerge. We can see this operating "in miniature," so to speak, in Luke's second volume when Peter recounts for the benefit of the Jerusalem community his experience in the house of the centurion Cornelius (Acts 11:1-17). He gives an "orderly account" (again *kathexēs*, v. 5) in the sense that he aims not simply to communicate facts but to tell the story in such a way that the hitherto hostile community (cf. v. 3) will share

---

[1] "Many" is conventional. There is no need to think much beyond the Gospel of Mark and a few other sources, written or oral, such as the Sayings Source "Q."

[2] He seems to be wrong, for example, regarding the dating of the census of Quirinius (Luke 2:1-2; Acts 5:37), the career of the rebel leaders Theudas and Judas the Galilean (Acts 5:36-37), and other matters; see Joseph A. Fitzmyer, *The Gospel according to Luke I-IX*, AB 28 (Garden City, NY: Doubleday, 1981), 15. Fitzmyer provides an excellent discussion regarding the historical value of the Lukan writings (pp. 14–18). In a postscript designed especially for Roman Catholic readers (pp. 17–18) he points out that it has never been church teaching that the inspired character of the biblical writings requires historicity as a necessary formal effect.

his own transformative experience and come to accept, as he has done, that Gentiles like Cornelius have a place within the new people of God.

What, then, is the "assurance" (*asphaleia*) that the narrative as a whole aims to produce? In the light of what we have said with respect to "orderly," it is not likely that simple historical reliability is in view. As I said in the introduction, Luke is very much concerned with human response. "Salvation" occurs not simply in outward events but when human beings own those events in their hearts, seeing them to fit into the framework of a wider purpose. Then they "know" salvation in the full Semitic sense of "knowing," where heart and soul are engaged as well as mind.

More specifically, "assurance" comes about when people find that things they had originally perceived to be out of joint with one another and clashing are in fact resolved within a wider, deeper understanding. Assurance is saying, "Yes, now I understand. I see how it all fits together. What I had hoped for and anticipated is not destroyed by these events but fulfilled in a deeper, more wonderful way." The classic instance of this in Luke's gospel occurs in the experience of the two disciples journeying to Emmaus on Easter Sunday. What had happened to Jesus on the Friday—his condemnation and gruesome execution—seemed totally incompatible with the hopes they had cherished for him as the one (Messiah) who would set Israel free (24:21). As the risen Jesus walks with them unrecognized, expounding the Scriptures that told how the Christ must suffer and (only then) enter his glory, the gap gradually closes. Later, they will remark how their "hearts burned within" them as they walked with him upon the way (v. 32). This is the experience of "assurance" that becomes complete when they know him in the "breaking of the bread" (v. 31, v. 35).

Luke's total project (the gospel and the Acts) wishes to communicate "assurance" in this sense on an even wider scale. As the first century drew to its close, two facts thrust themselves upon Christian consciousness with particular intensity. On the one hand—and happily—pagans (Gentiles) in remarkable numbers had responded positively to the Gospel and become believers. On the other hand, the vast bulk of Israel, the people chosen by God to be the recipients and bearers of the promises of salvation, had said "No" to the Gospel of the crucified Messiah. No other issue has left such a sharp impression upon all the major documents of the New Testament as this no of Israel. How to reconcile the paradoxical situation where Gentiles are in, Israel (seemingly) out of the renewed people of God? What has become of God's promises of salvation? God seems to have rather botched the job with respect to Israel. Will the divine promises be any more effective in seeing Gentile believers to the fullness of salvation? Somehow all this had to be fitted together within a wider, deeper understanding of salvation. Only then would "assurance" be forthcoming. Luke's aim is to project that vision and so communicate the assurance that would follow.

In this respect things do not simply "happen" for Luke. They are "fulfilled" (note the reference early in the prologue [v. 1] to "the events that have been fulfilled among us"). That is, behind all that happens, even the more dismaying things, seemingly incompatible with the process of salvation, lies the saving purpose of God. This has been revealed in the Scriptures, but only in the Scriptures as read in a particular way, informed by God's Spirit. Luke's essential aim is to tell the story of Jesus in a way that makes it part of the wider scriptural story. Later (in Acts) he will incorporate the story of the early church—particularly the great missionary outreach of Paul and the continuing, though less and less successful, mission to Israel—within the same scriptural vision. The "assurance" that comes from seeing how it does fit together so far engenders hope that all that remains to be achieved will, in the faithfulness of God, also be accomplished. Ultimately, then, Luke is writing a theodicy—a justification, in the face of what seems to be glaring evidence to the contrary, that God is indeed faithful and worthy of human trust.

Luke addresses the gospel to "most excellent Theophilus." Whether "Theophilus" denotes a real person or is just a literary personification of the audience Luke has in mind is not really necessary to determine. It is unlikely that a well-disposed and influential pagan is meant, since Theophilus has already had some instruction in Christianity. Taking into account the nature of the gospel (and Acts) that follows, it seems most likely that Theophilus stands in for an audience of believers of Gentile origin whose adherence to Christianity Luke wishes to confirm by communicating a new sense of their identity precisely as Gentile members of the people of God.

In this sense Luke's gospel is fundamentally an identity-articulating document. It is an attempt to state clearly and convincingly, in the face of confusing and contrary currents (such as the "no" of Israel): "This is who we are; this is where we have come from; this is your pedigree; this is why you (Gentiles) are fully members of the end-time people of God brought into being according to the divine plan articulated long ago in the Scriptures." Nothing communicates assurance so well as a strong sense of identity. Believers, secure in the knowledge of who they are, will deal with the surrounding world and its authorities in confidence and boldness—the kind of attitude typified by Paul in the later chapters of Acts.

The Infancy Stories I
Before the Birth of Jesus: 1:5-80

There was a time when the infancy stories were considered an optional extra in Luke's gospel, a pleasant overture to the real business of Jesus' public life. Now there is general agreement that they are essential to Luke's project. They form a bridge between the time of the promises and the actual drama of Jesus' life. They raise themes and issues central to the gospel.

The Infancy Stories: Introduction

The World of the Infancy Stories

In many respects, though, the infancy stories take us into a remote and strange world. We are not ordinarily visited by angels. Nor in our experience do people burst out in canticles of praise like the characters in these stories. Luke asks of us as readers to enter these scenes with a particular kind of awareness. Only then does their full meaning emerge.

What Luke presupposes is some familiarity with texts from the Old Testament describing the births of figures destined to be leaders and liberators of Israel. These biblical stories from the books of Samuel and Judges provide models for Luke's account. From them comes the idea that the birth of a significant figure should be announced beforehand by a messenger (angel) from God, as in the case of Samson (Judg 13:2-7). An even more prominent feature is that the mother in each case has been childless up till now. This is the situation of Hannah, the mother of Samuel (1 Sam 1:1-28; also Sara, wife of Abraham [Gen 16:1]), as it will be that of Elizabeth, mother of John the Baptist. The motif of childlessness implies a blockage on the human side that only God's power can overcome. If new life, leadership, and rescue for the people are to arise out of such a situation, it can only come about through the direct action of God. John's birth by a woman who up till then had been childless will be a final, climactic instance of God's intervention overcoming an obstacle on the human side (cf. Luke 1:37). Likewise, when John's father,

Zechariah, and Mary, the mother of Jesus, break into canticles (*Benedictus* and *Magnificat*), they follow a pattern established by Hannah (1 Sam 2:1-10). Besides these larger patterns, there are frequent echoes of words and phrases from the earlier stories.

In general, then, with considerable literary skill Luke tells his story in such a way as to suggest that the birth and childhood of Jesus comes as the climax of a long series of saving interventions of God. To the scripturally formed reader this signals a clear message: "Here, again, is sacred time, a moment of God's saving intervention, the fulfillment of promise."

Promise

This aspect of "promise" is very important. As I pointed out in the previous section, though we might think that the action of Luke's gospel begins with the annunciation to Zechariah (1:5-25), the reality of the promises and the expectation they have created form the essential background to the drama, from the beginning of the gospel to the end of Acts. The central players in the infancy story—Zechariah, Elizabeth, Mary, Simeon, Anna—all enter the story as devout Israelites who hang upon the hope of a liberation soon to come to Israel at the hands of a faithful God. Fulfillment of promise is, in fact, the main theme running through the stories. Again and again the leading characters find in the events surrounding Jesus' birth the dawn of the promised salvation.

But fulfillment is not all. In each episode, as we shall see, there is also a recognition of something fresh and unforeseen. This radically extends and ruptures the bounds of conventional expectation. There is continuity, yes, but also a measure of *dis*continuity as well. Something new, challenging, threatening even, takes place, causing wonder, disturbance, and surprise. And for Luke, surprise signals the hand of God.

The Canticles

As we have already noted, a feature of the infancy stories is the way in which the action stops for a while to give way to canticles placed on the lips of leading characters. Some of the canticles are quite long, for example, the *Benedictus* (1:68-79) and the *Magnificat* (1:46-55); some quite short, such as, Simeon's *Nunc Dimittis* (2:29-31) and the angels' *Gloria in Excelsis* (2:14). They are not optional extras. The canticles allow leading characters to reinforce the developing theme: God has been faithful to the promises but exercised that faithfulness in a challenging, open-ended way.

It has been suggested that the canticles in Luke's infancy story function somewhat like arias in an opera.[1] The whole action pauses while one character or another reflects upon and responds in song to the *inner meaning* of what is taking place. There are echoes of this later in the gospel when persons whom Jesus has healed or set free go away rejoicing and praising God. The world has become for them a more hospitable place. They want to share this knowledge in joy and celebration. In this way, what begins in private becomes a public, communal experience of salvation.

Structure of the Infancy Stories

Luke's habit of pairing off persons and episodes is nowhere more evident than in the infancy stories. (Medieval European art was faithful to the evangelist when it so frequently depicted scenes from the infancy in diptych form [pairing the annunciation to Mary with the visitation, and so forth].) The main pairing is that between episodes dealing with the infancy of John the Baptist and those dealing with Jesus. So we have an annunciation to John's father, Zechariah (1:5-23), followed by an annunciation to Mary, the mother of Jesus (1:26-38). The two story lines come together at the meeting of Mary and Elizabeth (the visitation, 1:39-45), where, in response to Elizabeth's distinctive greeting, Mary recites her canticle, the *Magnificat* (1:46-56). They divide again for the twin accounts of birth and circumcision (or naming).

The gospel describes John's birth briefly (1:57-58), but dwells at length upon his circumcision and naming (1:59-66), with Zechariah reciting his long canticle, the *Benedictus* (1:67-79). In the case of Jesus, on the other hand, there is a long and solemnly introduced account of his birth, including the angels' canticle *Gloria* (2:13-14), followed by a simple mention of his circumcision and naming (2:21). So the pairing has continued but with a balanced antithetical structure as regards length. There follow two separate stories concerning the childhood of Jesus alone: the presentation in the temple (2:22-38), with Simeon's *Nunc Dimittis* (2:29-32), and the finding in the temple when Jesus is twelve years old (2:41-50). A brief report concerning the growth and progress of John (1:80) is matched by more elaborate reports about the growth of Jesus (2:39-40; 2:52).

We can set it all out as follows:

---

[1] See Robert C. Tannehill, *The Narrative Unity of Luke-Acts: A Literary Interpretation: Volume One: The Gospel according to Luke* (Philadelphia: Fortress, 1986), 31 (especially with respect to the *Magnificat*).

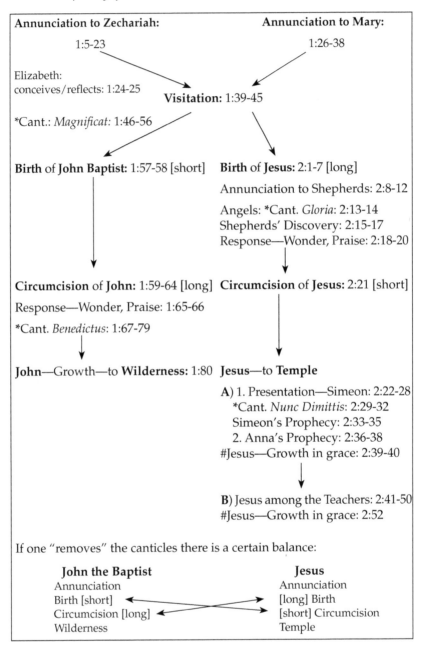

Annunciation to Zechariah: Annunciation to Mary:
          1:5-23   1:26-38

Elizabeth:
conceives/reflects: 1:24-25
                            Visitation: 1:39-45

*Cant.: *Magnificat*: 1:46-56

Birth of **John Baptist:** 1:57-58 [short]   **Birth** of **Jesus:** 2:1-7 [long]

                                              Annunciation to Shepherds: 2:8-12

                                              Angels: *Cant. *Gloria*: 2:13-14
                                              Shepherds' Discovery: 2:15-17
                                              Response—Wonder, Praise: 2:18-20

Circumcision of **John:** 1:59-64 [long]   **Circumcision** of **Jesus:** 2:21 [short]

Response—Wonder, Praise: 1:65-66

*Cant. *Benedictus*: 1:67-79

John—Growth—to **Wilderness:** 1:80   **Jesus**—to **Temple**

                                              A) 1. Presentation—Simeon: 2:22-28
                                                 *Cant. *Nunc Dimittis*: 2:29-32
                                                 Simeon's Prophecy: 2:33-35
                                                 2. Anna's Prophecy: 2:36-38
                                                 #Jesus—Growth in grace: 2:39-40

                                              B) Jesus among the Teachers: 2:41-50
                                                 #Jesus—Growth in grace: 2:52

If one "removes" the canticles there is a certain balance:

John the Baptist	**Jesus**
Annunciation	Annunciation
Birth [short]	[long] Birth
Circumcision [long]	[short] Circumcision
Wilderness	Temple

The pairing of episodes enables Luke to reinforce significant themes through repetition. More importantly, it allows him to play off events concerning Jesus against those concerning John in a way that brings out the superiority of Jesus. The circumstances of John's birth, wonderful though they are, do not depart all that radically from those surrounding the births of scriptural figures such as Samuel and Samson. In John's case the continuity with Old Testament precedents is strong. But, in the case of Jesus, while scriptural resonances persist, the comparison with John shows that something radically new has arrived in the process of salvation.

The Annunciations: 1:5-38

The Annunciation to Zechariah: 1:5-25

The action of the Gospel of Luke begins where it will also end (24:53): in the temple in Jerusalem, the traditional place of reconciliation between God and Israel. Beginning the story in this center of Israel's rituals and institutions shows continuity with the past. Likewise, the first characters to appear in the gospel, the elderly priest, Zechariah, and his wife, Elizabeth, enter upon the scene as people "righteous before God, walking blamelessly in all the commandments and ordinances of the Lord" (v. 6).

But there are *disturbing* things as well. This elderly couple are childless (v. 7). Their piety and observance has not shielded them from the great shame in their culture of being incapable of continuing the family line. So, for the first time, we sense a tension: on the one hand, conventional piety and righteousness; on the other, lack of blessing in a crucial area. The seed of a significant question is sown: What is God up to in the life of these people?

Outside the sanctuary, the people are praying (v. 10). The community is going to be involved in whatever happens to Zechariah. Their prayer shows openness to God. As so often in Luke's gospel, prayer forms the context for God's intervention.

Into this situation bursts an angel, later (v. 19) identified as Gabriel. After reassuring the terrified priest, the angel tells him that his wife will bear him a son whose name is to be John (vv. 11-13). In language rich with scriptural resonance, the angel describes the role the child is destined to play (vv. 14-17). He will be "great" (v. 15), and in two points in particular his ministry will recall that of the prophet Elijah. First, in the spirit and power of Elijah, he will exercise a ministry of conversion.[2]

---

[2] The sense of conversion emerges from the biblical idiom (based upon the Hebrew) of "turning": John will "*turn* many of the people of Israel to the Lord their God" (v. 16) and "*turn* the hearts of parents to their children" (v. 17a).

Secondly, he will "go before" the Lord to "make ready a people prepared for the Lord" (v. 17b).[3]

Zechariah's faith is not quite adequate to the announcement. "According to what (sign) shall I know this?" he asks (v. 18), pointing to the blockage on the human side: his own and his wife's advanced age. Reasonable as it seems, this query meets with a harsh response. For not believing what he has been told, Zechariah will be dumb, unable to speak until it all comes to pass.

How are we to interpret this infliction of dumbness? As a punishment? Granted the sequence, it is natural to take it in this way. But Luke probably means us to see it less as a punishment, more as a warning and a sign—a warning that something really new is breaking in here, requiring more than ordinary reserves of faith and trust. Being struck dumb is not so much a punishment as a consequence of the inadequacy of Zechariah's faith.[4] He asks for a sign and he himself becomes a sign—to himself and to the people waiting outside—that something very mysterious has taken place within the temple.

It is all very unfinished, ambiguous, frightening even. The problem is not at the level of reality, because what Gabriel says will happen does, in fact, occur: Elizabeth becomes pregnant (v. 24).[5] The inadequacy remains at the level of human response. A religious professional, a priest schooled in matters divine, must for a time remain simply dumb before the mystery. But Zechariah will have another day. Human rejection and failure rarely have the last word in Luke's gospel.

Elizabeth recognizes the action of the Lord in her becoming pregnant at such an advanced age (vv. 24-25). But for the time being it is a very private matter. For five months she hides herself away.

---

[3] The prophecy rests upon a Jewish tradition, based upon Mal 3:1 (and 4:6), according to which Elijah would return before the coming of the messianic age. In the original text, "Lord" refers to God. In the Lukan text, "the Lord" for whom John will prepare the way is clearly the Messiah, Jesus.

[4] Zechariah's experience is a bit like the temporary blindness that comes upon a person who has been sitting in a darkened room when someone enters and switches on the light.

[5] The narrative is careful to inform us that Zechariah returns to his house (v. 23), implying that Elizabeth becomes pregnant in the normal way. This sets up a contrast with the very different situation that will occur in Mary's case.

The Annunciation to Mary: 1:26-38

Paired off against the annunciation to Zechariah, the features of Gabriel's annunciation to Mary stand out in strong relief. Where before we had a high religious official (a senior priest) exercising his function at the very center of national life, here we have a young woman in a remote village in Galilee. We have moved from the center to the margins. Where the angel simply "appeared" to Zechariah and told him not to be afraid, here Gabriel has been "sent by God" and opens with an elaborate, respectful greeting: "Greetings, favored one [*kecharitōmenē*]![6] The Lord is with you" (v. 28). Where Zechariah had been troubled by the angelic apparition, what troubles Mary is the content of this greeting (v. 29).

The reassurance that follows (vv. 30-34) announces to Mary that she is to conceive and give birth to a child, who is to be named Jesus. Gabriel then provides a first description of the status and role of the child:

> He will be great, and will be called the Son of the Most High, and the Lord God will give to him the throne of his ancestor David. He will reign over the house of Jacob forever, and of his kingdom there will be no end. (vv. 32-33)

I say a "first description" because it is important to note that, following Mary's question (v. 34), there will be a second (v. 35). The first description makes clear that the child is to be the Messiah, the long-awaited descendant of David who will restore the glories of the Davidic kingdom and usher in for Israel a time of freedom, prosperity, and peace.[7] Similar expressions of the messianic hope appear in contemporary Jewish literature. So far, then, Gabriel has not spoken of anything going beyond the bounds of conventional messianic expectation.

Like Zechariah, Mary indicates a *problem* (v. 34): "How can this be, since I am a virgin?" The question does not draw a negative response

---

[6] The Greek perfect participle here, *kecharitōmenē*, expresses the sense of Mary's having been favored by God from the beginning of her existence and continuing in that favor up till now. If the Catholic doctrine of Mary's immaculate conception has any biblical foundation, it would be best indicated here.

[7] The text raises strong echoes of the throne oracle spoken by the prophet Nathan to David, which became a key carrier of the hope for a messiah of David's line: "When your days are fulfilled and you lie down with your ancestors, I will raise up your offspring after you, who shall come forth from your body, and I will establish his kingdom. He shall build a house for my name, and I will establish the throne of his kingdom forever. I will be a father to him, and he shall be a son to me" (2 Sam 7:12-14).

from the angel, as in the case of Zechariah. How is it different? In Zechariah's case, the problem had been the infertility of his wife, Elizabeth, and the fact that they were both well on in years. There were plenty of biblical precedents for God's overcoming a blockage of this kind; hence the severity when Zechariah asked for a sign. But here there is something quite different. Mary is not infertile or too old to have children, but she is only engaged. Her question does not so much express doubt about what was to happen but simply points out that she has not had sexual relations and that the time for taking up full marital life with her husband-to-be, Joseph, has not yet arrived (hence the present tense: "I am a virgin"). Presuming that the birth is to come about in the usual way (through sexual relations), how then, granted her current circumstances, is this to be achieved? Was she to go ahead and bring forward the time of her marriage to Joseph—something which in that culture would hardly be within her power? Or was it all to happen in some other way?[8]

Mary's difficulty sets up the dramatic context for the truly startling explanation, which Gabriel now proceeds to supply (v. 35):

> The Holy Spirit will come upon you, and the power of the Most High will overshadow you; therefore the child to be born will be holy; he will be called Son of God.

The new life to be born from her will come about through the direct agency of God's Spirit. The titles given ("holy," "Son of God") are not in fact all that different from those in which Gabriel had earlier described the messianic status of the child. But the explanation of the way in which the conception was to take place alters the picture entirely. "Son of God" now has a meaning going well beyond a merely messianic use of the phrase. The child is to be God's Son in a unique way. Intersected by Mary's question, the two-stage announcement of Jesus' birth and status highlights the note of discontinuity. Something new is breaking in, surpassing anything that has gone before.

---

[8] There has been much discussion concerning the meaning of Mary's question. Does it simply indicate that she has not yet had sexual relations or does the present tense point to some ongoing determination to avoid them in the future (a "vow" of virginity or the like)? The high esteem for virginity that arose in later Christian generations reinforced the latter view. But it is anachronistic. The question has a narrative function: it prepares the way for Gabriel's second, far more remarkable explanation.

At this point Mary receives a sign (vv. 36-37). Or, more accurately, she is given additional information that will function as a sign if she is prepared to believe and act upon it. Her cousin Elizabeth has in her old age also conceived a son and is now in her sixth month.

Mary believes both assurances—the one concerning herself and that concerning her aged cousin. Her concluding, "Here am I, the servant of the Lord; let it be with me according to your word" (v. 38), is at once an expression of faith and an insertion of herself into the long line of women who have, in the course of Israel's history, faithfully served the purposes of God. Her response, unlike that of Zechariah, is more than adequate to the display of divine power. In this young woman of Nazareth we see a first instance of what will become a constant pattern: the generous response of those on the margins to the outreach of God's grace.

Mary's Visit to Elizabeth: 1:39-56

Elizabeth's Testimony: 1:39-45

A favorite device of Luke, particularly prominent in Acts,[9] is to bring together two individuals, both of whom have had a religious experience that they only partly understand. When they share their experience, individual experience becomes community experience and in the process finds full meaning. The first instance of this in Luke's gospel occurs when Mary, prompted by the angel's message concerning the pregnancy of Elizabeth, hastens from Galilee to Judea to visit her cousin.

Mary enters Elizabeth's house (v. 39), where for several months she is to find hospitality. But immediately it becomes clear that she brings something very special as well. Note the repeated mention of "greeting." As the angel Gabriel had "greeted" her (v. 23; cf. v. 29), she now "greets" Elizabeth. Carrying as she does the Savior within her womb, her simple human greeting (presumably *Shalom* ["Peace!"]) becomes the good news that the "peace" of the messianic age is at hand (Isa 9:6-7; 52:7; 54:10; 55:12; 57:19). Anticipating his later role (3:4-6, 15-18), the infant John witnesses to the presence of the Messiah by "leaping" in his mother's womb (v. 41),[10] an action that releases within her a power of prophecy. Prompted by the Spirit, Elizabeth pronounces Mary blessed among all

---

[9] See Acts 8:26-40; 9:1-19; 10:1–11:18; 15:1-35.

[10] Biblical precedents (Gen 25:22 [LXX] and Ps 114:3, 6) suggest that the "leaping" (*skirptan*) has to do with joy at the onset of salvation.

women[11] and exclaims in wonder that she has been found worthy to give hospitality to the mother of her Lord (vv. 42-43). She is the first in a long line of characters in this gospel who give hospitality to Jesus only to find themselves drawn into the hospitality of God.

Elizabeth singles out Mary's faith as the instrument of her blessedness: "Blessed is she who has believed that there would be a fulfillment of what was promised her by the Lord" (v. 45). Mary believed in the angel's message concerning herself and, accepting the further assurance concerning her cousin, had set out in faith on her journey. Now, as the older woman recounts what *she* has just experienced, Mary *knows* that what she has hitherto held in faith has in fact been realized. The two women and the two stories have come together, and faith overflows in knowledge, testimony, and celebration. In the meeting of these two women, in the hospitality they exchange, we see the beginnings of the community that will share and celebrate the blessings of salvation.

The Canticle of Mary (Magnificat): 1:46-56

Mary expresses her testimony in the first of Luke's canticles, the *Magnificat*. The canticle has a discernible three-part structure. In its opening statements (vv. 46-50), Mary tells of what she has experienced personally. She rejoices in God as her "Savior" because God has "looked with favor upon the lowliness of his servant," whom all subsequent generations, like Elizabeth, will call "blessed" (v. 45). Mary's "lowliness" consists in being simply a young girl from a remote Galilean village. God's choice of her to be the mother of the Messiah begins a pattern of divine action that will recur throughout the gospel. God will bypass those at the center of power in favor of the marginalized and the lowly. The "lowly" yet "blessed" Mary becomes an emblem of the saving work now beginning.[12]

The central part of the canticle (vv. 51-53) expresses this even more vigorously. Moving on from her own experience, Mary sees the "proud scattered in the thoughts of their hearts,[13] the powerful dethroned, the

---

[11] The blessing recalls those bestowed on two heroines of the biblical tradition: Jael, as recorded in the Song of Deborah and Barak (Judg 5:24), and Judith (Jdt 13:18).

[12] Tannehill, *Narrative Unity*, 29.

[13] In Luke's gospel human "thoughts" generally are opposed to the action and revelation of God: 2:35; 5:22; 6:8; 7:39; 9:46; 24:38; see further Tannehill, *Narrative Unity*, 43–44.

lowly exalted, the hungry filled and the rich sent away empty."[14] The reversal and shake-up in values here announced foreshadow the Beatitudes (6:20-26) and in general become major themes of the gospel. The verbs are all in the past tense, as if the wholesale reversal had already occurred—which, of course, it has not. But the reversal that Mary has experienced personally is so sure a paradigm of what will happen on a wider scale that it is appropriate to celebrate the full presence of salvation. In this sense the *Magnificat* is not simply a beautiful religious hymn. It is a powerful challenge to existing structures of power and oppression. Mary speaks as one whose experience of God as "Savior" (v. 47) is paradigmatic for the poor and oppressed of all ages, especially women.

More immediately, however, Mary speaks on behalf of her people, Israel—in particular on behalf of that devout, poor, and lowly sector of her people that hangs upon the ancient promises, longing for the time of salvation. So the canticle ends (vv. 54-55) with Mary acknowledging in the name of this Israel that the longed-for era has come. What God has done for and in her represents the fulfillment of his promise to "our fathers," specifically Abraham. God has begun to fulfill promise.

Reflection: Magnificat

While traditionally interpreted in a primarily spiritual sense, the *Magnificat* has come into its own in a new way in recent years as a charter of hope for the materially marginalized and poor.[15] There is no need to drive a wedge between these two modes of interpretation. Mary is a model of liberation in a holistic sense, speaking out her song on behalf of the poor and offering a powerful challenge to entrenched structures of social and economic oppression. The *Magnificat* is a beautiful hymn but it is a beautiful hymn to the God of Israel whose partisanship for the poor is patent throughout the Hebrew Bible. In his adult ministry and especially in the Beatitudes, Mary's Son will take up and enact this

---

[14] "The couplets describe the dramatic reversal that is the signal of God's mighty acts" (R. Alan Culpepper, "The Gospel of Luke: Introduction, Commentary, and Reflections," in *New Interpreter's Bible* IX [Nashville: Abingdon, 1995], 55).

[15] See Gustavo Gutiérrez, *A Theology of Liberation: History, Politics, and Salvation*, rev. ed. (Maryknoll, NY: Orbis, 1988), 120; Elizabeth A. Johnson, *Truly Our Sister: A Theology of Mary in the Communion of Saints* (New York; London: Continuum, 2004), 263–74.

vision of God. We cannot pray her *Magnificat* without commitment to the same liberating mission.

After remaining with Elizabeth about three months (that is, up to but not including the time for the older woman to give birth), Mary returns to her own home (v. 56). The two sequences, one centering upon John and the other upon Jesus, have come together in the meeting of the two women. Now they go separate ways once more, the parallel between them serving, as always, to highlight the "superiority" of Jesus.

The Birth of John the Baptist: 1:57-80

The Birth and Naming of John: 1:57-66

As readers we have been left in suspense concerning the fate of Zechariah, left dumb "until the day these things occur" (v. 20). "These things" refer to the birth and naming of his child, the time for which has now arrived.

When Elizabeth gives birth to her son, her neighbors and relations share her joy (v. 58). Concentrating on the major players—Elizabeth, Zechariah, and John—it is easy to miss the role played by this unnamed surrounding group. They rejoice with Elizabeth, acknowledging that the Lord has shown great mercy to her but otherwise know nothing of the deeper significance of the birth. When the question of a name for the child arises, they take charge of the situation. They want to follow convention and name the child "Zechariah" after his father. Elizabeth, the mother, seems to have little say in the matter and has a struggle on her hands when she resists, insisting that the child be called "John," as the angel had commanded.[16] Zechariah breaks the deadlock with his authoritative written declaration, "His name *is* John" (v. 63)—a name that speaks of God's favor. The issue has long since been decided elsewhere, in the plan of God. Convention must give way to a new reality. This explains why the earlier general rejoicing at the birth (v. 58) now changes to "amazement" (v. 63; cf. v. 66).

---

[16] The significance of what is going on here came home to me when I taught this episode in an East African context in Kenya. In it the students recognized a "tyranny" of village tradition and collective control all too familiar to them.

The Canticle of Zechariah (Benedictus): *1:67-80*

Zechariah emerges from his long silence with a canticle that offers a fine summary of the theology of the gospel. Lengthy and rich as it is, I shall draw attention to a few features particularly relevant for our purpose.

In general, the *Benedictus* (vv. 68-79) responds to the question asked in amazement: "What then will this child become?" (v. 66). Toward the end (vv. 76-77), addressing his infant son directly, Zechariah does specify his future role. But the canticle encloses John's future within a broader theme: in the birth of this child God has set in motion the promised messianic liberation. As in the *Magnificat*, the canticle speaks of this liberation as something already arrived. The task is to communicate "knowledge" of it through the ministry of John and Jesus.

At the beginning of the canticle (v. 68) and again at the end (v. 78) there appears the notion of "visitation":

"God has visited [*epeskepsato*] his people and worked their redemption." (v. 68)

"[T]he Dawn from on high will visit [*episkepsetai*] us, to give light to those who sit in darkness and the shadow of death." (v. 78)[17]

By setting the canticle within this framework, Luke seems to be suggesting that the rich biblical idea of "visitation" best describes what God is about to do through the ministry of John and Jesus (see also 7:16). "Visitation" can imply judgment. For the most part, however, in the biblical tradition God "visits" the people to save them. The key issue is, How will the visit be received? Who will be hospitable to this visit and find salvation? Who will not? These are the questions that from now on dominate the narrative.

The role John is to play (vv. 76-77) recalls that already mentioned by Gabriel at the annunciation of his birth (1:17): he is to go before the Lord to prepare his path (v. 76). Now, however, there is a significant

---

[17] The NRSV completely obscures the inclusive use of the same verb in both instances in the Greek original by translating the first as "has looked favorably on" and the second as "will break upon us." The Jerusalem Bible helpfully translates "visit" in both cases. The phrase "Dawn from on high" (*anatolē ex hypsous*), subject of the second "visitation," is probably a title for the Messiah derived from references to the Davidic heir as a "righteous shoot" (*anatolēn dikaian*) in LXX Jer 23:5; see also Zech 3:8; 6:5; see further Joseph A. Fitzmyer, *The Gospel according to Luke I-IX*, AB 28 (Garden City, NY: Doubleday, 1981), 387.

specification: preparing the way of the Lord will consist in giving to the people "knowledge [*gnōsis*] of salvation through release [*aphesis*] from their sins" (v. 77). Here we come upon Luke's conviction that "salvation" is not simply something objective, "outside" people, so to speak. It has to do with conversion at depth. People are "saved" when they *know* reconciliation with God through and through in their hearts.

This more "internal" understanding of salvation sits in some tension with what appear to be more "external," "political" expressions in earlier parts of the canticle ("redemption" [v. 68]; "saved from our enemies and from the hand of those who hate us" [v. 71]; "rescued from the hands of our enemies . . . to serve him without fear" [v. 74]; also the strong expressions in the *Magnificat* [vv. 51-54]). Does the focus upon release from sin at the close of the canticle remove the sense of political liberation these earlier statements suggest?

We can draw such a conclusion too readily. The earlier statements are taken from traditional language in which generations of Israelites expressed their hopes for liberation. The great paradigm was always the (thoroughly political) liberation from slavery in Egypt at the time of the Exodus. Luke certainly places conversion of heart at the center of liberation. But there is no reason to doubt that he means the canticle to express Israel's hope for liberation on a more comprehensive scale: personal, moral, and political. As the drama of the gospel reaches its climax, what will emerge is that Israel's difficulty with Jesus' summons to inner conversion stands in the way of her achieving the wider (political) liberation for which she so understandably longs. Jesus will weep over a Jerusalem that does not know the time of its "visitation" (19:44). For the reader aware of what was to befall the city in 70 CE, there is already a tragic irony in Zechariah's celebration of the liberation of his people.

As regards Zechariah personally we at last have a satisfactory sense of closure. The elderly priest did not do too well at first and was upstaged by the originally more marginal Mary. In the end, the one marginalized through an inadequate first response returns to break out in richest praise.

The Infancy Stories II
The Birth and Childhood of Jesus: 2:1-52

The Birth of the Savior: 2:1-20

For most people the story of Jesus' birth would be the most familiar part of Luke's infancy narrative. The actual event itself Luke describes rather briefly (vv. 6-7). What he dwells upon at length is the announcement of the birth to shepherds (vv. 8-14) and their subsequent discovery of the child (vv. 15-20).

The Birth of Jesus: 2:1-7

It is important to note the context in which Luke sets the birth of Jesus (vv. 1-5). Caesar Augustus, ruler of the sole superpower of the time, has decreed a universal census.[1] Along with countless other subjects of Rome, the family of Jesus has to obey this worldly power. No matter. The edict of the greatest power on earth serves a divine purpose. The census means that Jesus will be born where Israel's Messiah should be born: in David's city, Bethlehem.

Well, almost but not quite. As it turns out (v. 6), there is no room for Joseph and Mary in the town caravansary, the place where travelers would normally find lodging.[2] So Mary gives birth to her child *outside*

---

[1] The reference to the worldwide census (v. 1) and, in particular, the added note (v. 2) that it took place while Quirinius was governor of Syria raises an acute historical problem. There is ample evidence that Quirinius was legate of Syria in 6–7 CE and that he conducted a census (Luke makes the Jewish teacher Gamaliel refer to it in Acts 5:37). But a census not conducted until 6–7 CE cannot form the context for the birth of Jesus located by Luke in the "days of Herod, King of Judea" (1:5), that is, Herod the Great, who died in 4 BCE (also Matt 2:1). The interested reader may consult the exhaustive discussion in Joseph A. Fitzmyer, *The Gospel according to Luke I-IX*, AB 28 (Garden City, NY: Doubleday, 1981), 399–405.

[2] It has been customary to think in terms of "no room at the inn." But "inn" or "hotel" is not a good translation for the Greek word *katalyma*. (Referring to

the town, the added detail about laying him in a manger suggesting a barn or stall for the housing of animals.[3] This "visitor from on high" (1:78) finds no "room," no hospitality, in the city that, as Son of David, he can rightly call his own. His birth takes place on the margins, beginning a pattern to be realized over and over in his life and ministry. The visitor from God, who could not find hospitality in his own city, will nonetheless institute in the world the hospitality of God. The poor, marginalized shepherds of Bethlehem will be the first to experience it.

The Annunciation to the Shepherds: 2:8-17

The marginal location of Jesus' birth renders it accessible to shepherds. As they watch their flocks by night, these marginalized ones become the subjects of a third annunciation from on high.[4] An angel announces to

---

the inn where the Good Samaritan takes the wounded traveler, Luke uses another word, *pandocheion* [10:34].) It is better to think of the public caravansary or khan where groups of travelers in the Middle East could spend the night with some degree of security.

[3] The allusions to being wrapped in swaddling bands and laid in the manger remain obscure. The wrapping is not unusual; it was what any devoted Palestinian mother would do. Luke may mention it here to stress that, though the birth took place in an exposed and open situation, Mary took precautions to protect the child from the cold. "Manger" could refer to either a feeding trough for animals or an enclosure where they could be penned. Some scholars (e.g., Raymond E. Brown, *The Birth of the Messiah*, rev. ed. [Garden City, NY: Doubleday, 1993], 399) consider the possibility of biblical allusions here. The Greek (LXX) version of Isa 1:3 reads: "The ox knows its owner and the donkey knows the manger of its Lord; but Israel has not known me; my people has not understood me." The point would be that when the shepherds, prompted by the angels, eventually find the child in the manger, this part of Israel at least (the shepherds) has now come to "know" its Lord. In Wis 7:4-5 Solomon, the son of David, says, "I was nursed with care in swaddling clothes," in a context where he is emphasizing the commonality of his lot with that of the rest of humankind. While the Lukan text is hardly alluding to Wis 7:4-5, the parallel could suggest an emphasis upon the lowly mode in which this new king is born. That the details concerning "wrapped in swaddling clothes and laid in a manger" are significant is shown by the fact that the text returns to them twice more: v. 12 and v. 16. They are part of the "sign" the shepherds are sent to find.

[4] Short as it is, the episode contains the chief elements of the "annunciation" pattern: appearance of a messenger from the heavenly realm, reaction of fear (v. 9), reassurance, announcement of birth, description of the status and role of

them good news for all the people: "Today, in the city of David, is born a Savior, who is Christ the Lord" (vv. 10-11).

We already know about the messianic status of the child through Gabriel's annunciation to Mary (1:32-33). Now the title "Savior" adds a new dimension. Zechariah in his canticle had proclaimed that God's "visitation" involved the raising up of a "horn of salvation" (v. 69) and indicated his son John as one who would communicate to the people a "knowledge of salvation." In the biblical tradition "savior" evokes the memory of Moses, God's instrument in liberating Israel from slavery in Egypt. In the Greco-Roman milieu "savior" was a title bestowed upon kings and rulers who brought peace and prosperity to their realms. In particular, the emperor Augustus, in whose reign Jesus was born (v. 1), was acclaimed paradigm savior on the grounds that his rule had brought peace—or at least the absence of war—to the entire world. Now, in the brief *Gloria* canticle, a multitude of the heavenly army signal the birth of a Savior bringing peace of a different kind:

> Glory to God in the highest heaven,
> and on earth peace
> to those who enjoy God's favor (v. 14).

Luke is not necessarily setting Jesus as Savior over against Rome in a hostile sense. But by placing the birth of Jesus within this context, he claims the notions of salvation and peace for the divine project now under way. The true peace for which the world longs can only flow from the divine favor that the ministry of Jesus will unleash. Though very much part of this world in its concrete manifestations and effects, the messianic peace he brings is ultimately the gift of heaven.

Like Mary, the shepherds are told to go in search of a sign: a baby wrapped in swaddling clothes and lying in a manger (v. 12). The sign describes something unusual but not in itself remarkable in the way, for instance, that the pregnancy of the aged and hitherto childless Elizabeth was remarkable. But when the shepherds—again like Mary (1:39)—go "with haste" to Bethlehem and find the child lying in the manger exactly as they had been told by the angels, the coming together of promise and reality constitutes for them "knowledge of salvation."

In this way the shepherds join Zechariah and Mary in modeling the reception of salvation as Luke understands it. One can experience

---

the child (vv. 10-11), announcement of a sign, commission to go and find the sign (v. 12).

salvation before receiving *all* the promised blessings. To see that the gap between promise and reality has been overcome in some lesser way gives confidence that God will in due course faithfully bring to pass the full measure. This is what the canticles of Mary and Zechariah affirm and what the shepherds also acknowledge when they return "glorifying and praising God" (v. 20). Salvation, then, has essentially to do with a sense that God is faithful. It connotes, to be sure, the attainment of eternal life. But it begins when people discern instances of God's faithfulness in their lives that become "signs" and pledges of a completion to come.

The Childhood of Jesus: 2:21-52

Luke devotes simply a single sentence to the circumcision and naming of Jesus (v. 21). But then come two lengthy episodes unparalleled in the story of John: the presentation of Jesus (2:22-40) and the loss and finding of him at the age of twelve (2:41-51). Both are located in the temple, forging a further link between the childhood of Jesus and that of the boy Samuel (1 Sam 1–2).

The Presentation of Jesus and the Oracles of Simeon: 2:22-40

In the episode of the presentation we find, once again, continuity and rupture. The parents of the infant Jesus bring him to Jerusalem to complete the ritual of purification "according to the law of Moses" (v. 22; also v. 27 and v. 39).[5] But a significant breaking-in of the new comes in the shape of two elderly Israelites, Simeon and Anna. Simeon is looking forward to the "consolation" of Israel (v. 25)—that is, the fulfillment of the salvation promised by God in scriptural passages such as Isaiah

---

[5] Luke seems to have had only a "book knowledge" of the relevant legal requirements: that is, one derived from reading the Greek Old Testament. In the construction of this scene he conflates two separate legal requirements. According to Exod 13:1 and 13:11-16, all firstborn males, animal and human, belonged to the Lord and had to be "redeemed," that is, bought back from the Lord through a sum paid to the temple. The sum could simply be forwarded; actually taking the child to the temple was not required. What did require presence in the temple was another rite: the purification of the mother of a child some forty days after childbirth as laid down in Lev 12:1-8. On this occasion an offering was to be made—in the case of the poor, as Luke notes, "a pair of turtle-doves or two young pigeons." Luke combines the two requirements. But, along with underlining the obedience of the family, the conflation provides a motive for bringing Jesus to Jerusalem and presenting him to the Lord.

40:1 and 49:13. Anna later (v. 38) speaks about the child to all who were looking for the "redemption of Jerusalem" (cf. 1:68; 24:21).[6] This elderly pair represent continuity with the great figures of Israel's past. They model faithful Israelites who hang upon the ancient promises and who, through prayer and fasting, are best equipped to recognize the promised salvation when it eventually comes. They can say authoritatively to Israel when they see the child, "Here is your salvation; God has fulfilled the promise." Like Zechariah and Mary in their canticles, like Elizabeth and the shepherds, in recognizing the fulfillment of promise they have come to "knowledge of salvation."

As the gospel describes the event, it is only the old man, Simeon, who expresses this directly. He does so in two rather different pronouncements.

The first (2:29-32) consists of the canticle known by its Latin title as the *Nunc Dimittis*. It is joyful and exultant, rich with echoes of (Second) Isaiah (40:5; 42:6; 46:13; 49:6; 52:9-10).

> Now, Master, you can let your servant go
> in peace according to your word.
> For my eyes have seen your salvation. (vv. 29-30)

Simeon had been assured by the Holy Spirit that he would not see death before he had seen the Lord's Messiah (v. 26). Now, moved by the same Spirit, he is able to discern in this otherwise very ordinary family from the poorer class the fulfillment of that promise. In his "knowledge of salvation" in this sense, Simeon has become the patron saint of those who, having found meaning at last in their lives, are able to let go and surrender all to the Lord.

But amid the strong note of fulfillment, there is a surprise in the final lines. The salvation that God has "prepared in the sight of all peoples" is to be

> a light for the revelation to the Gentiles and
> for the glory of your people Israel. (v. 32)

The novelty lies in the order: first, a "light for . . . the Gentiles," and only then, in *second* place, "for the glory of your people Israel." To mention

---

[6] While the pairing of two characters, one male and the other female, is typical of Luke, feminist critique can take no comfort here seeing that Anna plays a minor role compared to Simeon. Of course, as we have seen, in the case of Zechariah and Mary the situation has been quite the reverse. And we should also note that while Simeon speaks solely to Mary and Joseph, Anna makes a more public declaration (v. 38).

Israel after the Gentiles conveys the sense that her "glory" consists in having a role for others, to be the people who gave birth to the "Light of the nations." So, already in this exultant canticle there is a note of reversal, boundaries being extended, salvation widely cast. This is going to cause trouble, as we shall see.

Simeon's second statement (2:34-35) is a prophetic oracle stating the destiny of the child. It addresses Mary directly, telling her that her child

> is destined for the fall and the rising of many in Israel,
> and for a sign of contradiction—
> and a sword will pierce your own soul too—
> so that thoughts out of many hearts may be revealed.

As we have seen, shadows were not absent from earlier episodes in the infancy story. But here the note of foreboding is open and clear. The implication from the sequence of the oracles is that it is precisely the wide-ranging scope of salvation—the fact that it is not going to be confined to Israel but will be a light for the Gentiles—that will provide challenge and give rise to "contradiction."

Salvation is going to emerge from the child here present in a way that will "reveal the thoughts out of many hearts," and those "thoughts," when brought to the surface, will be shown to be narrow and ugly indeed. "Thoughts" in Luke's gospel (Greek: *dialogismoi*) are almost always "bad thoughts."[7] "Heart" refers to the depth of a person, the inner core that regulates attitude and action on the surface. The way in which Jesus is to bring salvation is not going to leave this inner core untouched.

In this reference to "thoughts" Simeon's second oracle provides an important signal of the direction Jesus' life and ministry will take and of the response that it will, in many circles, receive. Luke, as we have seen from the start, is interested not only in the proclamation of the Gospel but in the way human beings respond to it. To accept the message as "good news" requires conversion, a conversion at depth that shakes up and challenges conventional and comfortable assumptions about the way the promised salvation will run. Many will balk at the breadth of the hospitality God offers and react with rejection. Luke's gospel will explore the reasons for this rejection. In a particular way Simeon's ora-

---

[7] See Robert C. Tannehill, *The Narrative Unity of Luke-Acts: A Literary Interpretation: Volume One: The Gospel according to Luke* (Philadelphia: Fortress, 1986), 43–44.

cle is prophetic for what will occur when Jesus inaugurates his public ministry in the synagogue at Nazareth (4:16-30).

In a curious parenthesis cutting across the oracle, Simeon speaks of a "sword" that is to pierce Mary's soul (v. 35). Traditionally the "sword" has been associated with the suffering of Mary at the time of her Son's crucifixion. But Luke's account of Jesus' death makes no mention of his mother's presence at the cross, as in the Fourth Gospel (John 19:25-27). While allusion to Jesus' passion can hardly be excluded, I suspect that the "sword" has a broader reference. Mary will have to surrender her Son to a broader, more risky role—in effect to "his Father's business" (2:49) where "Father" refers not to Joseph but to God. The sword would refer, then, to the pain such surrender will involve. The following, final episode of the infancy story will bring this out.

Jesus Lost and Found at Age Twelve: 2:41-51

This scene forms a bridge to Jesus' adult ministry. Here we no longer have a passive infant but a young person beginning to grasp and shape his own adult identity. As is so often the case in adolescence, the process involves pain for his family.

The episode shows once again a strong element of continuity. As dutiful Israelites, the family of Jesus goes up to Jerusalem each year at the feast according to custom (vv. 41-42). Discontinuity emerges in the year Jesus turns twelve, that is, when he must begin to take on the responsibilities of an adult Jew. Instead of returning with the rest of the party to Nazareth, he secretly stays behind in Jerusalem. Mary and Joseph find him there in the temple only after three days of searching in great anxiety (v. 45, v. 48).

The way Luke tells the story brings out the element of misunderstanding between the boy and his parents. For all the intelligence that Jesus displays interacting with the teachers in the temple (vv. 46-47), his response to his mother's complaint ("Child, why have you treated us like this? Look, your father and I have been searching for you in great anxiety" [v. 48]) seems to reflect adolescent impatience with parental concern. "Why," he retorts, "were you searching for me? Did you not know that I must be about my Father's business?" (v. 49).[8] Nothing could express more sharply the gulf between them than the divergent ways

---

[8] The Greek expression is ambiguous: it could also mean "in my Father's house." The ambiguity may be deliberate on Luke's part. However, an allusion

in which mother and son are using the word "father." "Your father" on Mary's lips refers to her husband Joseph; Jesus means his Father in heaven. Into their tranquil family life (cf. v. 40) bursts a sharp reminder of Jesus' true status and destiny. Even if it is only for a moment (cf. v. 51), he is nonetheless ripped away from the family, his future determined by a divine imperative, expressed here for the first time by the characteristic Lukan "must" (Greek: *dei*). Jesus' family is going to have to surrender him, just as later his hometown (Nazareth) and his people (Israel) will have to surrender him, to a wider divine purpose.

Here is surely the moment when the sword begins to pass through Mary's spirit (2:35). Even the most faithful and privileged individuals, those closest to Jesus, are not going to be exempt from pain and misunderstanding as he goes about his mission. For a second time (cf. 2:19) we are told (v. 51b) that his mother kept all these things in her heart. She continues a journey of faith in which much remains obscure. In ways that she has yet to fully understand, "the servant of the Lord" (1:38) will have to surrender to his divine mission the child so mysteriously given her.

Conclusion

Let us draw a few of these threads together. As I said at the start, the infancy stories take us into an unfamiliar divine world, one featuring annunciations by angels, visions of angelic choirs, people breaking out into canticles and so forth. But along with all this specialness is a lot of *ordinariness* too: Zechariah dutifully fulfilling his priestly role; the sadness of an elderly couple unsuccessful in having children and now getting on in years; the dilemma of a young girl pregnant before she is married; the interference of friends and relations in the naming of a child; government decrees requiring travel at a most inconvenient time; finding no place to stay just when your wife is going to have a baby.

These two threads—the marvelous and the ordinary—are woven together in the narrative in a way that is surely intentional on Luke's part. The divine intervention, in fulfillment of the promise, comes about in the ordinary dilemmas of life. But it does so in surprising and unexpected ways. The mistakes, the failures (Zechariah's unbelief, no room in Bethlehem)—the dropped stitches, so to speak—are eventually picked up and sewn back into a broader divine purpose.

---

to the imperative of Jesus' wider vocation seems more appropriate to the context than the simple local sense referring to the temple.

As believers, we all live on a divine promise. We look for completion of that promise in the reality of our lives and in that of the communities and societies to which we belong. So often we find a painful gap between what we expected from the promise and the reality that we see. "*Knowledge* of salvation" (1:77) comes when human beings own the fulfillment of the promise in the actual reality of their lives, when faith is big enough to find the conjunction between the two. What is so consoling about Zechariah is that he got a second chance—and, in the end, is given the best lines (the *Benedictus*). Even Mary goes on a journey of faith and has much to contemplate and ponder as she surrenders her child to his role. The moment when she and Elizabeth shared their stories marked the beginning of the Christian community of faith. Later, she who was overshadowed by the Spirit (1:35) will be with the disciples as they await "the power from on high" (24:49; Acts 1:14). Her story and those of all the characters involved in the infancy of Jesus are our stories as well.

Prelude to the Ministry of Jesus
3:1–4:13

The dramatic action of the gospel now jumps ahead eighteen years to the time when Jesus, "about thirty years old" (3:23), is on the brink of his public ministry. A series of diverse scenes forms the prelude to the ministry proper:

> the preaching and public career of John the Baptist (3:1-20);
> the empowering of Jesus with the Spirit (3:21-22);
> the ancestry of Jesus (3:23-38);
> the temptation in the wilderness (4:1-13).

Within the scope of this book, I shall simply survey what I believe to be the main contribution of each to the drama of the gospel.

The Preaching and Public Career of John the Baptist: 3:1-20

In Luke as in the other three gospels, the prophetic ministry of the Baptist forms a prelude and preparation for that of Jesus. John's ministry fulfills the prophecy of Isaiah 40:3-5, where a "voice" cries in the wilderness, preparing a way for the Lord and proclaiming that all humanity shall "see the salvation of God" (v. 5). It also completes the role foreseen at his birth, according to which he is to proclaim "a baptism of repentance for the forgiveness (*aphesis*) of sins" (v. 3; see also 1:77).

Very remarkable is the way in which Luke sets the coming of God's word to John within the context of world history. The reigning Roman emperor, Tiberius, heads a long list of contemporary rulers (3:1-2a). This follows biblical precedent. It also continues a pattern (see also 2:1) whereby the "sacred" events of Jesus' life and ministry interact with the ordinary flow of affairs. The "saving events" are not a kind of "meta-history" running parallel to or divorced from everyday life. As we noted in connection with the prologue (1:1-4), there is in Luke a "hospitality" to secular culture and an "at-homeness" in the world that is part of his wider sense of the "hospitality of God."

John's message (vv. 7-9) is stark—a demand for repentance in view of the coming judgment: "You brood of vipers! Who warned you to flee from the wrath to come?" (v. 7). John even seems to sketch the future ministry of Jesus in a similar vein (vv. 15-18). When the crowds speculate as to whether he himself may not be the Messiah, John responds that, whereas he baptizes with water, the coming "stronger one" will baptize "with the Holy Spirit and with fire" (v. 16; cf. v. 17). "Baptism with fire" seems to point to a demanding, purifying judgment. But, as the gospel will make clear, any judging role that Jesus may exercise (17:22-37; 21:25-26) will take place in the indefinite future, following the "day of acceptance" (4:19, 21) that is the central focus of his mission. The "baptism" of the Spirit that the disciples are to receive at Pentecost will involve the appearance of tongues "as if of fire" (Acts 2:3). But this will not be a moment of judgment. The Spirit will empower them to take up the mission of Jesus and proclaim the "day of acceptance" to the ends of the earth.

Paradoxically, then, Jesus will not in fact take up the pattern of ministry John sketches out for him (which may explain why later, from prison, John sends messengers to ask whether he is truly the One to come [7:20]). Luke seems to want to highlight the distinction between the two. So, again, we have continuity—but also, in the case of Jesus, the strikingly new and unexpected.

There is a central portion of the Baptist's preaching (vv. 10-14) where he gives advice that is more down-to-earth and practical. He addresses members of three groups—the crowds, tax collectors, soldiers—who ask him, "What then should we do?" Beneath the advice in each case is a central Lukan concern: nothing so hinders relationship to God, dehumanizes human beings, and ruins life in community as attachment to wealth and possessions.[1] To accept and live within the hospitality of God always means detachment in this area.

The Empowering of Jesus with the Holy Spirit: 3:21-22

When the adult Jesus makes his first appearance, he simply emerges out of the crowds that come to John for baptism. Luke records no meeting or exchange between the Baptist and the young Galilean. Nor is the baptism in itself (v. 21a) all that significant. More important is what takes place

---

[1] When John tells soldiers to be content with their pay (v. 14), he is not advocating passivity in the matter of industrial rights. The policing role played by soldiers in an occupied country such as Palestine provided rich opportunity for extortion. John tells the soldiers not to seek to augment their regular pay in a way offensive to justice and charity.

immediately after (vv. 21b-22). While Jesus is at prayer—so often in Luke the context for human receptivity to the action of God—heaven is opened, the Holy Spirit descends in bodily form like a dove, and a voice from heaven declares: "You are my Son, the Beloved; with you I am well pleased." Jesus is here "anointed" with the Spirit in view of his messianic role (Isa 61:1). But the heavenly address suggests a status beyond that of the Messiah of conventional expectation. As in the case of Gabriel's description at the annunciation (1:35) and the response of the boy Jesus in the temple (2:49), there are overtones of a unique filial relationship to God.[2] Jesus is Israel's Messiah. But the messianic mission for which he is now empowered will principally consist in drawing human beings into the filial relationship with God that he enjoys as "Beloved Son" (see 10:21-24). To experience the Spirit is to know one is at home within the family of God (11:13).

The Ancestry of Jesus: 3:23-38

At this point the gospel provides a genealogy tracing Jesus' human origin back to Adam, the ancestor of the entire race. He too is a "child of Adam," who was himself "the son of God" (v. 38). The enclosure of the entire list within the framework of references to divine sonship at beginning (3:23)[3] and end (3:38) communicates the sense of the entire race, descended from Adam, as "the family of God," albeit a "lost family," the members of which it will be the Son's messianic mission to seek out and return to the hospitable home of the Father (see 19:10). His own special status (3:22) offers a pledge and paradigm of the dignity intended by the Creator not merely for Israel but for the human race as a whole. His messianic task will be to confront and overthrow all the forces that seek to thwart that dignity and the destiny to which it leads. The confrontation begins in the very next scene.

The Temptation in the Wilderness: 4:1-13

Jesus is armed for his mission with the power of the Spirit (4:1, alluding to 3:22). But before his public ministry gets under way, he has to

---

[2] The phrase, "with you I am well pleased" (see Isa 42:1) may also suggest that Jesus' ministry will follow lines marked out for the "Servant" figure in (Second) Isaiah (Isa 42:1-7; 49:1-7; 50:4-9; 52:13–53:12).

[3] The Lukan list begins by stating that Jesus "was the son (*as was thought*) of Joseph, son of Heli" (v. 23b). The parenthesis carefully safeguards and implies the divine sonship of Jesus, which has just been proclaimed in the preceding verse (v. 22).

undergo a private confrontation with opposing forces. This occurs in the wilderness—the place where, traditionally, conflict between good and evil is out in the open and clear. It was in the wilderness, too, that Israel— also called God's "Son" (Hos 11:1; see also Exod 4:22; Deut 14:1)—had undergone testing. Instead of passing the test, Israel constantly put the Lord to the test (Deut 8:2; Ps 95:8-11). In being tested as Son of God in the wilderness, Jesus relives the history of his people, proving victorious where they had so often failed.

All three temptations bear upon the same fundamental issue: the way in which the Son of God will go about his messianic mission. Each suggests a compromise that would not only make that mission less burdensome but would also seem appropriate in view of the special status above all other human beings that he, as Son of God, enjoys. The temptations, then, are subtle. Like all temptations to which the virtuous are vulnerable, they come under the guise of good.

So, in the first place (vv. 3-4), since Jesus is extremely hungry after forty days of fasting, it seems reasonable that he should use his miraculous powers for just one moment of self-interest, to provide bread for himself out of stone. His sharp response to the devil, "One does not live by bread alone" (quoting Deut 8:3b), gives little away. But it implies a clear determination to place his powers solely at the service of others (see Paul in Rom 15:3: "Christ did not please himself").

The second temptation (vv. 5-8) conjures up possession of all political authority and power throughout the world. Again, within the ambit of conventional messianic expectation (relying, for example, on Ps 2:8), this is not an inappropriate ambition for the messianic Son of God. In fact, early Christian preaching will subsequently acknowledge Jesus as "Lord of all" (Acts 10:36; see also 2:36).[4] The authority, then, is something he should one day possess. The issue is whether he should gain such authority now by worshiping the one (the devil) who claims to be able to give it, or whether he should not wait to receive it from the hands of God after fulfilling his mission in the way that God intends. The first is an easy and immediate path to lordship of the world. But choosing to go that route will simply preserve the present situation where rulers exercise authority in the world in oppressive and violent ways (see 22:25)—an authority reflective of the one ultimately calling the shots, namely, the devil. The second, much more difficult path to that lordship will mean

---

[4] See Robert C. Tannehill, *The Narrative Unity of Luke-Acts: A Literary Interpretation: Volume One: The Gospel according to Luke* (Philadelphia: Fortress, 1986), 59.

conflict with powerful entrenched forces. The authority it exercises will be one that serves rather than dominates (22:26-27). If God alone is to be worshiped (Deut 6:13) and all humanity made to feel at home in God's house, then this alone is the path that God's Son must take (v. 8).

Finally (vv. 9-12), the devil takes Jesus to the pinnacle of the temple in Jerusalem.[5] The invitation to cast himself down rests upon what appears to be a divine pledge of protection for the messianic king contained in Psalm 91:11-12. To emerge safely from this stunt would most effectively launch a messianic career. For Jesus, however, such feats amount to testing God, the very fault of Israel that he, as focus of a renewed Israel, is seeking to reverse. So, appealing once more to Scripture (Deut 6:16), he rebuts the suggestion (v. 12). What he will experience in Jerusalem will be not glory and recognition of this kind but rejection, shame, and humiliation.

So Jesus emerges from the conflict with the true direction of his mission irreversibly set. Son of God though he is, and "special" beyond all other human beings in this sense, he will not exempt himself from treading the ordinary path of human life. Precisely *as* God's Son, obedient to the pattern of divine love and grace that drives him, he will enter fully into the normal human lot of suffering and death. The salvation he brings will not be a magic wand waved miraculously from above over the ills of humankind. Son of Adam (3:23-38) as well as Son of God, he will enter into the pain and evil of the world to work the inner transformation that alone will render it hospitable to God.

Swift and unhesitating as Jesus' dismissal of the temptations has been, Luke hardly means us to conclude that it was all a pushover, that Jesus was not really drawn to go another way. As we read on through the scenes in the gospel, we should keep this episode in mind, aware that behind each act of service lies a fundamental choice to be this kind of Messiah and no other. There is, too, a final note in the Lukan version that we ought not fail to observe. The devil departs from Jesus until "an opportune time" (v. 13). The "opportune time" will be the hour just before his arrest on the Mount of Olives (22:39-46). Then the struggle with Satan will be renewed as Jesus confronts the full horror of the fate to which his costly choice has brought him.

---

[5] The order of the second and third temptations in Luke is the reverse to that in Matthew's parallel account (Matt 4:1-11). The fact that Luke's account has its climax in Jerusalem goes along with the climactic role the city plays in the drama of the gospel.

Hospitality and Inhospitality in Nazareth
Jesus Inaugurates His Mission: 4:14-30

It is hard to overstress the importance of this scene in Luke's gospel. In modern political terms this is where Jesus launches his campaign, announces his manifesto. The way he inaugurates his mission here in Nazareth and the response he receives set a pattern that will run throughout the gospel.

All three Synoptic Gospels record a visit of Jesus to his hometown Nazareth, a visit unsuccessful in terms of the response it evokes. Mark (6:1-6a), followed by Matthew (13:54-58), assigns this visit to a time when Jesus' ministry of calling disciples, teaching, and healing is well under way. Luke, however, brings forward the visit so that it becomes the true beginning of Jesus' public ministry. Such departures from the Markan order are uncharacteristic of Luke. The transposition signals the importance of this scene.

It is not quite accurate, though, to say that Jesus' ministry begins here. After telling us that "Jesus, filled with the power of the Spirit, returned to Galilee" (following his baptism and wilderness experience), the gospel goes on to add that "he began to teach in their synagogues and was praised by everyone" (4:14, 15). As will become clear, this brief notice of successful ministry elsewhere forms a significant backdrop to the drama at Nazareth.

The actual scene falls into two parts. Verses 16-21 give an account of Jesus' preaching. Verses 22-30 describe the response he receives—highly positive at first (v. 22), then in reaction to his further challenge (vv. 23-27), furiously negative, culminating in an unsuccessful attempt to lynch him (vv. 28-30).

Jesus' Sermon: 4:16-21

A curious aspect of this episode is that we hear virtually nothing of the content of Jesus' sermon. He quotes at length a passage from the prophet Isaiah (61:1-2) and then all we hear him say is, "Today this scripture has been fulfilled in your hearing" (v. 21). End of sermon, as far as we readers are concerned! Why do we not hear more—before the unhappy denouement that so swiftly follows? To appreciate what Luke is up to here we need to take note of the dramatic, tableau-like context that Luke establishes for the reading of this text and to attend closely to the Scripture passage as Jesus quotes it.

Jesus comes into the synagogue on the Sabbath day, as was his custom. (The note of continuity with the Jewish tradition rings once more.) Assuming his right as an adult Jew, he stands up to read, the prophetic scroll is given to him, he unrolls it, finds the place and reads the text. When finished, he rolls up the scroll, hands it back to the attendant, and sits down. We have a neat dramatic pattern, the elements corresponding with each other in reverse (chiastic) order:

stands	A
receives scroll	B
unrolls scroll	C
reads scroll [text: Isa 61:1-2]	D
rolls up scroll	C'
hands back scroll	B'
sits down	A'

The ascending-descending pattern lends maximum solemnity to the text read by Jesus. The drama continues in the subsequent note (v. 20b) that "the eyes of all in the synagogue were fixed on him," followed by the solemn pronouncement of the great "Today" (v. 21).

As regards the text itself, Jesus quotes Isaiah 61:1-2 according to the Greek translation of the Hebrew, the Septuagint. With respect to individual phrases there are some important divergences from the original, some omissions and one significant addition from an altogether separate passage. The text also contains words and phrases central to Luke's presentation of Jesus. It merits close examination. For this it will help to set side by side a translation of the original Septuagint (LXX) version and a translation of the passage as it appears in Luke.

Isaiah 61:1-2	Luke 4:18-19
1. The Spirit of the Lord is upon me,	18. The Spirit of the Lord is upon me,
because he has anointed me;	because he has anointed me;
he has sent me to bring good news to the poor,	he has sent me to bring good news to the poor,
to bind up the brokenhearted,	
to proclaim release (*aphesis*) to the captives	to proclaim release (*aphesis*) to the captives
and recovery of sight to the blind;	and recovery of sight to the blind,
	to let the oppressed go free (*en aphesei*),
2. to proclaim a year of acceptance on the part of the Lord (*eniauton kyriou dekton*),	19. to proclaim a year of acceptance on the part of the Lord (*eniauton kyriou dekton*).
and the day of vengeance of our God.	

The Scripture Jesus quotes, Isaiah 61:1-2, comes from the third part of the book of Isaiah ("Trito-Isaiah" [chaps. 56–66]) where, in phrases that echo the earlier "Songs of the Servant" (42:1-7; 49:1-7; 50:4-9; 52:13–53:12), the prophet announces his ministry and message to the returning exiles from Babylon. If we examine the two texts side by side, we note that, as regards the opening lines, the Lukan quotation is exact. Luke omits the fourth member of the Greek text, "to bind up the brokenhearted," but retains the phrases about proclaiming "release to the captives" and "recovery of sight to the blind." Then Luke has a phrase, "to let the oppressed go free," that does not occur in Isaiah 61:1-2 at all but is an import from a nearby passage: Isaiah 58:5-7. The Lukan quotation returns to quote in full the phrase about proclaiming "a year of acceptance" but omits altogether the threatening final proclamation of a "day of vengeance of our God."

How are we to interpret Jesus' quotation of the text, with all these omissions and inclusions? And, to return to our original question, what are we to make of the fact that the entire "sermon" preached by Jesus upon this text consists simply in the announcement that "Today" this Scripture has been fulfilled? What is so extraordinary about this passage that the bare statement of its fulfillment makes up the entire message?

First, we must remember that the dramatic action of Luke's gospel does not begin with the events surrounding the birth and childhood

of Jesus but way back in the promises made by God to Israel. For the
early Christian community, Scripture (the Old Testament) recorded not
so much what was happening "back there" in the history of Israel, but
what was to happen, in fulfillment of divine promise, in the messianic
era, that is, in their own day. From the moment of his empowerment with
the Spirit (3:22), Jesus can say, "The Spirit of the Lord is upon me," and
apply to the ministry he is about to launch the "program" announced
by the Isaian prophet centuries before. In this sense the prophet simply
wrote the script for Jesus. That is why the sermon need go no further
than the simple announcement: "Today this scripture has been fulfilled
in your hearing."

There is so much contained in that prophetic announcement. Even
to hear it is already to grasp salvation in the shape of the good news
proclaimed to the poor. And, for all the brevity of his words, Jesus does
provide here a model for all sermons: the essence of biblically based
preaching is to show how the words of Scripture are alive and applicable
"today"!

Omitting the phrase about binding up the brokenhearted, the text as
quoted by Luke jumps immediately to the idea of liberation: the proclamation of release to captives. This concept of "release," expressed by the
Greek word *aphesis*, is highly significant for Luke. Already Zechariah in
his canticle (*Benedictus* [1:68-79]) had spoken of "knowledge of salvation"
coming to God's people in the "release of (= "from") their sins" (1:77)
and John in fulfillment of this had proclaimed a "baptism of repentance
for the release (*aphesis*) of sin" (3:3). The ministry of Jesus, then, will have
much to do with freeing people from the captivity of sin. Sin is not so
much a situation of guilt that has to be forgiven as a plight from which
one needs to be set free.

Jesus in his ministry will literally fulfill the next promise, that of giving
sight to the blind (7:21; 18:35). The context suggests, however, the kind
of recovery of sight experienced by people finally released into the light
of day after long confinement in dark prisons.[1]

The next phrase, "to let the oppressed go free," does not, as we have
already noted, feature in the original of Isaiah 61:1-2. It is an import from
Isaiah 58:6, where it occurs in a very interesting context. The prophet
is complaining about Israel's readiness to be scrupulous about the ritual requirements of fasting while neglecting the duties of hospitality

---

[1] The Hebrew original is ambiguous. The LXX adopts one particular meaning, that of recovery of sight.

and social justice. These are far more important in God's sight; without them the ritual acts have no meaning. It is worth quoting the prophetic complaint in full:

> Is such the fast that I choose, a day to humble oneself? Is it to bow down the head like a bulrush, and to lie in sackcloth and ashes? Will you call this a fast, a day acceptable [LXX Greek: *dektos*] to the Lord?
>
> Is not this the fast that I choose: to loose the bonds of injustice, to undo the thongs of the yoke, to let the oppressed go free [LXX: *apostelle tethrausmenous en aphesei*] and to break every yoke? Is it not to share your bread with the hungry, and bring the homeless poor into your house; when you see the naked, to cover them, and not to hide yourself from your own kin? (Isa 58:5-7)[2]

The importing of a phrase from this passage into the text of Isaiah 61:1-2 quoted by Jesus brings with it the content of the wider passage from which it comes. It fills out the sense of releasing the oppressed with the wider program of social justice and hospitality to the poor announced in verse 7. Understood in this way, it implies that the ministry of Jesus will fulfill the program of social justice that, according to Isaiah 58, God required of Israel. This greatly enriches the significance of the whole.

What seems to have led to the importing of the phrase from Isaiah 58 is the fact that it contains the word "release" (*aphesis*) that also occurs in the primary text, Isaiah 61:1. In Jewish and early Christian scriptural interpretation it was common practice to seek to illuminate the meaning of a text by associating it with a second text with which it had a word in common. The two texts in question in the present case—Isaiah 58 and Isaiah 61—actually have a further term in common besides "release," namely, "acceptable" (*dektos*), and this may have reinforced the association, since the whole quotation comes to a climax with the idea of "acceptance," as we shall see. Meanwhile, "release" has a further connotation, which we ought not to neglect.

"Release" (*aphesis*) occurs again and again in connection with two related customs enshrined in Israel's Torah. According to Deuteronomy 15:1-18, in the seventh or sabbatical year the land had to lie fallow and

---

[2] The translation (NRSV) is based on the Hebrew of Isa 58:5-7. The Greek (LXX) expresses the same essential thought but in rather different syntax. At the point where the Lukan text quotes the Greek ("let the oppressed go free"), the latter follows the Hebrew quite closely.

there had to be remission of all debts and release from the bonds of slavery. Leviticus 25 prescribed that Israel celebrate the fiftieth, or jubilee, year as a "year of release" in which, along with release from slavery, land alienated through hardship from a clan or family had to return to its original owners. It seems clear that Isaiah 61:1-2 alludes to these customs.

Whether Luke's use of *aphesis* reflects a similarly deliberate allusion to them is not so certain. However, there are good grounds for finding this sense of "release" included in the program of liberation that Luke has Jesus inaugurate here.[3] The heart of that liberation is freedom from the bond of sin. But spiritual "release" is, in Luke's perspective, a beachhead and pledge of a liberation that will encompass the totality of human life, including the socio-economic structures of society. Such a vision has already appeared in Mary's *Magnificat* (1:46-55); we will see it powerfully restated in the Beatitudes (6:20-23). If those who inherit the Judeo-Christian tradition were to become familiar with the instructions in Deuteronomy 15 and Leviticus 25, if they were to take them to heart and seek ways to implement them in today's world, the implications on a global scale would be revolutionary. Luke 4:16-20 brings the followers of Jesus directly under the scope of this imperative.

As we noted above, the final element of the Lukan text (v. 19) quotes in full the phrase about proclaiming "a year of acceptance" but omits altogether the threatening final proclamation of a "day of vengeance of our God."[4] The omission is surely intentional. The idea of judgment and retribution to come is not lacking in Luke. It certainly appears in the preaching of John (3:7-9, 17) and will at times feature in Jesus' own prophetic preaching, especially when he is en route to Jerusalem (9:51–19:44). But in the preaching of Jesus the threat of judgment tends to be postponed to an indefinite future. The ministry that he is now inaugurating—and that will continue after his death, resurrection, and ascension

---

[3] See Sharon H. Ringe, *Jesus, Liberation, and the Biblical Jubilee* (Philadelphia: Fortress, 1985); Robert B. Sloan Jr., *The Favorable Year of the Lord: A Study of Jubilary Theology in the Gospel of Luke* (Austin, TX: Schola, 1977); Mark Allan Powell, *What Are They Saying About Luke?* (Mahwah, NJ: Paulist, 1989), 86–89; Robert J. Karris, "The Gospel According to Luke," in *New Jerome Biblical Commentary*, ed. Raymond E. Brown, Joseph A. Fitzmyer, Roland E. Murphy (43:675–721) §59 (Englewood Cliffs, NJ: Prentice-Hall, 1990), p. 690.

[4] In the original text of Isa 61:2 the "day of vengeance" most likely referred to the divine retribution that was to fall upon Israel's enemies and oppressors. Thus as regards Israel itself, the phrase had a positive, rather than a negative, meaning.

in the mission of the church—is not about vengeance but "acceptance." Between now and the judgment stretches a "space" of salvation history that Luke, following Isaiah, calls the "acceptable year of the Lord" (*eni-auton kyriou dekton*).[5]

This whole idea of "acceptance/nonacceptance" is pivotal to Luke's understanding of the ministry of Jesus. The "acceptable year of the Lord" is the season of God's "hospitality" to the human race, which it is Jesus' mission to proclaim and enact. It is a time when people are simply accepted, not judged. True, it is a summons to conversion—an urgent and insistent summons to a deep and transforming conversion. But before conversion there is acceptance, welcome, a hand held out to the afflicted, the trapped, and the bound. If, as I believe, the whole mission of Jesus according to Luke can be summed up in the phrase "the hospitality of God," then that summary has its foundation here in the text from Isaiah, which Jesus quotes to inaugurate his ministry and set the pattern it will follow.

Wherever Jesus will exercise his ministry, the "today" or "year" of God's acceptance—the welcome, the hospitality of God—prevails. The great question is, who will "accept" the "acceptance," and who will not? The one who brings the "acceptance" of God will find acceptance in surprising quarters and a great measure of "nonacceptance" in others. This is the issue around which the drama of Luke's gospel turns. It comes to a head for the first time in the events that now follow.

The Nazarenes Reject the One Who Brings Acceptance: 4:22-30

Initially the response of the Nazarenes to the sermon of Jesus is favorable. They speak well of him and are amazed at the gracious words (lit., "words of grace") that come from his lips.[6] With local village pride they begin to claim him for themselves: "This is Joseph's son, is it not?" (v. 22).

But Jesus will have none of this narrowness. Labeling him "Joseph's son," while true at one level, simply places him in a box with which they are comfortable and where they can take pride in him as local boy made good. But for readers of the gospel the issue of just whose son Jesus is

---

[5] We may recall that the idea of "acceptance" also occurs in the text from Isa 58 from which the quotation in Luke 4:18 has borrowed: "Will you call this a fast acceptable [*dektēn*] to the Lord?"

[6] There is much irony in the Nazarenes' finding "grace" in Jesus' words. It is precisely when he begins to remind them of the wide scope of God's grace that their response begins to turn ugly (vv. 25-29).

has been settled already—very painfully for the person closest to him, his mother Mary (2:48-49). He is Joseph's son, yes. But he is God's Son, too, and now more than ever must leave family and hometown ties to be about his "Father's business."

So immediately—in a way that may seem needlessly provocative to us—Jesus begins to challenge and lay into his Nazarene audience. Alluding to his earlier activity in other Galilean towns (cf. v. 15), he places upon their lips the request: "What you have done elsewhere (lit., "in Capernaum"), do here for our benefit" (v. 23). In other words, "Be our local prophet. Surely, we have first claim on you."

Jesus firmly resists this attempt to confine and control him. His mission is to range far beyond his own locality and its particular interests. As if writing the script for the scene about to occur, he reminds the Nazarenes of a saying, "No prophet is acceptable [Greek: *dektos*] in his own hometown" (v. 27). The gospel, with strong irony, is playing upon the notion of "acceptance": the one who proclaims the "acceptable year of the Lord" (v. 19), the time of the Lord's acceptance, is not himself destined to be accepted by his own. The only place where he is not going to receive hospitality is in his original home.

To reinforce the point, Jesus brings up two biblical precedents to his own prophetic career (vv. 25-27). Despite the pressing needs of Israel, the prophets Elijah and Elisha both exercised significant ministry to outsiders. At a time of severe famine in Israel, Elijah was sent to bring relief to a widow at Zarephath in Sidon (1 Kgs 17:8-24). Though there were many lepers in Israel, Elisha cleansed none of them but the Syrian general Naaman (2 Kgs 5:8-14). Jesus' outreaching acceptance follows a biblical pattern set long ago.

The townsfolk of Nazareth find this intolerable, and their mood turns ugly (v. 28). Seizing him, they drag him out of the town to throw him down the cliff (v. 29). But Jesus "passes through" their midst and goes on his way (v. 30). What had begun with such favor and acceptance ends in rejection and violence. Why is this so? Why has the reaction been so swift and so negative?

In the drama of the gospel the event looks both backward and forward. It looks backward to the second oracle of Simeon (2:34-35), where, as we noted earlier, the old man had prophesied that Jesus would be a sign of contradiction and that the thoughts of many hearts would be revealed. This is precisely what has happened in Nazareth. The Nazarenes' initial approval of Jesus was a superficial attitude involving no real conversion. The salvation that Jesus brings cannot rest simply on the surface, leaving the depths of human beings untouched, unexplored, and unhealed. The gospel suggests that he felt trapped and imprisoned by the narrowness he divined in his townsfolk. To be true to his mission and free to exercise it in the way God willed, he had to bring to the surface and expose the "thoughts" that lay in their hearts—a challenge the Nazarenes failed. Coming to "knowledge of salvation" means coming to self-knowledge as well—something that usually involves a painful discovery of the narrowness of one's "thoughts."

The episode also looks forward, in a symbolic way, to what will later happen when Jesus "visits," not his hometown, but the capital of his own people, Jerusalem. There, on a much larger scale, the same pattern will work itself out. Initially well received—at least by the people (19:48; 20:19; 21:38)—Jesus will end up being rejected by the leaders and, this time in reality, will be put to death. But in a true sense, he will also "pass through their midst" (4:30a) through his resurrection and ascension.[7] When his Spirit empowers his disciples (Acts 2:1-10), he will also "go on his way" (4:30b) as they begin to proclaim the Gospel beyond Jerusalem, in all Judea, Samaria, and "the ends of the earth" (Acts 1:8). And Israel, as Acts shows, will have its second chance.

Conclusion

So this all-important scene serves a twofold function in the gospel. It establishes once and for all that the heart of Jesus' message is the good news of acceptance, the invitation to all to come and be drawn into the hospitality of God. It also shows how this broad, inclusive outreach will meet with resistance and rejection on the part of those reluctant to undergo the conversion required. The prophet who comes as visitor offering the hospitality of God himself meets with inhospitality and rejection. But rejection does not have the last word: it, too, can be drawn into God's saving plan and made to further, rather than restrict, the outreach of grace.

---

[7] We may note in this connection the word "exodus" used with reference to what will befall Jesus in Jerusalem in the "conversation" Jesus holds with Moses and Elijah at his transfiguration (9:31).

The Early Galilean Ministry
4:31–6:11

Modeling the Ministry of Life: 4:31–5:11

The gospel now offers a series of scenes depicting Jesus carrying out the program he announced in Nazareth. Instructing and liberating human beings, he sets a pattern for the ministry to which he will shortly call his first associates. First we have a general notice to the effect that Jesus went down to Capernaum, where "he used to teach the people on the Sabbath" (4:31).[1] This repeats what Jesus did in Nazareth. However, the note of surprise and newness is also there: "They were astounded at his teaching, because he spoke with authority" (v. 32). The authority, of course, comes from his "anointing" with the Spirit (3:21-22).

Reclaiming Human Lives: 4:33-44

There follow three representative scenes: the exorcism in the Capernaum synagogue of a man possessed by a demon (4:33-37); the cure of Simon's (Peter's) mother-in-law (4:38-39); a summary account of an array of cures and exorcisms in the evening (4:40-41).

In the first scene in the synagogue, the actual exorcism (vv. 33-35) is enclosed within two descriptions of the audience's response to the power of Jesus' "word" (v. 32 and v. 36). The arrangement conveys the impression of continuity between the teaching of Jesus and his exorcistic power. His proclamation of the word is already a liberation of human beings from the power of the demonic. This is why, presumably, it provokes the demon to cry out in protest.

From the dramatic, public scene in the synagogue we move to the domestic sphere, where Simon's mother-in-law is ill with "a high fever" (v. 38). The way Luke describes the healing of Simon's mother-in-law, again, places it virtually in the category of exorcism as well. Jesus "re-

---

[1] Luke uses the imperfect form of the verb "to be" and the present participle to convey the habitual nature of this activity; see Joseph A. Fitzmyer, *The Gospel according to Luke I-IX*, AB 28 (Garden City, NY: Doubleday, 1981), 544.

bukes" the fever afflicting her (v. 39), just as he "rebukes" the demon in the synagogue (v. 35), and also the demons in the evening scene (v. 41). All three episodes, both the public and the more domestic, involve a conflict with demonic forces that oppress, stunt, and seek to control human lives. Jesus is employing his messianic power to reclaim human beings, physically and spiritually, for humanity and for God. This is the onset of the "kingdom" or "rule" of God (see 11:20).

A final scene evokes what is becoming a familiar pattern (4:42-44). At daybreak Jesus withdraws to a deserted place. But the crowds find him and "want to prevent him from leaving them" (v. 42b). In other words, like the people of Nazareth, they want to keep him for themselves. But Jesus insists upon his wider mission: "I must proclaim the good news of the kingdom of God to the other cities also; for I was sent for this purpose" (v. 43). For the first time we hear the adult Jesus give expression to the "must" (Greek: *dei*) that drives him on.[2] To be faithful to this divine imperative he must constantly go beyond the confines of family, hometown, locality, and, eventually, through the ministry of the disciples, his own people.[3]

The Call of Simon Peter and the First Disciples: 5:1-11

So far in Luke's account Jesus has exercised his ministry without assistance from others. Only when the ministry is under way and its pattern established does he move to select from the crowds a group of companions and assistants.[4]

Jesus is preaching by the Lake of Gennesaret to a crowd that presses in on him, eager to hear what he has to say. The press of the crowd leads him to get into a boat—the one belonging to Simon—and continue

---

[2] We first heard the "must" on the lips of the twelve-year-old Jesus in the temple: "I must be about my Father's business" (2:49b).

[3] Somewhat oddly in view of Jesus' present location (Galilee), Luke stresses the sense of outreach by reporting that "he continued proclaiming the message in the synagogues of Judea" (v. 44). Luke's theology seems to be driving his "geography" at this point.

[4] A notable contrast to the narratives of Mark and Matthew, where Jesus calls four disciples at the very beginning of his public preaching (Matt 4:18-22; Mark 1:16-20). Luke's account of the call of the first disciples follows the scheme of Mark (Mark 1:16-20) but greatly develops a moment of interaction between Jesus and the leading disciple Simon Peter. Mark 4:1 seems to provide the setting for the call: preaching to the crowds from a boat by the lakeshore.

teaching from there. At the time Luke wrote his gospel, a boat had become a symbol for the church. So from early on in this scene we are being given signals that Jesus is about to lay the foundations for the community that will extend his mission and carry it "to the ends of the earth" (Acts 1:8b). The narrative suggests that it is the press of the crowds that leads Jesus to seek assistants. The context of the call is humanity thirsting for life. The disciples are to become Jesus' apprentices in the project of drawing people to the hospitality of God.

Simon and his companions are fishers by trade. At the moment, however, while Jesus is teaching, they are not fishing but mending their nets. As we are soon to learn (v. 5), this is not a good time to go fishing. Night has yielded nothing, and prospects for a catch in the daytime are even worse.

Jesus has a different trade and presumably, as far as the disciples are concerned, knows nothing about catching fish. His teaching finished, he surprises Simon with a suggestion: "Put out into the deep water and let down your nets for a catch" (v. 4). Simon protests but eventually agrees to act as Jesus commands (v. 5). The result is a catch of such abundance that the nets they have been mending threaten to break with the strain. Their partners have to be brought in to help. Even then the boats are on the point of sinking with the mass of the catch (vv. 6-7).

So we have gone from a situation of fruitless fishing and no catch to one of reluctant fishing and abundant catch. The abundance appears miraculous. Yet we are still dealing with ordinary, everyday fish and fishing.

But the interaction between Jesus and Simon (now "Simon *Peter*") moves to a new level (v. 8). A miracle story is about to become a call or commissioning story. It follows a pattern familiar from stories in the biblical tradition, such as the call of Moses at the Burning Bush (Exod 3:1-6) and the call of the prophet Isaiah (Isa 6:1-13). At the sight of the miraculous draft, a sense of proximity to the divine overwhelms Simon. Like Isaiah ("I am a man of unclean lips and I live among a people of unclean lips" [6:5]), he protests his sinfulness and unworthiness. Paradoxically—comically, even, in view of the locale (a boat some way from the shore)—he begs Jesus ("Lord," now, rather than "Master" [v. 5]) to "depart" from him. His partners, James and John, share the same reaction (vv. 9-10a).

But it is just at this moment of painful self-knowledge and truth that the commission comes. "Do not be afraid," says Jesus (v. 10b), "from now on you will be catching people alive." Simon and his partners are to change from one occupation (fishing for fish) to a deeper, more personal one ("fishing" for people). In the context of divine generosity (the abundant catch when least expected) Simon has explored his own unworthiness and weakness. On the basis of that profound awareness he and his companions are ready to learn and become part of the "people-catching" trade of Jesus.

The curious phrase "catching people alive" conveys the sense of a Greek word—*zōgrein*—that Luke has undoubtedly used very deliberately.[5] When people catch fish, whether for livelihood or for leisure, the fish necessarily end up dead. Luke seems to be sensitive to this negative implication in the "fishing" image. So, in moving from the everyday sense of "fishing" to the symbolic sense that applies to the mission, he employs this special term—one used in connection with the catching of wild animals not for killing but for keeping in some protected way, like netting fish for an aquarium or fishpond. The Greek word resonates with the sense of "life" (*zōē*). The call communicates the sense of "capturing" people with the word and bringing them to the more abundant life of the kingdom of God.[6]

The response of Simon and his associates is immediate (v. 11). They bring their boats ashore and leave them and "all things" to follow Jesus. They enter upon the life of detachment from wealth and worldly possessions so central to the following of Jesus in this gospel (see 18:28-29). Set free from other pursuits and concerns, sharing the lifestyle of Jesus in this way, they are to learn the "people-fishing" trade that has been his from the start.

Simon Peter in particular has been singled out, set on the path to leadership. The experience of conversion he undergoes here anticipates a graver crisis when he will three times deny his Lord (22:54-62, esp. v. 62). That shocking failure will not destroy his leadership. On the contrary, as Jesus foretells (22:32), he will emerge from it all the better equipped, through deeper conversion (lit., "once you have turned"), to "strengthen" his brothers and sisters. The pattern set for Christian leadership is clear: only those who have plumbed their personal fragility in the context of God's generosity are apt for leadership in the community that celebrates the hospitality of God.[7]

---

[5] In contrast to Mark and Matthew, who in their parallel accounts (1:17 and 4:19 respectively) use the phrase "fishers of people."

[6] Luke's usage recalls Jesus' summary of his mission in the Fourth Gospel: "I have come that they may have life and have it to the full" (John 10:10).

[7] While all the accounts of Jesus' life in the gospels reflect post-Easter faith and knowledge, this seems particularly true in the case of Luke's descriptions

Healings and Controversies in Galilee: 5:12–6:11

After the call of the disciples comes a series of episodes further displaying Jesus' power to bring wholeness and healing to human life. Each involves going to people who are in some way on the margins of society, either because of their affliction or because they bear the stigma of public sinner. In bringing healing and welcome to such people Jesus encounters opposition from a new direction. Not the opposition of the demonic, as in the earlier scenes, but the opposition of those unwilling to move beyond conventional judgments and values.

Cure of a Leper: 5:12-16

This scene displays the outreach of God's hospitality most dramatically. Prevailing religious law could only banish lepers to the margins of society (see Lev 13–14; esp. 13:44-45). This man, the gravity of whose condition Luke accentuates ("covered with leprosy"), does not hesitate to approach Jesus ("Lord, if you choose, you can make me clean" [v. 12]). With an affirmation ("I do choose. Be made clean"), Jesus stretches out his hand and touches the ravaged creature. In the light of the social stigma attached to leprosy, the gesture is remarkable. But Jesus does not "catch" the disease from the man. On the contrary, at his touch and word of command the leprosy "departs," restoring the man to health and wholeness (v. 13d). Jesus tells the man to show himself to the priest and make an offering as the Law requires (v. 14). His works of compassion place pressure upon the law of Moses; they are not overthrowing it.

Cure of the Paralytic: 5:17-26

This episode brings together a number of Lukan themes. It is not only illness that marginalizes this man. He and those who assist him face the added problem of getting access to Jesus through the crush of the crowd.

---

of Peter's call. The evangelist appears to have retrojected back into Jesus' historical life a tradition originally located in a post-Easter setting, where the risen Jesus appears to Peter and "rehabilitates" him in his leadership role in view of his failure at the time of Jesus' trial. The final chapter of the Fourth Gospel records just such a post-Easter scene by the lake in Galilee, including the presence of other disciples and a miraculous catch of fish (John 21:1-19); see also Luke 24:34; 1 Cor 15:5 (where, in an early creedal fragment cited by Paul, "Cephas" heads a list of persons to whom the risen Lord appeared); see also Mark 16:7.

Like Zacchaeus up in his tree later in the gospel (19:4), they do something extravagant: they clamber up to the roof, displace the tiles, and lower the man down in front of Jesus (vv. 18-19). All this effort Jesus reads as an expression of faith ("When he saw their faith . . . " [v. 20a]). They "carry" the paralyzed man as much by their faith as by their physical strength, and this little community of faith creates the context for healing.

But something more than physical healing is called for. Jesus assures the paralyzed man that his sins are forgiven (v. 20b)—an assurance that provokes a negative response from Pharisees and teachers of the law also present at the scene. They play the role of the third party in the "triangular" pattern characteristic of a Lukan scene: the "they" who mutter and murmur. Does not such an assurance amount to blasphemy? (v. 21). Prophet that he is, Jesus becomes aware of what is going on in their hearts.[8] True to Simeon's oracle (2:35) and in line with his action at Nazareth (4:24-27), he moves to expose these dark thoughts and confront them.

Jesus does not argue his right to forgive sin. He simply makes his capacity to work a physical cure proof of his authority to pronounce forgiveness ("What is easier . . . ?" [v. 23]). At his command the man on the pallet rises, picks up his pallet, and, unaided (in contrast to his arrival), goes off to his house.

Modern readers may find the blend of the two issues—healing and forgiveness—disturbing. But there is no necessary suggestion that the man's paralysis is a consequence or punishment of his sin. It is just that, in his case, there were two issues to be addressed, and, in a polemical context, Jesus makes the more visible one (the healing) the sign and demonstration of the inner transformation (the reconciliation with God). The reaction of the crowd (v. 26) shows that they have seen the connection.

Through the power of God, in the face of opposition, Jesus has struck a blow for the total healing of human beings. Bodily healing and spiritual healing go together. The paralyzed man and his associates had to break through a physical barrier to access the first (physical healing). Jesus had to confront a more resistant barrier (the "thoughts" of the religious authorities) to communicate the other (forgiveness). In both areas, faith created the essential context for the outreach of the hospitality of God.

---

[8] The biblical and postbiblical tradition ascribed to prophets the ability to read people's thoughts: see 7:39; also 6:8; John 4:19.

Celebrating the Hospitality of God—the Call of Levi: 5:27-39

The note of controversy and hospitality continues when Jesus calls the tax collector Levi to be his companion (vv. 27-32). Tax collectors were unpopular because the payments they exacted included rich rake-offs for themselves. Though wealthy, they were marginalized because of their trade. It is this that made them special objects of Jesus' concern (see 3:12-13; 15:1-2; 18:9-14; 19:1-10). His calling of one of them to be an intimate disciple is a further instance of provocative inclusiveness on his part.

Levi's response captures so much that is characteristic of Luke. First, the call of Jesus frees him from attachment to his wealth. He rises, leaves all, and follows immediately (v. 28). He then uses his wealth to put on a great banquet where he and Jesus and all his tax collector friends can celebrate the newfound hospitality of God (v. 29).[9]

Once more, however—the Lukan "triangle"—the Pharisees and scribes complain about all this eating with "tax collectors and sinners" (v. 30). "Righteous" as they are, they cannot catch the sense of celebration (cf. 15:25-30). Jesus counters with an effective image: it is the sick, not the well, who need the physician (v. 31). The image has the effect of transforming the sense of sinfulness from something to be punished or forgiven into a condition, akin to sickness, from which one needs to be healed and set free. Repentance is certainly required (v. 32). But repentance is not a precondition for God's acceptance. Rather, it is something that a sense of God's acceptance makes possible, joy-filled and transformative in human lives.

The same adversaries now press a new line of attack (vv. 33-39).[10] They contrast unfavorably the celebratory behavior of Jesus' disciples with the more ascetic ways (frequent fasting and prayer) of John's disciples

---

[9] Only Luke (5:29) tells us that Levi put on a "great banquet" (*dochē megalē*); in Matt 9:10 and Mark 2:15, Jesus simply "sits at dinner." This goes along with the emphasis upon Jesus' presence at celebratory meals in Luke, anticipating the hospitality of the kingdom. François Bovon remarks, "It does not disturb Luke that Levi, who has left everything, still possesses a house and can throw a dinner party. According to Luke's ethical code, confirmed in Acts, Christians do not abandon everything in the literal sense, but place everything at the disposal of the church" (*A Commentary on the Gospel of Luke*, Hermeneia, vol. 1 [Minneapolis: Fortress, 2002], 190).

[10] Luke (contrast Mark 2:18-22 and Matt 9:14-17) makes the dispute about fasting a direct sequel to the call of Levi by having the contrast with John's disciples pointed out by the same adversaries (the Pharisees and scribes). In this way, the call of Levi, the celebratory banquet, and the dispute about fasting

and the Pharisees. In response Jesus draws on an image richly evocative of the time of salvation in the biblical tradition. His disciples celebrate rather than fast because this time of association with Jesus is a wedding feast with the bridegroom present. John and the Pharisees act in a way appropriate for a time of preparation, a day now passed (7:28; 16:16). In the ministry of Jesus the "day" of salvation (4:21) has arrived, the divine "visitation" is under way. Those who have received the acceptance it brings can only celebrate in gratitude, joy, and praise. As it would be perverse and an insult to the bridal party to fast at a wedding celebration, so, with Jesus, the Bridegroom present, this is not the time for fasting.[11]

The images that follow—patching a garment (v. 36) and putting wine in wineskins (vv. 37-38)—display once again Luke's fascination with human response. Old ideas, preconceived notions of God's mode of acting, are inadequate for the sharp new wine of salvation brought by Jesus. A humorous touch at the end (v. 39) states the problem Luke sees Jesus facing. Just as old wine is preferred to new, people—good religious people—are slow to surrender long-treasured expectations. Like the wine buff they say, "The old is good."

God's Hospitality on the Sabbath: 6:1-11

Strict observance of the Sabbath was a hallmark of Jewish culture. To touch the Sabbath was to strike at Israel's identity as chosen people of God. In the first of two Sabbath controversies (vv. 1-5), the Pharisees criticize Jesus for allowing his disciples, as they walk through the fields, to pluck heads of grain, rub them in their hands, and eat them (v. 2). The actions are tantamount to working in defiance of the Sabbath rest. Jesus' response (vv. 3-5) does not really address this issue at all. Rather, to justify what his disciples are doing, he points to a biblical episode that does not concern the Sabbath but involves comparable action contrary to the law. King David allowed his men, when hungry, to enter the "house of God" (the temple) and eat the bread of the presence legally reserved for the priest (1 Sam 21:1-6). He overrode the objection of the priest, insisting

---

(5:27-39) form one continuous sequence focused upon the celebration of the hospitality of God.

[11] Luke, following the Markan tradition (Mark 2:20), does of course note (v. 35) that there will be a time for fasting—when the Bridegroom (Jesus) is "taken away" (at the time of the passion). Thus the Christian church has found a place for fasting, associating it especially with the preparation for the celebration of the paschal mystery in the forty days of Lent.

that legal prescription had to yield to human need. So Jesus has biblical precedent for what he allows his disciples to do. Beyond this, invoking the case of David implies a strong christological claim: as Messiah, Son of David, and therefore "Lord" of the Sabbath (v. 5; cf. 20:41-44), Jesus has the authority to make legal prescription bow to human need.[12] The heart of his mission is to bring human beings to the fullness of life. For the messianic community, of which the disciples form the nucleus, that is what Sabbath celebration is all about.

Exactly the same principle stands at the center of the second Sabbath controversy (vv. 6-11). The presence of a man with a withered hand in the synagogue and the likelihood that Jesus would move to address the problem stir up hostile thoughts within the scribes and Pharisees. Once more Jesus moves to bring these thoughts to the surface, confronting the issue posed by the man's condition: "Is it lawful to do good or to do harm on the sabbath, to save life or to destroy it?" (v. 9). Since God is the God of life, religious ritual must be about the enhancement of life, or else it cannot be of God.

The miraculous restoration of the man's hand (v. 10) vindicates this principle and ends the controversy in favor of Jesus. It leaves, however, a lasting legacy of resentment (v. 11). Jesus' inclusive, life-enhancing ministry has challenged beyond endurance the authority of those who guarded more conventional ways. Now on a wider scale he has attracted the kind of murderous hostility foretold in Simeon's oracle (2:34-35) and displayed in his hometown Nazareth (4:28-30).

Reflection

The stories we have been considering regularly depict the scribes and Pharisees as the chief adversaries and critics of Jesus. It is all too easy, in interpretation, to derive from these a sense of Jesus as being in conflict with Judaism as such: to see him as attempting to bring life to human beings in the face of the dead hand of the law. Apart from being highly dangerous, such an inference fails to do justice to the subtlety of Luke's analysis of Jesus' relationship to his ancestral faith. We have noted throughout the gospel the stress upon continuity as well as on the

---

[12] We might regret that Luke, along with Matthew, has not seen fit to include the striking statement found in Mark: "The sabbath was made for humankind, and not humankind for the sabbath" (2:27). But the principle is implicit in Luke's account.

advent of the new. Moreover, the conflict depicted in Luke between Jesus and representative Jewish leaders reflects the conditions of Luke's own time—late in the first century—rather than those of Jesus in his historical life. Above all, we should remember that the attitudes here represented by Jewish figures are those to which adherents of any religious leadership—Christianity included—are prone. We have to be prepared to find something of "our story" in these adversaries as well as in those who respond positively to Jesus.

The Community of the Kingdom
6:12-49

For a considerable time Jesus has been carrying out the program he announced in Nazareth (4:18-19), proclaiming and enacting the "year of the Lord's acceptance." In the context of this ministry he has begun to call others—first Simon and his companions (5:1-11), then the tax collector Levi (5:27-28). He now moves to set this group of helpers and associates on a more formal basis. The way he does so suggests that what is at stake is nothing less than a refounding of Israel as the community of the kingdom. Then, in a long sermon, he outlines the attitudes and behavior that are to distinguish the new community.

The Choice of the Twelve Apostles: 6:12-16

Like the Israel of old descended from the twelve sons of Jacob, the community of the kingdom is to rest upon a foundation of twelve select individuals. Before choosing and appointing those who are to play this role, Jesus spends the night on a mountain in prayer (v. 12). This underlines the solemnity of the choice and makes it an extension of the mission he himself has received from the Father. Later, after his ascension, the early community, at Peter's instigation, will move to find a worthy replacement for the traitor Judas (Acts 1:15-26). The selection by lot will restore the symbolic Twelve before the Spirit comes upon the disciples at Pentecost, empowering them to take up the mission of Jesus. The Twelve are not simply static "pillars" or foundations. Jesus names them "apostles" (v. 13) because they are to be the spearhead of the church's mission.[1]

---

[1] It is to Luke, then, that we owe the designation "the twelve apostles." It joins together two categories—"the twelve" and "apostle"—originally distinct in the earliest days of the Christian community (e.g., at the time of Paul; cf. 1 Cor 15:5 ["the twelve"] and 1 Cor 15:7 ["all the apostles"]). Of course, in the case of certain individuals (e.g., Peter, James [son of Zebedee], John) the categories overlapped.

The Setting for the Sermon: 6:17-19

The narrative implies that, in selecting the Twelve, Jesus had called them up to the mountain where he had spent the night in prayer. It now tells us that "he came down with them and stood on a level place, with a great crowd of his disciples and a great multitude of people from all Judea, Jerusalem, and the coast of Tyre and Sidon" (v. 17). It is important to distinguish carefully the categories of people gathered on the level place. Out of these separate groups Luke constructs a striking tableau as a setting for the sermon that follows.[2]

Closest to Jesus are the twelve apostles he has just chosen, then comes the wider group of disciples from which they have been singled out, then the great multitude that has assembled from near and far. Their condition is vividly described: they have "come to hear him and to be healed of their diseases"; they were all "trying to touch him, for power came out from him and healed all of them" (vv. 18-19). It is before this array of burdened and afflicted humanity, longing to access his healing and liberating power, that Jesus instructs at length his immediate disciples. Luke wants us to hear the sermon in this carefully staged context. We can set it out graphically as follows:

\JESUS/

\The Twelve/

\The wider group of disciples/

\Crowds from Judea, Jerusalem, Tyre, and Sidon/

In this setting the sermon then becomes something like the charge given at an ordination. Candidates receive formal instruction regarding who they must be and how they must behave before the wider group they will serve.

---

[2] In a rare departure from the order in Mark, Luke places the choice of the Twelve (Luke 6:12-16) before the summary statement indicating the press of the crowd (Luke 6:17-19), whereas in Mark 4 the order of the two scenes is precisely the reverse. Luke's order more directly associates the choice of the Twelve with the "tableau" (6:17-19) and the sermon that follows.

The Sermon on the Plain: 6:20-49

Like Matthew (5:1–7:29), Luke presents Jesus, in the course of his Galilean ministry, imparting an extensive body of teaching in the form of a sermon. Luke's version is much shorter than Matthew's, since he reserves for later in the gospel (Jesus' "journey" to Jerusalem [9:51–19:44]) a good deal of material that Matthew includes in the sermon. Both versions, however, begin in the same striking way with a series of Beatitudes.

The Beatitudes and Woes: 6:20-26

In contrast to Matthew's nine Beatitudes (5:3-12), Luke has four, followed by four closely corresponding Woes. The formulation is blunt and unqualified: "Blessed are you poor." (Contrast Matt 5:3: "Blessed are the poor in spirit.") In the biblical tradition "blessed" does not, strictly speaking, indicate a moral attitude to be adopted. The formula declares a person to be in a fortunate or advantageous position in view of a coming action of God. It really amounts to "Congratulations"—the sort of thing one might say to a friend who had won the lottery.

The Beatitudes, then, are highly provocative. They constitute a series of oxymorons (the holding together of two clashing ideas), the sharpness of which centuries of familiarity have tended to soften. It is outrageous in any age to congratulate the poor on being poor, the hungry on being hungry, the weeping and the reviled on being in the condition they are in. Correspondingly, it appears foolish to declare unfortunate (for that is what "Woe!" signifies) the wealthy, the well-fed ("the full"), the laughing, and those who enjoy a good reputation. From a moral point of view these last four states are not in themselves bad. Other things being equal, they are perfectly desirable.

The point is, however, that in the vision of Jesus other things are not equal at all. The Beatitudes and the Woes make sense in the light of the coming reversal of fortune so prominent in Luke's view of salvation. Mary proclaimed this reversal in her *Magnificat* (esp. 1:51-53); it also lies behind the "good news for the poor" announced by Jesus at Nazareth (4:18). The prospect of a reversal to come makes it better to be poor, hungry, weeping, and reviled rather than rich, full, laughing, and well-spoken of. So imminent and so certain is the reversal that the thought of it overcomes the painfulness of the present. In the light of this expectation—and only in this light—it becomes reasonable to hold together "blessed" and "poor" and the other contradictory pairs. So Jesus is not endorsing poverty or hunger and so forth. He is insisting that what most people reckon to be advantages and disadvantages are relativized, and indeed reversed, in view of the coming action of God.

According to what the world values (the situations that the Woes address), it makes little sense to regard the poor as being in a favorable situation. Yet in the light of God's coming action, it makes very good sense indeed. All ultimately rests upon a particular vision of God—a God who has pledged to act on behalf of the poor and marginalized rather than the rich and well-off.

The Beatitudes (and the Woes) are provocative both for the poor and for the rich. But they do not suggest that the poor should be content with their lot and passively accept it. By calling the poor blessed, the Beatitudes maintain that God has adopted the side of the poor and will reverse the situation. The poor can only benefit from the action of God. The rich have much to lose. The great advantage is to have a capacity or lack that the God of overflowing generosity can fill, to be in a plight that attracts God's impulse to save. It is because God is as Jesus proclaims God to be, that the poor are blessed and the rich are not.

In relation to the Beatitudes (and Woes) it is often asked whether by the "poor" who are blessed Luke means the economically poor or the spiritually poor. It is misguided, I believe, to blunt the impact of Luke's Beatitudes by "importing" into them the more spiritualizing tendency evident in the Matthean parallel ("poor in spirit" [5:3], etc.). It is important to note the basic difference between the two sets. Luke's Beatitudes are pronounced upon people who are in the situations described ("poor," "hungry," "weeping," "hated") not through any choice on their part but because that is simply the condition they find themselves to be in. Matthew's Beatitudes, on the other hand, introduce an element of *choice* (to be "poor in spirit," to be "meek," "merciful," "to hunger and thirst for righteousness," etc.) and so move in a direction of spirituality: people who are not initially in the situations of vulnerability described can choose to adopt such values in imitation of Jesus and in response to the image of God and God's action that he proposes.[3] Bearing in mind this distinction between the two sets of Beatitudes, it is important to respect the Lukan perspective (which is probably closer to that of Jesus himself) and understand the "poor" as primarily the economically poor. The Beatitudes, like the similar pronouncements in Mary's *Magnificat*, ought

---

[3] On the distinction between the Matthean and Lukan Beatitudes, see further my article, Brendan Byrne, "The Beatitudes and Poverty of Spirit in the Ignatian Exercises," *The Way* 47/1–2 (January/April 2008): 29–46, esp. 33–42.

not to be spiritualized away so as to have no bearing upon economics or social justice.

At the same time, in Jesus' day "the poor" had become a standard self-description for the faithful in Israel who wait hopefully upon the Lord—as, for example, leading characters in the infancy story, especially Simeon and Anna. At the heart of their waiting for salvation—salvation in a total sense, including economic and structural salvation—lies a deep spiritual longing, something that may also be present in others whose plight is not primarily economic. In this perspective "the poor" can include the afflicted in general, whatever the cause or nature of the affliction they suffer. "The poor" are all whose emptiness and destitution provide scope for the generosity of God.

Let us keep in mind the context in which all this is said to the disciples—in front of the afflicted masses who have come to hear Jesus and be healed of their diseases (vv. 17-19). In the Beatitudes, as indeed in the sermon as a whole, Jesus depicts his community as vulnerable and as "blessed" in that vulnerability. Being vulnerable gives scope to God's power. A vulnerable community can become for the afflicted an instrument of the hospitality of God. It is the vulnerable who make the world safe for humanity.

Generosity in Relationships: 6:27-42

As if the Beatitudes were not radical enough, the sermon now pushes vulnerability to fresh extremes. A long instruction begins (v. 27) and ends (v. 35) with the extraordinary command to "love your enemies." This is the central theme. In between are concrete illustrations of what it might mean in practice: returning blessing for a curse (v. 28), turning the other cheek (v. 29a), not withholding one's shirt from a person who has taken one's coat (v. 29b), and so forth. All involve responding to injury or unreasonable demand with nothing but generosity and the abandonment of all claim to retribution or restitution (vv. 30-31).

In themselves such actions and attitudes make no sense—and, in fact, allowance has to be made, as so often in the gospels, for the exaggeration that often marks the prophetic speech of Jesus.[4] He is not laying

---

[4] Charles H. Talbert puts this very well: "Here [in sayings like this] we meet a 'focal instance.' In a focal instance the situation described is so specific it does not provide a very useful general rule when confined to its literal sense. The specificity is intended to shock the hearers with an extreme command, at strik-

down maxims to be followed literally. Rather, he is seeking to inculcate a fundamental attitude according to which one would be prepared to be vulnerable to a degree foolish by the standards of the world, because such vulnerability and generosity is what one both discerns in God and experiences from God. Once again, as in the case of the Beatitudes, everything makes sense only in the context of the distinctive vision of God and relationship to God that Jesus communicates to his own. So, he concludes, "you will be children of the Most High; for he is kind to the ungrateful and the wicked" (v. 35).

Again (vv. 36-38a), in view of this relationship with God, the members of the community are to be "merciful" as their Father is merciful (v. 36). If they refrain from judging (= condemning), they themselves will avoid being judged (= condemned [at the final judgment by God]). If they forgive, they will be forgiven (by God [v. 37]). If they are generous in giving, they will meet with an extraordinary measure of generosity in return ("a good measure, pressed down, shaken together and [still] overflowing will be poured into your lap" [v. 38a]). The principle is, "The measure you give will be the measure you get back" (v. 38b). The sense is not that God waits to see the level of human generosity before deciding how generous to be in return. God's aim from the start is to be as extravagantly generous as possible. But, just as the volume of water one can draw from a tank depends upon the capacity of the vessel one brings, so the human receptacle conditions the amount ("measure") God can give. Any limitation stems from the human side.

The Difficulty of Judging Other People: 6:39-42

The commands not to judge and not to condemn (v. 37) raise the issue of just how difficult it is for people to have the kind of understanding of others that would really allow them to make judgments. Jesus illustrates the matter with the images of one blind person leading another (v. 39) and with the (again outlandish and humorous) notion of attempting to remove the speck in a neighbor's eye when one has a log in one's own

---

ing variance with the way people usually behave in such a situation, to lead the hearer to think beyond the literal meaning of the words and to reflect on the whole pattern of behavior that dominates life. The specific command is not a rule of behavior which can be followed mechanically but is intended to stimulate the imagination to draw out the implications for life as a whole" (*Reading Luke: A Literary and Theological Commentary on the Third Gospel* [New York: Crossroads, 1989], 73).

(vv. 41-42). The point being made is that relations between human beings based on retribution, or even on strict justice, fail to take account of the extreme difficulty of really knowing what is going on inside another person. If God, who does see the heart, acts with such generosity, understanding, and compassion, that surely should be the model for human interaction—certainly within the community of the kingdom, but even in the response of members of the community to outsiders who persecute and maltreat them (see, e.g., Rom 12:17-21).

Integrity in Word and Deed: 6:43-49

The sermon concludes with reflections of a more general nature. These seem to take off from the accusation, "hypocrite," launched at the person who wants to remove a speck from a neighbor's eye (v. 42).[5] The image of a tree and its yield of fruit illustrates the continuity that must prevail between heart (the ultimate seat of human quality) and external action (vv. 43-45). The continuity must flow in the other direction too. Good intentions are no use if not put into practice (v. 46). The extended image drawn from contrasting modes of building a house (vv. 47-49) rounds off the sermon in the same vein. To take to heart and put into practice ideals such as loving one's enemies is to make oneself vulnerable before the wider world (see the Beatitudes). But those who do so are building the "house" of their existence upon a foundation of rock. Those who hear but fail to act build, by contrast, without foundation[6] and expose themselves to ruin. The paradox makes sense in the light of the expectation central to the sermon and implicit in this image that concludes it: an intervention of God is coming, which will be like floods that rise and beat against a house. In the light of that intervention it makes sense to heed the words of Jesus and adopt the vulnerable life he commends. To do so is to build upon the "rock" of divine power and faithfulness.

---

[5] The negative meaning of the Greek word *hypokritēs* arose out of its use to denote an actor in a play. An actor, by definition, plays and speaks out a role that differs from his or her own personal identity; see Joseph A. Fitzmyer, *The Gospel according to Luke I-IX*, AB 28 (Garden City, NY: Doubleday, 1981), 642–43.

[6] Luke (cf. Matt 7:49) does not mention "sand" in the negative case.

Response to the Ministry of Jesus
7:1–8:3

In the Sermon on the Plain Jesus laid down the spirituality required in the community of the kingdom. He now continues to gather that community in the cities and towns of Galilee. In the exercise of this ministry the gospel depicts Jesus very much in the guise of a prophet. We recall his provocative appeal in Nazareth to the precedents set by the prophets Elijah and Elisha (4:25-27). Now, like them, he moves from place to place in a wide-ranging ministry, preaching conversion, working miracles, showing an ability to read the heart. As always, we find Luke particularly concerned with human response—noting who responds positively to this prophet and who does not, exploring in each case the reason.

Two Prophetic Miracles: 7:1-17

2 Kings 5:1-14 tells how Elisha the prophet cured Naaman, the commander of the army of the king of Syria, from leprosy. The cure came about at the suggestion of an Israelite slave girl who served Naaman's wife. There was no direct contact between the prophet and the Syrian foreigner. Elisha simply issued instructions from within his house that the general was to go and bathe seven times in the river Jordan, an instruction that Naaman was initially very reluctant to carry out.

This biblical story provides a model for Luke's description of Jesus' cure of a Roman centurion's slave (vv. 1-10).[1] The person who seeks Jesus' help is a foreigner whose case is argued by a Jewish delegation (vv. 3-5).[2] In contrast to the version in Matthew, the centurion sends a second delegation after the first to forestall Jesus' coming to his house

---

[1] The tradition underlying this story also appears in Matthew (8:5-13) and John (4:46-53).

[2] The very favorable recommendation characterizes the kind of "God-fearing" Gentile Luke-Acts presents as most amenable to the gospel (see Acts 10:2 [the centurion Cornelius]).

(v. 6). It is this delegation that brings the message containing the expression of faith (vv. 7-8) that Jesus finds so remarkable (v. 9). The centurion recognizes that Jesus has power similar to his own: he gets things done by those subservient to him because of the higher authority vested in him. Jesus does not, then, need to come to his house, something that for a Jew would involve a measure of defilement (see Acts 10:28).

This conforms to the general schema in Luke where Jesus, in his historical life, does not deal with the Gentile world but models patterns of outreach later to be played out when, after Pentecost, the disciples carry the good news to that world. The episode invites Gentile hearers of the gospel to identify with the centurion and his commendable faith. Like the centurion, they do not enjoy physical contact with Jesus, but faith enables them to access the hospitality of God reaching out to them and their households. Jesus' concluding comment, "I tell you, not even in Israel have I found such faith" (v. 9b), restates the theme that had so contentious a beginning at Nazareth: those on the margins of Israel—in this case a Gentile centurion—respond more readily to the good news.

The following episode (vv. 11-17), located in the village of Nain, is peculiar to Luke's gospel. Once again we have an account highly colored by a biblical story concerning a prophet—this time the episode in 1 Kings 17:8-24 where Elijah restores to life the son of the widow of Zarephath. Here Jesus makes the first move. Jewish society considered widows particularly vulnerable; the law singled them out for concern (Exod 22:22-24; Deut 24:17-21; etc.). But the situation of a woman who had lost not only her husband but her only son as well was extreme. It is the plight of the woman rather than her son that draws Jesus' concern. "Moved with compassion" (Greek: *esplagchnisthē* [see also 10:33]), he bids her not to weep (v. 13) and commands the young man to rise. Then he "gives him back to his mother" (v. 15).[3] The restoration of life to the young man, remarkable though it be,[4] is subsumed into ministry to the bereft and grieving mother. Nothing is said about her faith, and in this respect the young man, too, is necessarily passive. The episode simply instances Jesus' reaching out to human beings, his compassion drawn by nothing else save their state of affliction.

---

[3] This last phrase seems to be an explicit echo of 2 Kgs 17:23.

[4] On a possible historical background to this story in the life of Jesus, see John P. Meier, *A Marginal Jew: Rethinking the Historical Jesus*, vol. 2: *Mentor, Message, and Miracles* (New York: Doubleday, 1994), 788–98.

While it is usual for Luke to mention the response of bystanders, their words in this case are notably significant: "A great prophet has risen among us" and "God has visited [Greek: *epeskepsato*] his people" (v. 16). The exclamation recalls the canticle of Zechariah, where "knowledge of salvation" is linked to God's "visitation" of Israel (1:68, 77-78). Jesus' ministry of healing fulfills the divine visitation pledged in the ancient promises. Those most particularly benefiting from the ministry are people on the margins—like the foreign (Gentile) centurion and the poor widow of Nain. People like them are most notably hospitable to the visitor from God.

The Inquiry of John the Baptist; Jesus' Response and Reflection: 7:18-28

John the Baptist reenters the story at this point. Or at least he does so in the person of two disciples he sends to Jesus to inquire whether he is the One to come or whether another is to be expected (vv. 18-20). The inquiry may seem strange in view of the association of Jesus and John in the infancy story. It becomes more understandable when we recall the kind of messianic visitation John himself foresaw: a threatening visitation of judgment and wrath (3:7-9, 15-18). When Jesus took up his messianic ministry, what he announced and enacted was, on the contrary, "a day of the Lord's acceptance" (4:19). As Luke tells the story, it is understandable that John should have doubts as to whether Jesus really does correspond to the figure he himself had envisaged and proclaimed.[5]

Jesus does not directly answer yes or no to the question. Instead, occupied as he is "at that hour" (v. 21)[6] with a great deal of healing and liberating activity, he simply points the messengers to what they should be able to see and hear:

> Go and tell John what you have seen and heard: the blind receive their sight, the lame walk, the lepers are cleansed, the deaf hear, the dead are raised, the poor have good news brought to them. (v. 22)

The description, drawing largely upon Isaiah 61:1 (with some allusions to Isa 35:5 ["the ears of the deaf will hear"] and Isa 26:19 ["the dead will be raised"]), shows Jesus to be fulfilling the prophetic promises concerning

---

[5] See further Joseph A. Fitzmyer, *The Gospel according to Luke I-IX*, AB 28 (Garden City, NY: Doubleday, 1981), 666–67.

[6] The distinct temporal reference "at that hour" reminds us that we are in the great "day" ("Today") of God's acceptance announced by Jesus at Nazareth (4:21).

the messianic age.[7] The messengers can draw their own conclusions and take them back to John.

Apparently in reference to John, Jesus adds, "Blessed is anyone who takes no offense at me" (v. 23). John has "taken offense" at Jesus in the sense that he has found the pattern of his ministry to be counter to what he had himself expected. In this way, for all his greatness, he betrays that he belongs to those of the previous age who have difficulty adjusting to the "new wine" of the kingdom. This provides the lead-in for the passage that follows, where Jesus, after the messengers have departed, offers a reflection upon John (vv. 24-28). The commendation of John is unstinting: he is "a prophet and more than a prophet" (v. 26); he is "the forerunner" of the Lord that Malachi had announced (v. 27; see Mal 3:1; and, already, Luke 1:17, 76); "of all those born of women, no one is greater than John" (v. 28). And yet—"the least in the kingdom of God is greater than he" (v. 29). In this way John the Baptist is respectfully, but firmly, put in his place as belonging to an era now past.[8] Implied, by contrast, is the extraordinary "blessedness" of those who belong to the community of the kingdom.

Varying Responses to the Ministry of Jesus: 7:29-35

In line with its interest in human response, the gospel now pauses to reflect upon the kind of persons who respond positively to Jesus and those who do not. First there is a comment from the evangelist, then a reflection from Jesus himself.

The evangelist's comment (vv. 29-30) focuses upon the mission of John and points to a crucial division in the response it evoked. In the divine plan of salvation John's ministry was meant to prepare for that of Jesus by breaking the outer shell, as it were, of human resistance. The common people, by and large, including outcasts like the tax collectors, accepted John's message and the baptism of repentance he offered; they thereby

---

[7] The so-called "Messianic Apocalypse" (4Q521) from Qumran provides a remarkable contemporary parallel to these words of Jesus (stemming from "Q" [see Matt 11:4-5]); it too mentions raising of the dead amongst other miraculous activity listed. Text in F. García Martinez, *The Dead Sea Scrolls Translated: The Qumran Texts in English*, 2nd ed. (Grand Rapids, MI; Eerdmans, 1996), 394–95.

[8] Whereas in Mark and Matthew, John plays the role of Elijah *redivivus* who comes before Jesus as Messiah (see Mark 9:11-13; Matt 17:10-13), the Gospel of Luke is ambivalent about associating John with Elijah because it so strongly wishes to reserve that association for Jesus, the messianic prophet *par excellence*.

came under the scope of God's saving plan.[9] The Pharisees and the lawyers, on the other hand, frustrated that plan by refusing to submit to it.

Jesus, in his reflection on their response (vv. 31-35), appeals to a striking image: a taunting chant set up by children in the marketplace:

> "We played the flute for you, and you did not dance;
>   we wailed, and you did not weep."

> For John the Baptist has come eating no bread and drinking no wine, and you say, "He has a demon"; the Son of Man has come eating and drinking, and you say, "Look, a glutton and a drunkard, a friend of tax collectors and sinners!"[10]

It seems that we have to think of two separate groups of children sitting in the marketplace. One group, looking for something to do, invites the other group to join in their games but receives no response. So the first group complains, "We played weddings (flute) for you and you would not dance; we tried playing funerals (wailing) for you and you wouldn't weep," leading to an implied complaint, "What use are you!" John's demeanor was austere and his message threatening. "Weeping" was an appropriate response. Jesus, on the contrary, "partied on," celebrating the acceptance (hospitality) of God. In both cases the Pharisees and lawyers reacted negatively. They would not weep with John ("he has a demon" [v. 33]). They would not celebrate with Jesus ("a glutton and a drunkard, a friend of tax collectors and sinners" [v. 34]).

Jesus does not deny that his demeanor is celebratory. If his adversaries wish to call him a glutton and a drunkard, so be it. The holding of celebratory meals is essential to his ministry because, as the tax collectors and sinners are discovering, there is a great deal to celebrate: the love and acceptance of God. The Pharisees and lawyers are not so much condemned as pitied. Like the older brother in the parable of the Lost Son (15:11-32), they hear the music and dancing but are unable to join in. There are times

---

[9] Literally, "justified God" or "acknowledged the justice of God" (NRSV). "Justify/justice" appears to be used here in a biblical sense referring to the divine plan of salvation. It probably appears here in anticipation of the statement in v. 35: "Wisdom is vindicated (= "justified") by all her children" (NRSV).

[10] The text flow is chiastic (the outer and inner elements corresponding to each other in reverse order):
   A: celebration (flute playing/dancing)
   B: wailing/weeping
   B': austere ministry of John
   A': celebratory ministry of Jesus.

and seasons when it is appropriate to hear the austere message of John. But a community that never experiences as a group the joyful celebration of God's love has hardly heard the good news proclaimed by Jesus.

The sequence ends with a mysterious comment: "Nevertheless, wisdom is vindicated by all her children" (v. 35). "Wisdom" refers to the saving plan of God personified as a woman. Her "children" are probably, in the first instance, John and Jesus. But, by responding appropriately to their preaching, the tax collectors and sinners also become her "children." Their positive response vindicates the divine plan of salvation.

Hospitality and Inhospitality in the House of Simon: 7:36-50

The preceding reflection has thrown up a distinction between those who respond positively to Jesus and those who do not. Very effectively from a narrative point of view Luke goes on to dramatize this distinction with the story of the woman who anoints Jesus in the house of a Pharisee. Hardly any other scene in the gospel illustrates the "hospitality" theme as well as this one.

Like so many important scenes in Luke's gospel, the episode takes place at a meal. Jesus has been invited to dine by a leading Pharisee named Simon (v. 36). The invitation immediately sets up a context of hospitality. But, as will soon emerge, Simon the host does not offer even the most basic gestures of hospitality: he does not wash Jesus' feet, he fails to greet him with a kiss, he does not anoint his head with oil. Instead, an unnamed woman, with the reputation of being a public sinner, gatecrashes the party and begins to supply in a most extravagant way the duties of hospitality Simon has ignored (vv. 37-38).[11]

Christian interpretation of this episode through the ages has tended to focus upon Jesus and the woman (often wrongly identifying her as Mary Magdalene). Much is made of Jesus' kindness to this repentant sinner and edifying reflections drawn from it. But this "comfortable" interpretation misses the whole point. Here, as in so many other places

---

[11] The scene is, of course, in many ways reminiscent of the tradition in Mark (14:3-9), Matthew (26:6-13), and John (12:1-8) where a woman (Mary of Bethany in John's account) anoints the head of Jesus in the week before his death. While there are similarities between this tradition and the episode in the house of Simon that Luke locates so much earlier, there are also marked differences. It is not at all certain that all are drawing upon the same basic tradition. See further, Luke Timothy Johnson, *The Gospel of Luke*, Sacra Pagina 3 (Collegeville, MN: Liturgical Press, 1991), 128–29.

in Luke's gospel, a "triangular" pattern is operative. Simon the host is equally the focus of attention. The woman's bold action in respect of Jesus stirs up within him the kind of negative thoughts that are so frequently the object of Luke's concern (2:34-35; 5:21-22; 6:8; etc.): "If this man were really a prophet, he would know who this is and what sort of woman is touching him—namely, a sinner" (v. 39). Presupposed, once again, is the view that prophets are possessed of more than ordinary knowledge. We note too the *label*, "sinner," that Simon, unconsciously reflecting the more general estimation, pins on the woman.

Ironically, precisely because Jesus *is* a prophet, he knows what is going on in Simon's heart, and, as so often in Luke, he moves to bring it to the surface—this time employing a parable:

> A certain moneylender had two debtors. One owed him five hundred pieces of silver, the other fifty. Since they could not pay it back, he graciously canceled both debts. Now which of them will love him more? (vv. 41-42)

The parable neatly hoists Simon on his own petard. He cannot deny that the debtor released from the greater sum will from now on love the moneylender more than the one released from less (v. 43).

So then, point by point, Jesus goes in order through the duties of hospitality omitted by Simon and supplied so extravagantly by the woman. If we set out the responses side by side, we can see how effectively the narrative brings the point home (vv. 44-46).

[Simon]	[The Woman]
I came into your house and you offered me no water for my feet (= did not **bathe**),	yet she has **bathed** my feet with her tears and wiped them dry with her hair.
You gave me no **kiss**,	yet ever since I arrived, she has not ceased **kissing** my feet.
You did not **anoint** my head with oil,	yet she has **anointed** my feet with perfume.

Jesus then draws the inevitable conclusion: "For this reason, I tell you, her sins, many though they are, must have been forgiven her, seeing that she has shown so much love. Whereas, the one to whom little is forgiven loves little" (v. 47).

There is an alternative way of translating this last verse—a way that makes the forgiveness received by the woman follow her gesture of love:

"I tell you, her many sins have been forgiven her for this reason: because she has so much loved." This interpretation is open to the suggestion that her gesture of repentance somehow "earns" or merits the forgiveness she subsequently receives (see v. 48). Along with most recent interpreters and translations, I would argue that the thrust of the parable points inevitably to the alternative interpretation where acceptance and forgiveness come first and the love of the woman follows.[12] Then Jesus' concluding words to the woman, "Your sins are forgiven. . . . Your faith has saved you; go in peace" (vv. 48, 50), represent simply an explicit and public assurance of the forgiveness already imparted without words. They remove the label, "sinner," that Simon, and doubtless others present, had pinned upon the woman.

This episode illustrates perfectly Luke's theme of the hospitality of God. Jesus, the divine visitor to the world, comes as guest to this house but receives little or no hospitality from the one who as host ought to have provided it. A person publicly labeled "a sinner"—one, therefore, on the margins—is drawn to the occasion. Though certainly not welcomed by the Pharisee, she has sensed—correctly, as it turns out—that a wider, deeper welcome ("acceptance") awaits her. Boldly, she breaks through the barrier of hostility to herself and her kind. She, not the Pharisee, gives hospitality to Jesus (recall Luke's comment in vv. 29-30). In return, she receives from him a new outflow of the "hospitality of God" as, publicly and authoritatively, he declares her forgiven and at home in the community, removing the label (v. 48).

Introducing a christological note, "those at table with him" ask, "*Who* is this who even forgives sins?" (v. 49). Well might they do so! Their fellow guest is the "Visitor from high" (1:78), one who personally embodies and communicates the forgiveness of God.

Jesus' final assurance, "Your faith has saved you; go in peace" (v. 50), sheds light on the meaning of "salvation" in Luke. Taken as a dramatic whole, the episode shows that salvation consists not only in forgiveness but also in the human transformation the experience of forgiveness has brought about. Simon, who has neither experienced this forgiveness nor

---

[12] From a syntactical point of view, the Greek sentence is open to both interpretations. The decision in favor of one over the other rests upon the flow of thought in the passage. The interpretation opted for here takes the Greek conjunction *hoti* in a logical rather than a causal sense: it expresses what can be deduced from seeing the woman's action (see Matt 8:27; Gal 4:6; 1 John 3:14). See further, Fitzmyer, *Luke I-IX*, 692.

felt the need for it, comes across as cold, distant, and unloving. By contrast, the previously marginalized woman is free to supply gestures of love and service on a most extravagant scale: the alabaster jar containing precious rather than common oil, sufficient tears to "bathe" the feet of Jesus, using her hair to dry them, "not ceasing" to kiss them. So, when finally (v. 50) Jesus bids her "go in peace," she carries with her the messianic peace of one transformed by Jesus' power to save.

The scene displays Luke's genius for bringing together two people's experience in a single scene—save that here he does not so much bring them together as hold them in mutually illuminative contrast. Simon is not necessarily judged or condemned. Jesus simply points to outcomes: Who's getting something here? Who's missing out? The drama puts to readers of the gospel a similar challenge: Are you going to go with Simon or with the woman? We shall find a similar pattern in chapter 15.

Women Who Minister to Jesus: 8:1-3

After the story of the unnamed woman's gesture of hospitality, Luke mentions that Jesus went about proclaiming the good news of the kingdom (v. 1), accompanied not only by the Twelve but also by a number of women, several of whom he names, beginning with Mary Magdalene (vv. 2-3).[13] These women are said to have been cured of evil spirits and infirmities, and of Mary we learn besides that "seven demons had gone out of her" (v. 2b). The women not only accompany Jesus, they also provide financial support (v. 3b).[14]

From a feminist perspective, this brief notice will not be particularly appealing. There is a suggestion that women are prone to mental illness; their role seems to be the auxiliary one of providing for Jesus and those (the male disciples) who had "left all and followed him" (5:11). At the

---

[13] Luke locates here the list of women that Matthew (27:55-56) and Mark (15:40-41) name as watching from a distance the crucifixion of Jesus.

[14] The total phrase in Greek, including the verb *diakonein*, seems best understood in this context to refer principally to financial support, rather than more domestic service like cooking, washing, mending, etc. This is supported by the fact that one of them, Johanna, is stated to be the wife of a high official in Herod's court, which suggests a person of some means. The Acts of the Apostles describes women of means supporting the local house churches, the classic example being Lydia of Philippi (Acts 16:14-15). Luke probably wishes to show that such support continues a pattern established during the ministry of Jesus.

level of interpretation, these problems cannot be denied.[15] At the same time, it is important to note what is likely to have been Luke's intention at this point. In comparison with men, women in the ancient world belonged to the margins of society. What Luke seems to be suggesting here, in continuity with the scene immediately preceding, is that among the marginalized who received healing from Jesus and responded with generous service were a significant number of women.[16]

---

[15] For an excellent discussion of these issues in regard to this episode, see Barbara E. Reid, *Choosing the Better Part? Women in the Gospel of Luke* (Collegeville, MN: Liturgical Press, 1996), 124–34.

[16] Two of the three women named here, Mary Magdalene and Johanna, will be witnesses to the death (23:49) and the burial (23:55) of Jesus; they will also be the first to hear the news of his resurrection (24:10). The male disciples will not believe their report, dismissing it as "an idle tale" (24:11). The women will be vindicated in the end by the appearances of the risen Jesus (see 24:22-23, 25).

Later Galilean Ministry

8:4–9:17

Hearing and Living the Word: 8:4-21

The preceding section has shown the differing responses (positive and negative) that various groups make to the message of Jesus and to the divine acceptance he brings. Now, as Jesus' ministry in Galilee approaches its final stage, the gospel explores what is required if an initial positive response is to be lasting and truly effective. The chief vehicle for this is the parable of the sower and its accompanying explanation.[1]

Parable of the Sower: 8:4-18

The original purpose of the parable as told by Jesus[2] seems to have been to counter disappointment at the meager response the preaching of the kingdom has evoked so far. Jesus points to the way the sower goes about his work. The sower throws the seed around extravagantly in the wind, heedless, it would seem, that so much falls where it will be lost. How can he afford to be so careless and wild? Because he knows that the yield from the seed that falls into good ground will abundantly compensate for all that is lost (the "hundredfold"). The parable suggests that God operates with a similar extravagant carelessness in respect to the good news of the kingdom.[3]

---

[1] The Gospel of Luke at this point rejoins the narrative of Mark (left off for the purpose of Luke's "lesser insertion" [6:12–8:3]). Of the three extended parables in Mark 4 (the sower, the seed growing secretly, and the mustard seed), Luke retains only the first. Luke also transfers the story of Jesus' family seeking him from its Markan location (Mark 3:22-35) before the sequence of parables (Mark 4:1-33) to the end of that sequence (Luke 8:19-21).

[2] The actual parable, like most of the parables, almost certainly goes back to Jesus himself. Most scholars view the interpretation (Mark 4:14-20 and parallels) as reflecting the situation of the early Christian community.

[3] Between the parable and the interpretation, in line with Mark (4:10-12) and Matthew (13:10-15), Luke retains the disciples' question about the meaning of

Luke simplifies the parable (vv. 5-8) and the interpretation that follows (vv. 11-15). The focus lies more intentionally and narrowly upon factors in human life that make for success or failure with respect to the word. Like the seed that falls upon the path, the word simply bounces off some people, evoking no response at all (v. 5, v. 12). Those whose disposition corresponds to the seed on the rock initially hear the word with joy, but their conversion is only temporary; lacking root, their grasp of the word does not survive a time of testing (v. 6, v. 13).[4] In the case of others still—the seed among thorns—there is a more gradual erosion of the word stemming from "the cares, the riches and pleasures of life" (v. 7, v. 14), a theme to become ever more prominent as the gospel proceeds. Finally, there are those "who, having heard the word in an honest and good heart, hold it fast and bear fruit with patient endurance" (v. 8, v. 15).

Here Luke provides a point-by-point summary of Christian spirituality. The word has to be heard, not on the surface but deep down in the heart—the wellspring of human life and action; the heart itself must be "honest and good" (see 6:45). As life proceeds, the word must be "held fast" in the heart as a living force warding off threats from other attachments, other interests, and simple boredom. Finally, with the inevitable ups and downs of life, a measure of "endurance" is required. Beyond the joy of initial discovery Christianity is something for the long haul.

The sayings that follow (vv. 16-18) attend to this aspect of perseverance and the ongoing effect of the word. If the lamp of faith is lit in a human

---

the parable (though restricting the question to the meaning of *this* parable rather than to the parables in general) and Jesus' enigmatic and pessimistic response (8:9-10). The response plays upon the broader meaning of "parable" in the biblical tradition, which can include the sense of a "puzzle" or "riddle" that obscures rather than facilitates understanding. It seems that the early Christian tradition exploited this sense of "parable" in order to account for the failure of so many Jewish contemporaries to accept Jesus as Messiah of Israel: to accept his parabolic utterance as intelligible divine communication required being "gifted" by God to know the "secrets of the kingdom" (v. 10); otherwise, his teaching came across as simply "parable" in the obscuring rather than illuminating sense. Biblical thought in general was less troubled by the tension between divine action and human responsibility that such an explanation sets up for us. See further, François Bovon, *A Commentary on the Gospel of Luke*, Hermeneia, vol. 1 (Minneapolis: Fortress, 2002), 312–13.

[4] "Test" here probably refers to the instances of persecution or petty harassment that believers had to endure from time to time from the authorities or unsympathetic fellow-citizens.

life, it is not meant to be covered or hidden but to keep on shining and shed light in Christian witness to others (vv. 16-17). When persons have responded positively to the word, God's grace invades their lives ever and ever more abundantly, whereas an initial refusal cuts things off from the start (v. 18).

The True Family of Jesus: 8:19-21

The sequence ends with a report about Jesus' mother and brothers seeking to reach him. Jesus' response ("My mother and my brothers are those who hear the word of God and do it" [v. 21]) is not a tribute to his mother's faith; nor, on the other hand, is it a put-down or slight. Jesus uses the occasion of his family's approach to make a wonderful point: those who hear the word that he is preaching and keep it in the way the parable (the sower) commends, make up his new family (see 2:49; also 2:35a). They become members of the household of God, celebrating and embodying in the world the "at-homeness" with God that God intended for the human race from the start (3:22-38).

Further Displays of God's Saving Power: 8:22-56

At this point Luke describes four incidents (the last two intertwined), each of which displays Jesus' power to reclaim human lives from demonic and destructive forces. His more immediate disciples are closely involved in each case. This is appropriate because at the end of the sequence (9:1) he will communicate his power to the Twelve and send them out on their own saving mission (9:2-6). In the four incidents, Jesus creates, as it were, a beachhead from which their own mission can proceed.

Overcoming the Storm on the Lake: 8:22-25

In this dramatic episode there is a remarkable contrast between the picture of Jesus at the start and at the close. Jesus, it is true, initiates the voyage across the lake (v. 22). But, once in this sphere where the fishermen disciples are competent and he a mere passenger, he leaves them to it and, in a very human way, simply falls asleep. When the windstorm (v. 23b) creates a crisis that they cannot manage, suddenly, majestically, he is exercising more than human power. In the ancient world water out of control was a standard symbol of chaos. In rebuking and calming the sea (v. 24), Jesus exercises a power that the biblical tradition accords to the Creator alone (see Pss 65:7; 89:9; 106:9; 107:23-30; Job 26:11-12;

38:8-11; Isa 51:10). So the scene ends with the disciples, not so much relieved and grateful, as afraid, amazed, and asking, "Who then is this . . . ?" (v. 25b). The one who can be quite passively asleep in the boat is also one who rebukes the winds and the waves with the power of God.

Jesus' question, "Where is your faith?" (v. 25a), does not mean that the disciples lack faith altogether. Rather, a new reality has suddenly placed their current level of faith under severe strain. Their understanding of Jesus has a long way to go as it struggles to come to terms with his identity and the future pattern of his mission.

Reclaiming a Profoundly Disturbed Human Being at Gerasa: 8:26-39

A new crisis awaits Jesus and the disciples as they disembark on the opposite shore: an encounter with a person possessed by an extremely destructive demon.[5] Exceptionally for Luke, Jesus here enters a region inhabited by Gentiles (pigs would not be raised in a Jewish area). The possessed man is originally "from the city" but for a long time has been an outcast, wearing no clothes, living in tombs rather than a house (v. 27). People had tried to restrain him with chains and shackles but to no avail; the demonic force would inevitably drive him back into the wilds (v. 29). The picture is that of a totally dehumanized person, driven out of society (house and city), forced to live in the abode of the dead. This is indeed a powerful demon.

Ignoring the man's plea to be left alone (v. 28), Jesus forces the evil power to name itself ("Legion") and so submit to his power (v. 30). The stratagem of seeking to enter the herd of pigs and their subsequent fatal rush to the sea (vv. 32-33) underlines the destructive nature of the force from which the man is set free.

So far the encounter has been simply between Jesus and the possessed man. Now a third party appears on the scene (the Lukan "triangle" once more). A report from the swineherds brings the people from the city out to see for themselves what has happened (vv. 34-35). They find the creature

---

[5] The episode is one of the most curious in the gospels. Taking it on a historical level to any degree unleashes a whole host of issues (such as, Jesus' apparent indifference to the loss incurred by the owners of the pigs). Variations in the manuscript tradition as to the location of the incident ("Gerasa," "Gadara," "Gergesa"), together with so many aspects that seem inflated in the way of folklore, render difficult any attempt to reconstruct a historical basis for the tradition; see Joseph A. Fitzmyer, *The Gospel according to Luke I-IX*, AB 28 (Garden City, NY: Doubleday, 1981), 734–35, 737.

whom they had failed to control seated peacefully at the feet of Jesus, clothed and in his right mind: the very picture of humanity regained. Their reaction is curious. Overcome with fear, they ask Jesus to leave them (v. 37). They can cope better, it seems, with the presence of the demonic than with a power that has reclaimed one of their number by confronting and naming the evil.

As Jesus prepares to leave, the liberated man wants to go with him (v. 38). But Jesus tells him, "Return to your home, and declare how much God has done for you" (v. 39). The one who before had no home save the abode of the dead is sent back to his home and told to make it a little beachhead of the hospitality of God. Through his living witness, the people of the city will have a second chance to access God's grace.

Reflection

Strange as many of its features are, the scene invites us to enter its drama. With which character or group should we identify? The disciples who simply observe? The townsfolk who cannot cope and ask Jesus to go away? Or can we indeed find something of our story in the plight of the possessed person himself? Each of us has demons that rend and tear at us and make us want to dwell "in the tombs" rather than in the house of life. Perhaps the parts of ourselves, our character or our experience of life, that most readily attract the freeing power of God are those where we are most inclined to say to the Lord, "What have you to do with me? Why have you come to torment me?" Is Jesus trying to get us to name our demons and acknowledge their destructive power? What would it mean for us to be later "sitting at his feet, clothed and in our right mind" or sent back "to our home" to proclaim "how much Jesus has done for us"?

Two Journeys of Faith: Jairus and the Woman with Hemorrhages: 8:40-56

These intertwined stories mutually illuminate one another. They show Jesus confronting, respectively, incurable illness and death. They also underline very strongly the link between faith and the experience of salvation.[6]

---

[6] These features are already present in the Markan parallel (5:21-43). But Luke, while not greatly modifying Mark, has characteristic touches of his own. Thus the young girl for whose life her father pleads is an "only daughter"—

Desperate for the life of his daughter, the synagogue ruler Jairus approaches Jesus in faith and persuades him to come immediately to his house (vv. 41-42). He then has to stand by helplessly while Jesus stops to attend to the woman (vv. 43-48). Finally he is told that it is all too late: his daughter, in the meantime, has died; why trouble the Master further? (v. 49). First the delay, now death. Jairus's faith must leap to an entirely new level as Jesus assures him, "Do not fear. Only believe, and she will be saved" (v. 50). At the end of this long journey of faith and in the context it provides, Jesus overcomes death, restoring the little girl to her father and mother (vv. 54-55a). Very humanly, he suggests they resume their parental duties by giving her something to eat (v. 55b). Their "house" (only Luke mentions the house [v. 41, v. 51]) has become the venue of the life-giving hospitality of God.

In contrast to the influential ruler of the synagogue, how different the situation of the nameless woman (vv. 43-48). As far as the community is concerned, she is as good as dead; according to Leviticus 15:25-31, her condition renders her permanently unclean, and she in turn renders unclean any person or object she touches. It is scarcely possible to grasp the loneliness and isolation of her situation—accentuated now by poverty, since she has spent all she had on physicians (v. 43).[7] She is in many ways one of the most marginalized figures in the gospel.

She has, then, to break through a vast barrier to gain access to Jesus. To touch him publicly would render him unclean. So, amidst the press of the crowd (v. 42b, v. 45), she contrives to touch secretly the fringe of his clothes. The crowd "presses in" upon Jesus, but she touches him with faith. And her faith becomes a channel for his healing power to take effect.

We might well ask why Jesus, aware that power has gone out from him, goes on to bring the whole matter out into the open (vv. 45-48). Would it not be more sensitive to let the woman go away quietly and reenter the community in her own good time? But healing is never a purely private matter in the gospel. Salvation includes restoring this per-

---

just as the young man at Nain was an "only son" (7:12). The two raising stories balance one another: father—only daughter//mother—only son.

[7] Luke's gospel omits Mark's added comment (5:26c) that the medical attention the woman had received had served not to improve her condition but to make it worse. This omission has intrigued the Christian tradition in view of the fact that Paul in Col 4:14 refers to a disciple called Luke as "the beloved physician."

son to social status in the community, making her faith and her healing a community experience as well. So Jesus calls her forward to acknowledge what has happened. He publicly commends her faith and sends her away, a living witness to the onset of salvation (v. 48).

New Ministers of the Hospitality of God: 9:1-17

The Twelve Sent Out on Mission: 9:1-6

The four demonstrations of the messianic power of Jesus provide the context for apprenticing the Twelve for leadership and service. He confers upon them some measure of his own power and sends them out, armed with authority over demons and the gift of healing, to proclaim the good news of the kingdom (9:1-6).[8] In human terms they are to travel very lightly, taking nothing for the journey (no staff, bag, bread, money, or extra tunic); they are to remain in the house where they first find welcome, not moving about. If they experience rejection, they are to respond with a prophetic gesture, shaking the dust off their feet as a testimony (v. 5).[9] They are, in other words, to go out in great vulnerability, relying upon whatever hospitality they may find. In this, of course, they follow the pattern of Jesus, who, as "visitor from on high" (1:78), has exposed himself to the risk of human inhospitality in order to draw human beings into the hospitality of God.

A notice about Herod's interest in Jesus and the death of John the Baptist (9:7-9) provides a narrative interlude allowing for the activity of the Twelve.[10] When they return (9:10) and make a report to Jesus, he withdraws with them privately to Bethsaida. But the crowds, discovering

---

[8] This is the first of two such sendings in Luke, the second (sending of seventy disciples) occurring in 10:1-16. The first is modeled upon Mark 6:6b-13; the second has much in common with Matt 10:1-16 and so seems drawn from a "Q" tradition.

[9] In Acts 13:51 Paul and Barnabas perform this same gesture on being expelled from Antioch in Pisidia.

[10] Herod's question makes explicit once more the issue of the identity of Jesus (see 8:25b); it prepares the way for the question he will soon put to his disciples (9:18-20). More remotely, the notice about Herod's interest explains his later satisfaction when Pilate remits the case of Jesus to him (23:8). It is characteristic of Luke to weave advance signals of this kind into his narrative. The sequence also informs us that John the Baptist has been beheaded by Herod (see Mark 6:17-29; Matt 14:3-12). John has faded from view as far as Luke is concerned; he belongs to a past epoch (recall 7:28).

his whereabouts, follow him. He "welcomes" them, speaks to them about the kingdom of God, and attends to those who need to be healed (v. 11). The press of the crowd impels him once more to offer the hospitality of God.[11]

Feeding the Five Thousand: 9:10-17

But a far greater exercise of hospitality now follows. Practical people as they are and aware that the day is fast drawing to a close, the Twelve remind Jesus that the people who have followed him to a lonely place[12] have nothing to eat and nowhere to stay for the night.[13] They urge him to send them away. But for Jesus the duties of hospitality are not so swiftly ended. He challenges the disciples, "You give them something to eat" (v. 13a). Baffled, they protest: they have only five loaves and two fish—or does he mean that they should go and buy food for all the people, five thousand no less? (v. 13b).

Jesus has other plans. He makes the disciples initiate the provision of hospitality by getting the people to sit down in groups—a clear signal that they are going to be fed. Then, taking the loaves and the fishes, invoking heaven, blessing, breaking, and giving them, he miraculously makes it possible for the Twelve to feed the entire multitude (v. 16). And feed them they do—not merely adequately but so abundantly that even after all were filled they were able to gather twelve basketfuls of broken pieces (v. 17).

Noteworthy in the episode is that Jesus does not himself deal directly with the crowd. Rather, he makes it possible for the Twelve to provide the hospitality that initially they had found so daunting. In this and many other aspects the episode is loaded with symbolism for the life of the later church. It happens as the "day" is coming to a close (v. 12). When the "day" of Jesus' historical life comes to a close, it will be these disciples who will carry on the "day" of his hospitality and mission. The gestures of Jesus as he multiplies the loaves and fishes (taking, blessing,

---

[11] In Mark (6:32-34) and Matthew (14:13-14) Jesus withdraws not to a city but to a deserted place. Luke, characteristically, has Jesus in a domestic setting; see Luke Timothy Johnson, *The Gospel of Luke*, Sacra Pagina 3 (Collegeville, MN: Liturgical Press, 1991), 146.

[12] Luke does not mention that Jesus has gone out from Bethsaida but, in view of the disciples' warning (v. 12 [end]), the narrative seems to presuppose this.

[13] It is characteristic of Luke (contrast Mark and Matthew) to mention the need to find lodging as well as provisions.

breaking, and giving) echo the eucharistic institution narrative at the Last Supper (22:19-20) and the fleeting post-Easter meal at Emmaus (24:30 [when, again, the "day" is far spent; v. 20]). The feeding thus anticipates the Eucharist, where sacramentally the church will celebrate and offer the hospitality of God in the long "day" of Jesus' absence until its fulfillment in the kingdom of God (22:15-18). There is indeed a very rich "apprenticeship" going on in this scene. The Twelve now have authority over demons (9:1). But, with respect to the community of faith, their primary task is to minister the hospitality of God.

Climax of the Galilean Ministry
9:18-50[1]

Jesus' ministry in Galilee comes to a climax around the great questions of his identity and the direction his ministry is to take from this point on. After he had calmed the storm on the lake, the disciples asked themselves, "Who is this . . . ?" (8:25); King Herod had also been putting to himself the same question (9:9). Now, as the focus begins to fall more directly upon the disciples and less upon the crowds, it is time to raise the issue more explicitly. A new phase of the disciples' education begins. They have to learn what following Jesus and sharing his mission will really involve.

The Identity and Destiny of Jesus: 9:18-27

As so often in Luke's gospel, an important new development begins with Jesus at prayer (9:18a). Then he puts before his disciples the great question, "Who do the crowds say that I am?" (v. 18b). The various identities listed (v. 19) all see him as a prophet come back to life (John the Baptist, Elijah, or one of the ancient prophets). Jesus has, it is true, played the role of prophet in many respects and so these views have some foundation. But they are far from adequate. He looks to his disciples for a more appropriate response: "Who do you say that I am?" (v. 20a). Speaking on behalf of all, Peter gets it right: "You are the Christ" (v. 20b). Jesus is more than a prophet: he is the long-awaited Son of David, destined to usher in the messianic age.

[1] In Luke's gospel at this point there is nothing corresponding to the large block making up Mark 6:45–8:26, where, after a long discourse on what is meant by clean and unclean, Jesus journeys in areas beyond the confines of Galilee, venturing into Gentile regions. If this so-called "great omission" was intentional on Luke's part, it probably reflects reluctance to portray Jesus interacting with Gentiles during his historical life; for Luke the Gentile mission belongs to the time of the church; see Acts 1:8.

As readers of the gospel, we have known this truth from the start; it was central to the infancy stories. But the disciples have had to deduce it from what they have seen Jesus say and do. Even now they are to keep this knowledge to themselves (v. 21). They are to do so because the truth that Jesus is the Messiah can never stand alone. It must immediately be qualified by awareness of the kind of Messiah he is destined to be: not the Messiah of conventional expectation but a Messiah destined to suffer and die and *so* (through suffering and death) enter his messianic glory (see 24:26, 46-47).

We have seen Jesus wrestling with this paradox at the time of his temptation (4:1-13): Will he take advantage of his messianic status and follow an exalted and easy road to world dominion? Or will he go the way marked out by God, treading the ordinary human path of suffering and death? The disciples must now confront this issue. It will dominate the rest of the gospel. No sooner, then, is Jesus' identity as Messiah out in the open than it is immediately qualified in a first prophecy of the passion: "The Son of Man must undergo great suffering, and be rejected by the elders, chief priests, and scribes, and be killed, and on the third day be raised" (v. 22).

In the Lukan account (contrast Mark 8:32-33; Matt 16:22-23) neither Peter nor any of the other disciples contest this juxtaposition of messiahship and suffering. The gospel moves immediately to the short instruction (9:23-27) where, having foretold his own destiny to suffer, Jesus makes clear that suffering will be the lot of his disciples as well. They must deny themselves, take up their cross daily, and follow in his steps.

The qualifier "daily" (v. 23) is peculiar to Luke—an instance once again of his sense of Christianity as a spirituality for the long haul. In the ancient world the cross was nothing but an instrument of death. What is at stake is a daily dying to self, a loss of the "life" created by the self's superficial desires, in order to gain the life that fulfills the self's deepest longing—to love and be loved, to give and receive in a communion of love, both human and divine.[2]

The instruction ends (vv. 26-27) with a glance to the future—to the coming great reversal that is so constantly the background to Jesus' teaching (6:20-26). Those who now find the prospect of the cross "shameful"—certainly the general human view of the cross—will find themselves an

---

[2] This is not to deny that instruction may also have in mind actual physical loss of life for the sake of the gospel. Luke is well aware that Christians suffered persecution (6:22; 12:2-12; 21:12-19; see also 2 Cor 4:7-15).

object of shame to the Son of Man when he comes in the glory of the Father and of the holy angels. The choice is stark: to be vindicated now in the sight of the world or to share in Jesus' heavenly vindication, one that will be definitive and lasting.[3]

The Transfiguration: 9:28-36

The mysterious episode of the transfiguration anticipates that divine vindication.[4] While it certainly describes an experience of Jesus, its location in the gospel at this point seems designed to help the disciples come to terms with the difficult message they have received: Jesus may be the Messiah, but following this Messiah will mean for the present a life of "daily dying."

Once again the experience occurs while Jesus is at prayer (v. 28, v. 29). The three select disciples (Peter, John, and James) see the appearance of his face changed. His clothes, too, are transformed into dazzling whiteness, a feature regularly associated with heavenly reality in the biblical tradition. Two leading figures of that tradition, Moses and Elijah, appear in similar glory and converse with him (v. 30). The appearance of these two fulfills the expectation that both would in some sense return to earth in the messianic age.[5] Their presence completes the picture of messianic glory.

In contrast to Mark (9:4) and Matthew (17:3), Luke tells us the subject of the heavenly conversation. It has to do with the "departure" (Greek: *exodos*) that Jesus is to "accomplish" in Jerusalem (v. 31).[6] "Exodus," of

---

[3] The promise in v. 27 ("But truly I tell you, there are some standing here who will not taste death before they see the kingdom of God") presumably referred originally—on the lips of Jesus himself—to the coming of the Son of Man at the end of time. In the Gospel of Luke, and perhaps already in Mark (9:1), the saying probably refers to the anticipatory glimpse of that coming that three of the disciples receive in the following scene of the transfiguration.

[4] It seems better to see the transfiguration as an anticipation of Jesus' return in glory at the end of time (Parousia), rather than to his resurrection. On this see Joseph A. Fitzmyer, *The Gospel according to Luke I-IX*, AB 28 (Garden City, NY: Doubleday, 1981), 786, 789–90.

[5] With regard to Moses, the tradition is based upon his promise in Deut 18:15-18 that God would raise up a prophet like himself. The tradition concerning Elijah's return stems from Mal 3:1; 4:4-5.

[6] Both figures are well qualified to speak about the mysterious end of Jesus' life since, according to the biblical tradition, both experienced mysterious conclusions to their own lives upon earth. According to 2 Kgs 2:9-11, Elijah did not

course, recalls God's liberation of Israel from slavery in Egypt. Here the
allusion is clearly to Jesus' own death, of which he had just been speaking (v. 22). It is called "exodus" because, although at one level it will
be an act of injustice brought about by hostile human authorities, on a
deeper plane it will be a divine liberation comparable with, and indeed
fulfilling, the Exodus of old.[7] It will also be an "exodus" in that, through
resurrection and ascension, Jesus will "pass through" the bonds of death
to messianic glory—just as earlier at Nazareth he had "passed through"
the crowd intent on lynching him and gone on his way (4:29-30).

As the vision begins to wane (v. 33), Peter proposes the building of
three "booths," one for each of the figures. "Booths" probably alludes to
the feast of Tabernacles, a joyous harvest feast that featured in popular
imagination as an anticipation or symbol of the messianic age. The sense,
then, would be that Peter correctly discerns the messianic nature of the
vision and seeks to hold on to it. But, as the note about his "not knowing" makes clear, this aspiration is misguided on two accounts. First,
by seeking to build "three booths," Peter is placing all three messianic
figures on the same level; he has not grasped that Jesus' status is unique.
Secondly, in seeking to hold on to the experience, he shows that he has
failed to hear what Jesus has been saying: that before messianic glory
there has to be the shame and suffering of the cross.

The intensification of the experience that follows (vv. 34-35) addresses
this misunderstanding. The overshadowing cloud signals the presence of
God.[8] The voice that the terrified disciples hear from heaven proclaims
the true identity and status of Jesus ("My Son, my Chosen One")[9] and
enjoins full attention to his words ("listen to him!"). What they have to

---

die but was taken up to heaven in a fiery chariot. Deut 34:5-6 notes briefly that
Moses died but then adds that to this day no one knows where he was buried.
This mysterious comment gave rise to speculation, reflected in post-biblical
Jewish literature, concerning the "assumption" of Moses (into heaven).

[7] Luke uses the word "accomplish" with reference to events that occur
in fulfillment of a long-standing divine plan preannounced in the Scriptures
(cf. 1:1).

[8] In the biblical tradition a cloud frequently serves to indicate the proximity
or presence of the unseen God (Exod 13:21-22; 24:16-18; 33:9-10). Significantly,
the last time Luke has used the word "overshadow" (Greek: *episkiazein*) has
been with reference to the "overshadowing" of Mary by the Holy Spirit to
bring about the conception of Jesus (1:35).

[9] Jesus, of course, had received a similar assurance from heaven at his
"anointing" with the Spirit immediately following his baptism (3:22). Luke's

"listen" to is the prediction of the passion and the instruction on the conditions of discipleship that he has just been giving. Had they really taken that to heart, they would not now be seeking to retain the vision. They would understand it as an assurance that the messianic glory will one day come but only via the route that Jesus had described.

So the disciples have to hold two truths about Jesus in mysterious tension. On the one hand, as God's Son and Chosen One, he has a status totally outstripping that of conventional messianic expectation (recall Gabriel's "two-stage" explanation to Mary at the annunciation of his birth [1:32-33 and 1:35]). On the other hand, precisely as God's obedient Son, his messianic mission will be that of bringing freedom ("exodus"), to Israel and ultimately to the world, through a costly entry into its pain and suffering. Messianic glory, of which they have now caught a glimpse, will come only after that. This is the tension Jesus had wrestled with in the time of temptation that followed his baptism (3:21-22; 4:1-13). Now it is something that the disciples have to grapple with as well.[10]

Further Misunderstandings and Clarifications: 9:37-50

Following the transfiguration, the instruction of the disciples continues in a swift flow of rather disparate scenes.[11] The exalted experience on the mountain gives way to down-to-earth reality in the shape of a distraught father and his gravely afflicted son (vv. 37-43a). What would almost certainly be recognized as epilepsy today, the biblical narrative presents as demonic possession. Jesus rebukes the spirit, heals the boy, and, in a typical Lukan touch, gives him back to his father (v. 42; cf. 7:15). Once again a family finds healing.

The main point of the episode in this place, however, is not simply to record another mighty work of Jesus. The focus is upon the disciples and, more precisely, on their inability to deal with the situation. Hence the force of Jesus' complaint when the father explains this to him (vv. 40-41). The incident, as Luke describes it, also comes immediately before

---

gospel, like that of Mark (1:11; contrast Matt 3:17), describes this as a private communication to Jesus.

[10] At this point it is only for them, as the notice at the end of v. 36 makes clear.

[11] Nothing in Luke corresponds to the discussion about Elijah that takes place according to Mark (9:9-13) and Matthew (17:9-13) immediately after Jesus and the three disciples descend from the mountain. In those accounts Jesus identifies John the Baptist with Elijah. Luke has already finished with John and, in any case, he prefers to depict Jesus rather than John in the guise of Elijah.

a second prophecy of the passion (9:43b-44), which, again, meets with incomprehension and fear on the part of disciples (v. 45).

Putting all this together, the upshot seems to be that the disciples will be helpless to "exorcise" the evil in the world—exemplified by this case of possession before them—unless they are prepared to come to terms with and follow the suffering of Jesus. Jesus is not going to deal with the world's evil by being a Messiah in a triumphant and worldly way—that was what the temptation was all about. He is confronting and overcoming evil by entering into the suffering of the world, effecting healing and liberation from within. That is his way because it is God's way. The disciples will share his effectiveness against evil only insofar as they are prepared to follow the same path.

The gap between what Jesus has just been trying to impart and the disciples' understanding is again clear when they argue about which one of them is the greatest (vv. 46-48). Once more he shows a prophetic awareness of "inner thoughts" (see also 5:22; 6:8; 7:40) and brings them to the surface (v. 47). He disarms their pretensions by taking a little child and speaking of what we might call a "chain of welcome," running from the child, to himself, to his Father ("the One who sent me" [v. 48]). In Jesus' perspective, the route to the welcoming of God into one's life and community runs through the little ones represented by this child. It is they who access and channel the hospitality of God.

The activity of an exorcist who, though not one of Jesus' followers, uses his name to cast out demons provides a further opportunity for the disciples to learn (9:49-50). Their inclination is to put a stop to such independent activity. But in this they are misguided. The community of the kingdom does not have to cling to its prerogatives in an exclusivist way. If God's grace, which has been shown to be so effective on the margins of the community, can also operate beyond them, that is something to welcome rather than deplore. The narrative of Acts will show the Spirit constantly out in front of the church's understanding (see esp. Acts 10:1–11:18).

The Journey to Jerusalem Begins
9:51–10:24

At this point (9:51) Luke's gospel adopts the form of a long journey to Jerusalem on the part of Jesus.[1] It was in Jerusalem that the entire drama began: with the annunciation to Zechariah in the temple (1:5-22). The temple was also the scene of Simeon's prediction concerning the role and destiny of Jesus (2:34-35). At age twelve, in an initiative of startling independence, Jesus again visited the temple, dubbing it "my Father's house" (2:49). If Jesus is the Messiah, as his closest disciples have acknowledged (9:20), there must come a time when he will leave Galilee to "visit" and take possession of Jerusalem, the city of the Messiah, Son of David.

The time to set out on that project has arrived. However, as we have seen, Jesus has only allowed his disciples to become aware of his status as Messiah in the context of a more somber truth: that he is destined to be betrayed, to suffer grievously, and to be put to death (9:22; 9:44). The transfiguration held these two paradoxical truths together. In particular, the conversation between Jesus and the two prophetic figures, Moses and Elijah, had as its subject the "exodus" that Jesus is to "accomplish" in Jerusalem. So Jesus' journey to take possession of David's city is also a journey laden with tension and foreboding. That is why, presumably, it begins with solemn and striking language: "When the days drew near for him to be taken up,[2] [Jesus] set his face to go to Jerusalem" (9:51).

---

[1] Luke has chosen to gather together in this section most of the sayings material he derived from the source he shares with Matthew ("Q") and also his own special tradition ("L"). The section comprising 9:51–18:14, then, makes up a large block ("Luke's Great Insertion") where Luke departs from Mark. At 18:15 (corresponding to Mark 10:13) Luke takes up once more the Markan account of Jesus' journey.

[2] "Taken up" recalls precisely what happened to Elijah (2 Kgs 2:1) and (in a looser sense according to the postbiblical Jewish tradition) to Moses—the conversation partners of Jesus at the transfiguration.

"Set his face" communicates the sense of a fixed determination against a strong temptation to do the opposite.[3] The phrase strikes a note that will sound throughout the gospel from here on. Something of the aura of joyful celebration that attended the early ministry in Galilee falls away. A tougher, more demanding Jesus now emerges, a person on the way to a difficult destiny. As well as acceptance, there are warnings of judgment and a heightening sense of crisis. Will the city of David be "hospitable" to its messianic "visitor" or not? And, if not, what will be the outcome within the wider design of God?[4]

For most of the journey Jesus is speaking rather than acting. Those whom he addresses fall basically into three groups.[5] First, there are the disciples, the inner circle who for the most part receive positive instruction. Then there are the crowds, who must be summoned in more threatening tones to repentance and conversion. Finally, there are those increasingly emerging as adversaries, especially the Pharisees and lawyers; Jesus confronts their hostility with prophetic utterances and parables. Luke is careful to indicate the audience in each case. Taking account of this helps interpret the variety of tones in which Jesus speaks in this part of the gospel.

Setting a Pattern for the Journey: 9:52-56

Two episodes, each in its own way, set a tone or "direction" for the journey that now begins. In the first (9:52-56), a Samaritan village proves inhospitable to messengers sent ahead by Jesus. James and John propose a drastic response: Why not, like the prophet Elijah (2 Kgs 1:10, 12), call down upon the village destructive fire from heaven? But Jesus will have none of it. This is not his way to deal with inhospitality. Nor, happily, is

---

[3] "Set his face" recalls the statement of the Servant figure in Isa 50:7: "I have set my face like flint, and I know that I shall not be put to shame."

[4] After the initial indication in 9:51 there are, to be sure, occasional further hints that Jesus is on a journey (9:57; 10:38; 13:22, 33; 14:25; 17:11; 18:3; 19:11, 28). But it is impossible to trace the journey in any strict geographical sense nor does there appear to be some master plan organizing the great mass of material contained within the ambit of the "journey" (9:51–19:44). While Luke locates much of the traditional material that came to him within the framework of a journey, my sense is that it is not precisely the journey as such that is important (as it is indeed for Mark) but rather the fact that Jesus is on a journey to *Jerusalem*.

[5] Here I am indebted especially to Luke Timothy Johnson, *The Gospel of Luke*, Sacra Pagina 3 (Collegeville, MN: Liturgical Press, 1991), 164–65.

it the last word on Samaria and Samaritans in the gospel; they will have a better day (10:29-37; 17:11-19; also Acts 8:4-25). The episode signals the approach Jesus will take in the face of much more serious inhospitality from Jerusalem.

Jesus' response to three people who would be his companions on the journey (9:57-62) sets a pattern in a rather different direction. He makes clear to the first who offers that following him means a life of wandering with no guaranteed lodging (vv. 57-58). The second and the third—one called by Jesus (vv. 59-60), the other offering himself (vv. 61-62)—both want a little space before coming along; each has important family duties to attend to. In contrast again to Elijah, who did allow his disciple Elisha to say goodbye to his parents (1 Kgs 19:19-21), Jesus insists that the urgency of the kingdom has priority over family ties. The kingdom is about rescuing human beings for life in a world fast sliding to destruction.

Missionaries of the Kingdom: 10:1-20

The same sense of urgency pervades a second sending-out of disciples on the part of Jesus. Earlier, in Galilee, Jesus had sent out the Twelve to heal and proclaim the kingdom (9:1-6). Now Jesus sends ahead of him seventy[6] disciples in pairs (vv. 1-16).[7]

The instructions for the missionaries are similar to those already given to the Twelve: lightness of equipment, reliance upon hospitality, and so forth (vv. 4-7). This time, however, there is far greater premonition of hostility and rejection.[8] The missionaries who go before Jesus will be vulnerable—like lambs sent among wolves (v. 3). Like him (4:18-30),

---

[6] The textual tradition is divided upon whether the number is seventy or seventy-two. Most interpreters believe it is virtually impossible to decide for one figure over against the other.

[7] The apprenticing of this wider group may reflect Moses' selection of seventy elders to assist him in the governance of Israel (Exod 24:1; Num 11:16, 24), further reinforcing the portrayal of Jesus in this part of the gospel as a prophet like Moses. The number may also reflect the number of the nations of the world according to the table in Gen 10:2-31. In this case the sending may anticipate and model the post-Pentecost evangelization of the world; see Robert C. Tannehill, *The Narrative Unity of Luke-Acts: A Literary Interpretation: Volume One: The Gospel according to Luke* (Philadelphia: Fortress, 1986), 233.

[8] The curious injunction "greet no one on the way" (v. 4) may be in view of travel through hostile areas—e.g., Samaria (see 9:53)—or it may reflect the need for total single-mindedness in view of the urgency of the task (the proclamation of the imminent kingdom).

they will experience both hospitality and inhospitality, acceptance and rejection. Rejection they are to counter with prophetic gestures signaling the imminence of the kingdom (v. 11). When rejected they can be secure in the knowledge that proverbially inhospitable Sodom will fare better at the judgment than towns that are inhospitable to them (v. 13)[9]—an allusion that leads to a series of woes pronounced upon Galilean cities resistant to the summons to conversion (vv. 13-15).

The tone, then, is grim. But the narrative prepares Christian missionaries for the rejection that will inevitably be their lot as emissaries of the kingdom. It is all part of Luke's wider theme of seeking to incorporate the rejection of Jesus in Jerusalem and the subsequent rejection of the Christian gospel by most of Israel within the wider saving plan of God. Rejection of the missionaries is also rejection of Jesus and ultimately rejection of the One who sent him into the world to offer it the hospitality of God (v. 16). Rejection is painful, but God's grace can overcome it and ultimately win through.

This time, however, the mission is a great success. The seventy return in joy, announcing their victory over demonic power (10:17-20). Jesus acknowledges their success ("I watched Satan fall from heaven like a flash of lightning" [v. 18][10]) and teaches them to draw confidence from it (v. 19). But he points to a greater reason for joy: that their "names are written in heaven" (v. 20).[11] Christian joy does not ultimately rest upon achievement. It rests upon a deep sense of relationship with God and a knowledge of the destiny to which that relationship leads.

---

[9] While Sodom was a byword for immorality in general, the narrative of Gen 19:1-25 interprets its destruction as punishment for the betrayal of hospitality toward the two messengers (angels) of God whom Lot had taken in.

[10] The sense here seems to be that, while the missionaries have been at work, Jesus has viewed their successful exorcising efforts as a wholesale dethroning of Satan, the prince of demons. At this point in the narrative the assertion seems overdrawn—Satan is far from conquered. It is probably meant in an open-ended way in the sense that not only the work of these missionaries but also that of their successors in the Christian church entails a cosmic dethroning of Satan, which will be definitive only at the end of time.

[11] The image behind the phrase "written in heaven" derives from the custom in the ancient world for cities and kingdoms to draw up lists of those enjoying rights of citizenship within them. The sense, then, is that of being "citizens of heaven" (God's kingdom) with all the rights and privileges and prospects that this holds out; see Phil 3:20; 4:3; see further Joseph A. Fitzmyer, *The Gospel according to Luke X-XXIV*, AB 28A (Garden City, NY: Doubleday, 1985), 863–64.

A Moment of Joy Shared with the Disciples: 10:21-24

If the disciples have this grounds for joy, Jesus has it in a preeminent degree. In a singular passage[12] the gospel gives us entrance for a moment into the experience of Jesus where he rejoices in the Holy Spirit and thanks the Father for the "revelation" that has been hidden from the wise and intelligent and revealed to "mere infants" (v. 21). What has been revealed is nothing less than the knowledge Father and Son have of each other within the relationship that is theirs (v. 22). The knowledge involved is not so much intellectual knowledge as "knowledge" in the biblical sense, meaning intimate experience of another person with whom one is in relationship. The Fourth Gospel presents the human life of Jesus as an enactment in the world of the eternal relationship between Father and Son—something that renders this relationship accessible to human beings so that, being drawn into it, they may share the (eternal) life and love that Jesus has from the Father.[13] What is so remarkable about the present passage (and its parallel in Matthew [11:25-27]) is that here in the Synoptic tradition we seem to have a fleeting glimpse of what in the Fourth Gospel is a sustained theme (climaxing in the "Priestly Prayer" of Jesus in John 17). It may be only a glimpse but, taken along with Jesus' enigmatic words in the temple at age twelve (2:49b) and the moments of divine assurance following the baptism (3:22) and transfiguration (9:35), it suggests that primary in Luke's presentation of Jesus is also the sense of a unique relationship with God into which he wishes to draw human beings.

This relationship is the ultimate basis for the hospitality of God and for the joy that those who discover it experience. It lies at the heart of the kingdom of God as proclaimed by Jesus and is in this sense prior to any social or political program that the arrival of the kingdom entails—while not excluding, and in many respects requiring, radical sociopolitical transformation of present structures (recall the *Magnificat*, the Beatitudes, etc.).

---

[12] Once dubbed a "bolt from the Johannine heaven," this sequence (paralleled in Matt 11:25-27 and therefore from the source "Q") seems to reflect the Christology of the Fourth Gospel rather than the Synoptic tradition (see esp. John 10:15). I see no firm grounds for excluding its provenance from the lips of Jesus himself—other than a priori prejudice against the possibility that Jesus might have expressed relationship to God in such terms. For a thorough discussion, see Fitzmyer, *Luke X-XXIV*, 870.

[13] See C. H. Dodd, *The Interpretation of the Fourth Gospel* (Cambridge [UK]: Cambridge University, 1953), 262.

This "knowledge" is something to which the little ones ("infants") have privileged access, while for the "wise and intelligent" it remains "hidden" (v. 21b). The statement goes along with the constant insistence throughout the gospel that the poor and marginalized are particularly the objects and beneficiaries of God's saving design. It does not mean that education and theological formation, in particular, are barriers to relationship with God; faith necessarily seeks understanding. But faith must go beyond understanding, into a realm where understanding falters and one is simply led, unknowing, into the deeper mystery of God.

It is in view of this that Jesus concludes the sequence by turning to the disciples and pronouncing a blessing upon them (10:23-24). In many ways representative of the little ones of the world, grasped by the kingdom and the relationship it brings, they see and hear what was denied to many prophets and kings: the knowledge of God communicated by Jesus. One recalls Jesus' reflection upon John the Baptist (7:28): he may be greater than all born of women, but the least in the kingdom of God is greater than he.

A sequence, then, that began with mission (10:1-16) concludes on this joyful note of highly privileged and intimate relationship with God. There is no tension in this development. Jesus' own mission flows entirely out of his relationship with the Father revealed here for a moment. Those who are being apprenticed to this mission must understand that the same intimacy and relationship is there for them. Only this knowledge will keep them going along with Jesus toward the difficult and conflictual destiny awaiting him in Jerusalem.

The Way to Eternal Life

10:25–11:13

Jesus' assurance that the missionaries' names are "written in heaven" (10:20) has introduced the theme of eternal life with God. The section that follows seems to catch up and develop this theme as it begins with a lawyer's question: "Teacher, . . . what must I do to inherit eternal life?" (10:25). Jesus' counter question (v. 26) about what the lawyer "reads in the law" elicits a response (v. 27) in terms of fulfilling the twin commandments: to love God and to love one's neighbor. The parable of the Good Samaritan (10:29-37) addresses the second part of the commandment, while the episode with Martha and Mary (10:38-42) can be seen as addressing the first. There is, then, a natural progression to the instruction on prayer that follows (11:1-13). This gives some principle of organization for the entire sequence in 10:25–11:13.

How to Inherit Eternal Life: 10:25-42

The Lawyer's Question: 10:25-28

The question concerning eternal life is put by a "lawyer" (v. 25). To modern ears "lawyer" suggests a professional expert in the secular legal system. Jewish law, however, embraced the whole of life without distinction between the secular and religious spheres. What we have here is a question from an expert in the law of Moses. The question is hostile, designed to "test" Jesus (v. 25). It seeks to pit him in some way over against the law, to draw out from him a suggestion that one can inherit eternal life while bypassing the law.

Jesus will not have this for a moment. As so often, he throws the question back to the questioner (v. 26) and draws from him a perfectly satisfactory answer in terms of the law (v. 27). The lawyer cites as a single commandment the injunction to "love the Lord your God with all your heart, and with all your soul, and with all your strength, and with all your mind" from Deuteronomy 6:5 and the command to "love your neighbor as yourself" from Leviticus 19:18.[1] "Do this," says Jesus, "and you will live" (v. 28b). In other words, the law itself, understood holistically, with the separate commandments to love God and to love one's neighbor brought into unity and mutual interaction, provides the path to life. Jesus is not outside or bypassing the law.

But the expert is not satisfied. He suspects—rightly as it turns out—that Jesus may be pushing the term "neighbor" further than the conventional understanding where it was restricted basically to fellow Israelites.[2] So he presses his case: "Who is my neighbor?" (v. 29).

The Parable of the Good Samaritan: 10:30-37

The lawyer's persistence prompts Jesus to tell one of his most famous parables. It is traditionally known as the "Good Samaritan," a title that immediately blunts its impact for the reader. Centuries of holding together the adjective "good" and the noun "Samaritan" have dulled us to the explosive tension of the phrase in the world of Jesus. The hostility between Jews and Samaritans at the time makes the phrase an oxymoron—as a phrase like "good terrorist" would be for us.

As originally told by Jesus (abstracted, that is, from the setting Luke has provided), the parable draws the hearer into the perspective of the wounded, half-dead traveler. The passing parade of three persons sets up a pattern that cumulatively builds up expectation. A *certain class of persons* on a journey *arrives* at that place, *sees* (the wounded traveler), and *responds*. In the first two cases—that of the priest and the Levite—the response is "to see" and then "pass by on the other side." This is to avoid the defilement from contact with the dead—or soon to be dead—which

---

[1] In the Matthean (22:34-40) and Markan (12:28-31) parallels the lawyer ("scribe" in Mark) asks Jesus which of the commandments is the greatest and Jesus provides the answer himself, dividing what is in Luke a single double commandment into the "greatest" (Matthew) or "first" (Mark) commandment (Deut 6:5) and "the second" (Lev 19:18). Whether the two commandments (love of God/love of neighbor) had been brought together in this way in Judaism prior to Jesus is not clear; see further, Joseph A. Fitzmyer, *The Gospel according to Luke X-XXIV*, AB 28A (Garden City, NY: Doubleday, 1985), 879; John P. Meier, *A Marginal Jew: Rethinking the Historical Jesus*, vol. 4: *Law and Love* (New Haven, CT: Yale University Press, 2009), 499–528, esp. the positive conclusion regarding historicity expressed on p. 519 and pp. 526–27.

[2] Lev 19:33-34 extended "neighbor" to the resident alien in the land but this was understood fairly restrictively; see further, Fitzmyer, *Luke X-XXIV*, 880–81.

would prevent them, according to the law, from carrying out their religious duties. Who does the audience expect the third passerby to be? In view of the pattern of descending order of dignity—from priest to Levite—now set up, the expectation would probably be a Jewish layperson—like Jesus and the bulk of his audience: this one will do the right thing, pick up the dirty work from which the law exempts the other two. So the audience is probably expecting something of an "anti-clerical" ending at the expense of the religious functionaries.

That the third person arriving on the scene should be a Samaritan creates a frisson in the hearers. Surely this alien will also "see" and "pass by on the other side"—or even see if there is anything further to rob from the man! Instead, when he "sees" he is "overcome with compassion" (*esplagchnisthē*)[3] and sets about fulfilling in a most extravagant way the duties of mercy and hospitality the other two had ignored (vv. 33-34). Beyond "first aid," he draws generously on his own funds to ensure that the innkeeper will be unstinting in his care for the man until his own return (v. 35).

The story compels its (Jewish) audience to disentangle from the word "Samaritan" the inevitable label "bad," to hold together the previously antipathetic notions "Samaritan" and "good." Set worlds of conviction and prejudice crash down. If the law—or a particular understanding of it—prevented the priest and Levite from rescuing human life in this way, then there is something flawed about that understanding. It cuts against the heart of the law as found in the twofold commandment binding together love of God and love of neighbor. Jesus, in the parable, has not overthrown or bypassed the law. He has simply shown that to fulfill the law's true intent the notion of "neighbor" has to be drastically revised.

In Luke's setting (vv. 36-37), when the parable proper is over, Jesus takes the offensive, as it were, and makes the lawyer draw the application (v. 36).[4] But in so doing he changes the terms of reference. The lawyer had asked, "Who is my neighbor?" (v. 29). Jesus asks, "Which

---

[3] The Greek word communicates (even in its sound!) the sense of a great wave breaking over one. The same word describes Jesus' reaction to the plight of the widow of Nain (7:13) and that of the father on seeing his returning younger son in the parable of the Lost Son (15:20).

[4] It is often said that Luke has turned Jesus' parable into an example story—especially because the lawyer is told in the end "Go and do likewise" (v. 37b). But in its Lukan setting the story still functions as a parable: it blows apart old understandings and creates new meaning. See further on the understanding of the parable presented here, John Dominic Crossan, *The Dark Interval: Towards*

of the three . . . proved neighbor to the man who fell into the hands of robbers?" (v. 36). At the end of the parable it is not a question of where and how far I should draw the limits of the notion "neighbor"—to see how far my obligations of "love" extend. It is a question of imitating the hospitality shown by the despised alien who broke through the barriers of ethnic and religious prejudice to minister to a fellow human being in need.[5] The concept of "neighbor" shifts from being a tag that I may or may not apply to another, to being a quality or a vocation that I take upon myself and actively live out.

This is the way to inherit eternal life. The God whom one is attempting to love with all one's heart is the God who reaches out to the world in compassion in the same way as the Good Samaritan did.[6] In the ministry of Jesus, which the church has to continue, God offers extravagant, life-giving hospitality to wounded and half-dead humanity. The way to eternal life is to allow oneself to become an active instrument and channel of that same boundary-breaking hospitality.

Centuries of repetition of the phrase "Good Samaritan" has dulled Christian sensitivity to the "bite" of this parable. We are so accustomed to putting the two words "good" and "Samaritan" together that the force of the oxymoron in its Palestinian setting has been lost.[7] Even in general parlance "Good Samaritan" has become a byword for anyone who performs a notably philanthropic act. If the parable is to regain its power in preaching and more general Christian discourse, something of the original oxymoron has to be recaptured or at least illustrated in a

---

a Theology of Story (Niles, IL: Argus Communications, 1975), 104–8; John R. Donahue, *The Gospel in Parable* (Philadelphia: Fortress, 1988), 128–34.

[5] "The point, we learn, is not who deserves to be cared for, but rather the demand to become a person who treats everyone encountered—however frightening, alien, naked or defenseless—with compassion: 'you go and do the same.' Jesus does not clarify a point of law, but transmutes law to gospel" (Luke Timothy Johnson, *The Gospel of Luke*, Sacra Pagina 3 [Collegeville, MN: Liturgical Press, 1991], 175).

[6] As Donahue notes (*Gospel in Parable*, 133–34), "Patristic allegory, though fanciful in detail, was perhaps not too far afield when it identified the Samaritan with Christ coming to the aid of wounded humanity." For a history of interpretation see also, François Bovon, *A Commentary on the Gospel of Luke*, Hermeneia, vol. 2 (Minneapolis: Fortress, 2013), 60–65.

[7] In Australia, for over a century and a half, a much loved congregation of Catholic religious women have served the education of the poor under the name "The Good Samaritans."

contemporary way. In particular, we have to see how, as so often in Luke, it challenges the "label" that conventional societal understanding places upon the other, the different, the "not one of us," to keep them at a safe distance. The Samaritan in the parable did not see "a Jew" or an alien. He simply saw a fellow human being in dire need. His multiple actions of care and kindness flowed from that vision. This is the fundamental transformation that the parable, then as now, seeks to promote.

The Hospitality of Martha and Mary: 10:38-42

Interpretation of the following episode, where Jesus receives hospital-ity in the house of two sisters, Martha and Mary, has been controversial in recent times. Understandably, the scene has been a focus of feminist concern and, on this score, has received a mixed evaluation. A good deal depends upon the way in which one understands the activity of Martha. If what she is "busy about" is simply traditional woman's work in the kitchen, then Jesus can be seen as defending, in Mary, the right of women disciples to be free from such duties in order to receive from him the kind of instruction that will equip them for leadership in the community, to be no different from male disciples in this respect. If, on the other hand, Martha instances effective and leading action in the community, then the commendation of Mary looks like a stratagem on Luke's part to return women in the community to a passive role more in keeping with traditional views. If the latter is the case, then Luke is no feminist hero.[8]

While I understand feminist interest in the passage, I am not sure that Luke's main point here is to say something—positive or negative—about the status of women. The fact that the two persons who give hospitality to Jesus are women may not be central. The presence of patterns familiar from other places in Luke points in a rather different direction.

The passage presents Martha as the dominant figure, the one who welcomes ("receives") Jesus into her home and offers hospitality (v. 38b).[9] Mary is simply "her sister"—very much the junior partner, one suspects. But now, characteristically for Luke, it is Mary, the more marginalized figure, who offers the kind of hospitality that Jesus commends.

---

[8] For a thorough review of feminist criticism of the passage, see Barbara E. Reid, *Choosing the Better Part? Women in the Gospel of Luke* (Collegeville, MN: Liturgical Press, 1996), 144–62.

[9] In the sequence featuring the two sisters in John 12:1-8, Martha again does the serving (v. 2) while Mary attends to Jesus—in this case anointing his feet with precious ointment (v. 3).

Once again, we have a "triangular" situation. Mary simply listens to Jesus, sitting at his feet in the attitude of a disciple. Martha complains about this and asks Jesus to send Mary back to the more customary role of serving. As in the case of the woman who gate-crashed the banquet in the house of Simon the Pharisee (7:36-50), Jesus first admonishes the one who criticizes and then defends the one attacked. Martha has gone overboard in the duties of hospitality; in the way of traditional Middle Eastern hospitality, she is busy about preparing many dishes when, as far as Jesus is concerned, only one is needed.[10] Mary has "chosen" (she is not passive; her action is the result of a free choice) "the better portion" (v. 42b). "Portion" (*meris*) here should, I believe, not be generalized but understood quite literally to refer to a portion of food being offered. This means that what Jesus is doing, in characteristic mode, is taking the meal context and transforming it into an image of what *he*, as distinct from the sisters, has to offer. Martha is busy about offering hospitality to him. But he has a deeper hospitality to set before them: the hospitality of his word, "the better portion," which Mary has recognized and chosen to take.

So again, then, we have the hospitality "exchange" that is a feature of Luke. Jesus receives hospitality but has himself a deeper hospitality to provide. Where Martha is too "busy" providing the former, Mary has recognized who this visitor is and received him with a hospitality of loving attention and listening that is truly appropriate. The way she has chosen will not be "taken away from her" (v. 42c)—in the sense of her being sent out into the kitchen—because this would destroy the hospitality that she, the more marginal one, is both receiving and offering in turn. The implication is that Martha should be content with preparing the one dish that ordinary hospitality requires and join Mary in her deeper hospitality. In this way she will experience what her sister is experiencing: their visitor's welcome into the hospitality of God.

The episode makes a subtle point. Frenetic service, even service of the Lord, can be a deceptive distraction from what the Lord really wants. Luke has already warned that the grasp of the word can be choked by the cares and worries of life (8:14 [application of the parable of the Sower]). Here the cares and worries seem well justified—are they not in the service of the Lord? But precisely therein lies the power of the temptation, the great deceit under the guise of good. True hospitality—even

---

[10] "Only one" seems to be the best choice in what is a very confused manuscript tradition at this point (v. 42): "only one"; "few things"; "few things . . . or even only one"; see further, Fitzmyer, *Luke X-XXIV*, 894.

that given directly to the Lord—attends to what the guest really wants and has to give.

Praying to a Hospitable God: 11:1-13

The commendation of Mary's single-minded attention to the Lord leads naturally into a request by the disciples that Jesus should teach them how to pray (11:1). Once again, they see him at prayer (v. 1a) and they know that John the Baptist had taught his disciples about prayer. So it is natural that they should look to Jesus for guidance in this matter. Jesus responds by giving them a form of words (the Lord's Prayer [11:2-4]). But this is not all—or even the main thing. Jesus goes on to give them a lengthy instruction on the attitude of confidence with which the disciples must approach God in prayer (vv. 5-13).

The Lord's Prayer: 11:2-4

Luke's gospel provides a more concise form of the Lord's Prayer than the version found in Matthew (6:9-13) that liturgical usage has rendered so familiar. The basic content, however, is the same. The additional elements in Matthew largely repeat, in alternative phrases, petitions common to both versions.

The prayer begins by invoking God as "Father" (v. 2). The disciples speak as members of the "household" or "family" of God into which they have been introduced by Jesus (cf. 8:19-21). They have heard Jesus thanking the "Lord of heaven and earth" as "Father" (10:21-22)[11] and have been assured of the blessedness they enjoy in the relationship with God that is now theirs (10:23-24). Now they are being taught to pray out of that relationship, calling God "Father" in their own turn.

The particular petitions come across in translation as wishes ("May . . . "). But in the original language of Jesus (Aramaic) they were probably far stronger—in effect telling God to bring about what they propose.

---

[11] Behind the simple Greek address *pater* would seem to lie the Aramaic *Abba*, the address to the male parent in the Jewish family—not quite as formal as "Father" and not so babyish as "Daddy," but lying somewhere between ("Dad"?). "*Abba*" seems to have been Jesus' characteristic way of addressing God; see Mark 14:36. In Rom 8:15 and Gal 4:6 Paul refers to the Spirit's prompting believers to address God in this way. On the connection between this and the likely practice of Jesus, see further, Brendan Byrne, *A Costly Freedom: A Theological Reading of Mark's Gospel* (Collegeville, MN: Liturgical Press, 2008), 224, n. 30.

As such they follow a distinct logic: from a focus solely upon God in the first ("Bring it about that your name is sanctified"), to what God ought to achieve in the world ("Make your kingdom come"), to what the community needs from God—sustenance, forgiveness, rescue from overwhelming tribulation. The community that prays the prayer sees itself as a beachhead of the kingdom in the present world, reclaiming it for life and humanity. Since, like its Israelite ancestor of old, the community is on a journey, it looks to God for sustenance—that God will provide day by day the food needed for life (v. 3).[12] Likewise, because it is a community not yet arrived at the perfection of the kingdom, it is a community that needs continual forgiveness—both from God and mutually among its members (v. 4a). The sense is not that God waits to see whether humans forgive before offering forgiveness, but that human beings block the flow of God's forgiveness if they do not themselves lead forgiving lives. The final petition acknowledges that the world in which the community lives is very frequently a place of trial, persecution, and temptation.[13] The community prays that such troubles will not prove overwhelming, causing it to fall away from its high vocation (v. 4b).[14]

The community that prays the Lord's Prayer is, then, a community very conscious of its privileged closeness to God. But it prays the prayer in the world, as part of the world, on behalf of the world, to which it testifies the onset of the kingdom. It is praying for food, for reconciliation,

---

[12] Luke's version of this third petition suggests a continual (see the present imperative *didou*), day by day (*to kath'hēmeran*) provision, whereas Matthew (6:11) conveys more the sense of a once-for-all giving "today" (*dos . . . sēmeron*). The phrase "food needed for life" translates a Greek word, *epiousios*, notoriously difficult to interpret since it is not found in any Greek text independent of its appearance in both versions of the Lord's Prayer. It could mean "bread necessary for survival" (the interpretation I adopt here); "bread for today"; "bread for tomorrow." The latter two interpretations fit better with the Matthean than the Lukan form of the total phrase.

[13] In its original meaning on the lips of Jesus this petition probably had a more distinctive eschatological reference: praying for deliverance from the intensification of evil that was foreseen as destined to occur just before the final liberation; see further, Fitzmyer, *Luke X-XXIV*, 898–99.

[14] This admittedly is a somewhat adapted interpretation of the stark "do not bring us to the time of trial." The suggestion of God's direct agency in the original expression reflects a time when the distinction between God's absolute will (what God wants and effects) and God's permissive will (what God does not directly will but simply allows) was not formulated; see further, Fitzmyer, *Luke X-XXIV*, 906–7.

for deliverance from evil, not just for itself but for the entire human family, whose dignity and destiny as children of God it tries to model and proclaim. In short, it prays that the entire human race may return to the hospitable home of the Father.

The Friend at Midnight and Further Instruction on Prayer: 11:5-13

Having taught the disciples what to pray, in the parable of the friend at midnight (vv. 5-8) and its accompanying instruction (vv. 9-13), Jesus inculcates the attitude that must go with the words. The parable leaps right out of village life in Palestine in a wonderfully fresh way.[15] To grasp its meaning we have to appreciate that no less than three "friends" are involved. There is a central figure, whom Jesus addresses directly ("you") and makes the chief subject of the story. This person then has friends in two "directions," as it were: a friend who is a fellow villager (Friend A) and a friend from somewhere else who suddenly turns up as a guest (Friend B). The arrival of Friend B causes a crisis in hospitality: the main character ("you") has nothing to set before him. So, though it is midnight, "you" go to your fellow villager (Friend A), seeking three loaves of bread. The logic of the parable depends heavily on the sense of "shame" so powerful in the culture. In effect, the story puts this suggestion to its audience: Is it really conceivable that the man (Friend A) would respond in the way described (unwilling to get up and help because the door has been locked and the children are in bed, etc.)? Is it not certain that even if he won't get up for friendship's sake, he certainly will to avoid shame, the shame he would inevitably feel before the entire village the next day because he caused it to fail in hospitality?

As seen occasionally in Jesus' parables (see 16:1-8; 18:1-8), the character chiefly in focus is something of a rogue—someone forced to do the right thing against personal inclination or interest. The logic then works on an *a fortiori* basis. If this rogue will most certainly act and provide what is required, how much more certainly will the God of all goodness move to hear the petitions of those who approach in prayer.

That seems to have been the thrust of the parable on the lips of Jesus. But something of the original meaning seems to have slipped away in the course of its transmission. Or, rather, the sense of "shame" has been

---

[15] K. E. Bailey's discussion of the parable (*Poet and Peasant: A Literary-cultural Approach to the Parables in Luke* [Grand Rapids, MI: Eerdmans, 1976], 119–33) brings this out well.

subsumed into a note of persistence. Now, the shame is not something that puts pressure directly upon the man who has gone to bed (Friend A). It has been transferred to the one ("you") who comes to him for assistance. What causes Friend A to get up is not personal shame but a shamelessly persistent knocking that he simply cannot ignore. So the parable, rather like that of the unjust judge and the widow (18:1-8), becomes an instruction on the need to persevere in prayer.[16]

I would argue, however, that despite the problems of language, the context in which Luke sets the parable—notably the triple instruction that follows (11:9-13)—preserves the original *a fortiori* logic. Why can one be certain that if one searches, one will find; if one asks, one will receive; if one knocks, the door will be opened (v. 10)? Because, if it is inconceivable that as human parents you would give your children a snake when they ask for a fish, or a scorpion when they ask for an egg; if, on the contrary, "evil" as you are (that is, as human beings in comparison with the goodness of God), you know how to give good and not evil things to your children, how *much more* will the Father of infinite goodness give good things (here, the gift of the Holy Spirit) to you!

The genius of the parable and of the sequence that draws from it is that it engages intense human feeling (the sense of shame; the sense of parental love and responsibility) and draws these directly into an attitude toward God. Jesus does not *tell* his hearers about God. He makes them *feel* something very deeply and then says, "That—multiplied a thousand and more times over—is how God feels about you! It is in the light of this knowledge that you should come before God in prayer."

---

[16] There is actually no word connoting the idea of "persistence" in the text. The Greek word expressing the reason that the friend gets up and attends to the request is *anaideia*, which literally means "shamelessness." The phrase then literally reads "because of his shamelessness . . . ." The idea of "persistence" has to be imported from a sense of parallel with the parable of the unjust judge and the widow (18:1-8) and then the sense of "shamelessly persistent" knocking constructed. It seems more accurate to remain solely with the idea of "shame" (applicable to the householder rather than the one who knocks) and not import the notion of persistence. The problem, then, is to account for the negative form "shamelessness," when one would expect simply "shame." Also, the possessive pronoun "his" more naturally refers to the one who knocks. There are, then, serious problems attending both interpretations. Best discussion in Bailey, *Poet and Peasant*, 119–33.

It may seem surprising that the text nominates the Spirit as the gift of the Father.[17] In the Lukan schema the community will receive the Spirit from heaven following the resurrection and ascension of Jesus at Pentecost (Acts 2:1-13). In the narrative of the gospel this teaching anticipates that event. But readers of subsequent generations are encouraged to pray that what the early community experienced at Pentecost will be their gift as well. We should recall that not long before this particular sequence the gospel presented a glimpse of Jesus' inner life where he "rejoiced in the Holy Spirit" and thanked the Father for the relationship of knowledge and revelation, which he was sharing with his disciples (10:21-24). The gift of the Spirit is ultimately a communication of the sense of being enfolded by God's love, a sense that Jesus has in the supreme degree (also, Paul: see Rom 5:5 and 8:15). It is this sense that convinces disciples that they enjoy here and now the relationship with God characteristic of the kingdom.

---

[17] The Matthean parallel (7:11) has simply "good things."

The Prophet Continues His Way I
11:14–12:53

At this point on the journey to Jerusalem the gospel confronts us with a long sequence, 11:14–14:35, that is perhaps the most difficult for the modern reader and preacher. No meek or mild Jesus speaks here but rather a prophet confronting a difficult destiny. This presses in upon him, adding sharpness and severity to his message. The "day of acceptance" continues. But there is also the sense that the space of time before the judgment is running out.

Interpreting the Prophetic Preaching of Jesus

It is the sense of a looming judgment that creates most difficulty for contemporary interpretation. By and large, unless they belong to sects of a fundamentalist nature, present readers of the gospels are not at ease with the apocalyptic expectation that formed the background to the preaching of Jesus. We do not live expecting the final reckoning to come any day soon. Nor in fact, it must be said, did the early Christians. The New Testament provides abundant evidence of attempts to modify intense expectation of "the end" and to make sense of the time "in-between," which now looked like stretching on indefinitely. The whole project of Luke-Acts is one attempt in this direction; the Gospel of John is another. From almost the very start, then, Christianity found it necessary to interpret the eschatological preaching of Jesus in other than literal ways.[1]

But the sense of things one day coming to an end has never been entirely surrendered. Creeds and liturgical statements still affirm that Christ

---

[1] A number of scholars—especially members of the Jesus Seminar—dispute that eschatology was central to Jesus' preaching of the kingdom; they see him essentially as a purveyor of wisdom. Along with many others, I cannot read the evidence in this way; see esp. John P. Meier, *A Marginal Jew: Rethinking the Historical Jesus*, vol. 2: *Mentor, Message, and Miracles* (New York: Doubleday, 1994), 243–70.

will come to judge the living and the dead. Essential to Christianity is the sense that believers and all human beings are morally accountable for the pattern of their lives in the world and for the state of the world in which they live. There are values that will receive ultimate vindication; there are evils that will not go unrequited. If there is indeed a God—the God that Jesus proclaimed—there is also a higher justice calling all to account.

There is a sense, too, in which the apocalyptic threat of all things coming to an end can be quite literally brought down to earth. Never before have members of the earth community been so aware of a global crisis in economic, social, and ecological terms. The threat of total devastation through weapons of mass destruction may have receded with the end of the Cold War, but the preservation and enhancement of the world as a healthy shared habitat for the total earth community remains a pressing challenge. In terms of the theme of this book, we have some time to make this world a hospitable place for its inhabitants, but that time is running out.

I am not pretending that there is any easy shortcut between the prophetic preaching of Jesus in this part of the gospel and our current situation. I am simply suggesting that the urgency and insistence that attends the message is not something we can simply dismiss as part of the disposable apocalyptic "baggage" of early New Testament thought. It is in view of our own social and global situation, as well as personal moral deportment, that Jesus summons us to conversion.

Returning more immediately to the gospel itself, let us keep in mind, with regard to each episode, that interpretation requires us to be aware of the audience Jesus is addressing. For the most part, in this section he addresses the as-yet-unconverted crowds. In the way of a prophet, he summons them to conversion with warnings and denunciation. Alongside the crowds are those who represent the religious leadership—especially the Pharisees and lawyers. More and more explicitly, members of these groups emerge as the antagonists of Jesus. Fearlessly and savagely, he denounces their leadership, exposing it as self-serving and burdensome to the people. Finally, interspersed with confrontation are sequences where, in the context of this growing hostility, Jesus reminds his disciples of the cost of following him and where alone their security lies.

I propose to move fairly swiftly across the section in question, omitting detailed commentary. My hope is that the more general remarks I have just made will provide an orientation that will make particular sections of Jesus' prophetic preaching somewhat more accessible.

Controversies, Warnings, and Denunciations: 11:14-54

The Beelzebul Accusation: 11:14-26

Jesus has cast out a demon that had rendered a person unable to speak. While the crowd for the most part is "amazed" (v. 14), some attribute the expulsion to alliance with the evil power itself—namely, with Beelzebul the prince of demons (v. 15). Jesus refutes the charge with the image of a kingdom or house divided against itself (vv. 17-18). He then goes on the offensive, asking why the same interpretation could not equally apply to their own exorcists (v. 19). Moreover, they had better arrive at the right interpretation in this matter, because if in fact Jesus is expelling demons through the "finger of God," then the kingdom of God has already come upon them and they are missing out (v. 20).[2] Though they want "signs from heaven" (v. 16), they are failing to advert to the signs already present—not dramatic stunts and marvels but the reclaiming of human lives for the fullness of life and humanity in the context of a renewed relationship with God. Jesus is that "stronger one," who successfully attacks and overcomes the strongly armed and defended realm of Satan (vv. 21-22). The decisive battle is engaged; this is no time for hesitation or half-hearted adherence (v. 23). The train of the kingdom of God is already leaving the station; decide once and for all whether you want to climb on board!

The mysterious short passage (vv. 24-26) about the return of the evil spirit has been understood in various ways. In the immediate context, where Jesus does seem to acknowledge that Jewish exorcists expel evil spirits (v. 19), the image of the "house" all tidied up and in order, yet open to "reinvasion" by an even larger number of evil spirits, could suggest that mere expulsion is not sufficient; the ensuing "emptiness," lest

---

[2] We meet here the sense that the rule of Satan and the rule or "kingdom" of God are correlative opposites: the expulsion of Satan from any area of life connotes the onset of the rule of God into that area; there is no neutral or uncontested space. The striking phrase "finger of God" (paralleled in Matthew [12:28] by "Spirit of God") may be an echo of an acknowledgment ("This is the finger of God") wrung from Egyptian sorcerers when Aaron was able to produce the plague of gnats in the face of their own impotence to do so (Exod 8:19; see also Exod 31:18; Deut 9:10). The use of the word "finger" suggests instrumentality and skill: as God employed Aaron for this purpose, so Jesus portrays himself as the effective instrument for the setting up of God's rule on earth; see further, François Bovon, *A Commentary on the Gospel of Luke*, Hermeneia, vol. 2 (Minneapolis: Fortress, 2013), 121–22.

it be reinvaded by an even greater measure of evil, must be filled with the power of God brought by Jesus.[3] On a more ethical tack, the parable could suggest that an initial liberation from evil and acquisition of virtue is no grounds for spiritual complacency. So long as the kingdom is not fully arrived, even the believer remains open to the attack of evil—and virtue itself, far from providing immunity, can be especially vulnerable to that attack in its more subtle form of spiritual pride. The only true safeguard is that the "house" of one's life be filled with rule of God (v. 20) and constant attention and obedience to the word.[4]

Questionable Enthusiasm: 11:27-36

Jesus' attack on his critics in the preceding controversy receives an enthusiastic response—first in the shape of an interjection from a woman in the crowd (vv. 27-28),[5] then from the crowds more generally (v. 29). Jesus takes no comfort from this enthusiasm. As at Nazareth at the opening of his ministry (4:22-24), he moves to challenge it and probe its depths: "This is an evil generation; it is asking for a sign" (v. 29a). It is a generation that wishes to deal with God on its own terms rather than being prepared to see the signs being performed in its midst. Again, as at Nazareth (4:25-27), Jesus points (vv. 29b-32) to biblical examples of people outside Israel (the citizens of Nineveh, the Queen of the South [Queen of Sheba]) who responded more positively to the preaching and wisdom before them (of Jonah and Solomon, respectively) than do the Israelites of the present generation—even though "something greater" (= "Someone greater") than Jonah or Solomon is here.

God has placed Jesus in the world to be its light (v. 33; cf. 1:79; 2:32). But, to benefit from the light, the organ of reception—the eye—must be healthy (v. 34).[6] If Jesus' hearers are not benefiting from the light, they must ask themselves whether it is not because their organ of reception—

---

[3] See I. Howard Marshall, *The Gospel of Luke: A Commentary on the Greek Text*, NIGTC (Grand Rapids, MI: Eerdmans, 1978, repr. 1987), 479.

[4] See Robert C. Tannehill, *The Narrative Unity of Luke-Acts: A Literary Interpretation: Volume One: The Gospel according to Luke* (Philadelphia: Fortress, 1986), 242, 244–45.

[5] Jesus corrects the woman's praise ("Blessed is the womb that bore you . . .") by responding, as in 8:21, that the true family of God is realized in those who hear and obey God's word.

[6] Presupposed here is the ancient view of the eye as a kind of gateway allowing light to enter the body from outside.

their readiness to hear the word—is faulty (lit., "not healthy"; vv. 34-35). If, on the other hand, they do receive the light, they will themselves be light bearers (v. 36).[7]

Critique of the Pharisees and Lawyers: 11:37-54

At this point the focus of Jesus' address turns from the crowds to the groups that are now becoming directly hostile—the Pharisees and the lawyers (the experts in the law of Moses, otherwise called "the scribes"). The sequence begins innocuously enough with an invitation from one of the Pharisees for Jesus to dine with him at table. We have, then, a situation of hospitality. But Jesus is no comfortable guest. When his failure to wash before dinner causes his host to be amazed, Jesus brings this private amazement to the surface in what becomes a sustained prophetic discourse severely critical, first of the Pharisees, then (from v. 45) of the lawyers. While it seems clear that Jesus criticized religious authorities in his own lifetime, the sharpness of the polemic reflects conditions of a later generation when conflict between the early Christians and the Jewish synagogue had greatly intensified. In no sense should it be construed as an attack on Judaism as such. What we have is a prophetic critique from within Israel, with many biblical precedents among the prophets of old.

Against the Pharisees (vv. 39-44) Jesus targets in turn three practices, all of which frustrate the true purpose of religious law and offend against deeper moral values, particularly justice and charity. In the first instance (vv. 39-41) preoccupation with external cleanliness neglects the fact that the cleanliness of utensils is a symbol of the cleanliness of human beings.[8] Real uncleanliness has to do with the inner life of persons—with moral failings such as greed and wickedness. Material objects such as cups and dishes best serve as occasions for almsgiving (v. 41). That is what brings about true cleanliness in God's sight. Likewise (v. 42), preoccupation with the minutiae of tithing (setting aside a tenth of one's produce) neglects the fact that Deuteronomy 14:22-29 prescribes tithing as an acknowledgment that the produce of the fields is the gift of God; it also served as a

---

[7] The thought, then, would be similar to that in Phil 2:15-16: "so that you may be blameless and innocent, children of God without blemish in the midst of a crooked and perverse generation, in which you shine like stars in the world, holding out to it the word of life." But the sense of v. 36 is obscure nor is there any Matthean parallel to it. See further Joseph A. Fitzmyer, *The Gospel according to Luke X–XXIV*, AB 28A (Garden City, NY: Doubleday, 1985), 941.

[8] See Fitzmyer, *Luke X–XXIV*, 944–45.

relief measure for the poor (v. 29). How wrong, then, to tithe all kinds of small herbs to the neglect of justice and the love of God—the absolutely central religious duties upon which life depends (see 10:27).

Finally (vv. 43-44), the Pharisees look to gain personal honor (the best seats in the synagogue and respectful greetings in the marketplace). This renders them like unmarked graves that people walk over without realizing it, thereby incurring defilement from the bones within.[9] The suggestion is that the Pharisees, who give the public appearance of seeking to keep the populace as clean as possible from pollution by hedging the law with all kinds of minute prescriptions, are themselves a source of pollution for those they seek to influence—pollution, that is, from what is truly unclean in the sight of God: neglect of justice and charity. In line with the prophets of Israel, Jesus works from a wholly different view of the kind of "cleanliness" required of God's people.

The critique of the lawyers (vv. 45-52) chiefly fastens upon the fact that they are using their expertise not to lift burdens but to increase them. The true test of religious law is whether it serves to increase the burdens that life brings to most people or whether, in the context of a vital and hope-giving relationship with God, it serves to lift burdens and enhance human dignity. Expertise in the law provides lawyers with a key to this truth ("key of knowledge" [v. 52]). But they have not used it either to enter in themselves or to allow others to have access. Instead, they continue the murderous hostility of their "ancestors" (their predecessors as legal experts) to prophets who point out these unpalatable truths (vv. 47-51).

In this critique Jesus seems to be writing a script linking himself and his fate with that of the prophets who suffered of old.[10] The sequence concludes with a notice (vv. 53-54) concerning the (understandable) growth of hostility toward him on the part of the scribes and Pharisees. From now on they will constantly seek to catch him out in something he might say.

---

[9] The Matthean parallel (23:27) is even more colorful and detailed ("whitewashed tombs," etc.). It is important not to "import" these Matthean overtones into one's reading of the text of Luke, which is severe enough as it stands.

[10] The reference in v. 51 to a Zechariah who was slain "between the altar and the sanctuary" is obscure. As the father of John the Baptist is hardly in view, the most obvious candidate would be a priest Zechariah who was slain in the temple during the reign of King Joash according to 2 Chr 24:20-22. If Chronicles was the last book in the Hebrew canon at the time, this would give the sense of a line of figures who paid with their lives for their righteousness from the very first, Abel, according to Gen 4:1-12, to the one last mentioned in the Scriptures. See further, Fitzmyer, *Luke X–XXIV*, 951; Marshall, *Gospel of Luke*, 506.

Life and Discipleship in Troubled Times: 12:1-53

Jesus has been in dispute with the Pharisees and scribes. Nonetheless the crowds continue to press upon him in great numbers (12:1). In the context of this mixed response, he once again turns to instruct his immediate disciples.

All Will Be Revealed: 12:1-3

First (12:1-3) they are to beware of the "leaven" of the Pharisees, the lack of correspondence between their external behavior and what they are inside (the "hypocrisy" exposed in 11:43-44). The disciples, on the contrary, must be open and sincere, with true correspondence between "inside" and "out." The reason is that one day all will be made clear (vv. 2-3).

False Fear and Salutary Fear: 12:4-12

The instruction then (vv. 4-9) looks to a situation of physical persecution and addresses the fear that, naturally, it will provoke. There is a false fear and a true fear. Disciples need not fear those (human persecutors) who can kill the body, because their entire physical existence is held within the hands of God. If God values even sparrows that are sold five for two pennies, how much more precious in God's sight are they (vv. 6-7). Even if their confession of Jesus should bring them to the point of death, their cause is secure in heaven (v. 8). Dragged before human tribunals, they should not even prepare their defense. The Holy Spirit will teach them what they have to say (v. 12).[11]

So much for false fear. But there is also a salutary fear (v. 5): fear of the One (that is, God) who (unlike mere human persecutors) can threaten not only physical existence but also the grasp on eternal life. In one breath, almost, the sequence commends two attitudes to God: unbounded confidence and salutary fear. But the latter only becomes operative as a

---

[11] The sayings about the Holy Spirit in vv. 10-12 are mysterious; for a survey of interpretations, see Fitzmyer, *Luke X-XXIV*, 964. The difference between the "forgivable" blasphemy against the Son of Man (Jesus) and the "unforgivable" blasphemy against the Holy Spirit seems to lie in the fact that those who reject the preaching of Jesus in his earthly life will get a "second chance" through the preaching of the apostles after Pentecost (Acts 2:14-36; 3:12-26), but those who reject the Spirit at this later time choose their own (now irrevocable) fate; the time for further chances will have run out.

kind of saving backstop when major unfaithfulness, such as apostasy, is contemplated. The point is that it is only God's favor or displeasure that really counts. If one opts continually for God, there is no cause for fear in any circumstance whatsoever.

False Security (Parable of the Rich Fool): 12:13-21

An interruption (v. 13) from a man who wants Jesus to arbitrate in a family dispute over inheritance triggers an instruction about where people should place their security. First, in a negative vein and addressing the crowds in general, Jesus warns about greed (Greek: *pleonexia* [lit., "the desire of gaining more and more"]) and placing one's security (lit., "life") in "abundance of possessions" (vv. 14-15). To support this he tells a parable.

Presupposed in the parable is a sense of the fragility and uncertainty of this present life. For the rich man, his abundant crop will provide security for years to come. His only worry is how to store it all. The parable vividly depicts his preoccupation with this problem ("What should I do . . . ?" [v. 17])—to the total neglect of more important areas of concern (human and religious values). With his storage problem solved (by building bigger barns), he can sit back and take his ease, sure in the knowledge that his wealth has guaranteed ease and comfort for years to come. Alas, his absorption in the storage problem has masked from him the fact that wealth provides no security against the possibility that life may be short. The only security that is truly lasting consists in being "rich with God" (v. 21).

The parable initiates a theme that becomes very prominent in the gospel from now on: nothing is more destructive of life and humanity than preoccupation with acquiring, holding on to, and increasing wealth. The problem is not so much the possession of riches as such. It is that the desire to acquire and enhance them, fed by insecurity, prevents people from attending to the relationship with God that brings the only security that counts. Luke Timothy Johnson puts this very well:

> It is out of deep fear that the acquisitive instinct grows monstrous. Life seems so frail and contingent that many possessions are required to secure it, even though the possessions are frailer still than the life.[12]

---

[12] *The Gospel of Luke*, Sacra Pagina 3 (Collegeville, MN: Liturgical Press, 1991), 201.

Such desire also erodes the concern for the other that is the basis of true community. Attachment to wealth is incompatible with living, sharing, and celebrating the hospitality of God.

True Security ("Do Not Be Anxious"): 12:22-34

Now that he has exposed the folly of placing security in wealth, Jesus develops the theme more subtly. In an instruction directed to the disciples he probes the kind of anxiety that leads to such behavior. It is quite incompatible with the understanding of God that he proclaims.

There is a clear pattern to the instruction. The general theme, stated at the beginning (v. 22a) and returning at the end (v. 29), is "Do not be anxious." That is, do not be so absorbed by the worries and cares of this life as to neglect what is really necessary: relationship with God. Such worries arise in two areas in particular (vv. 22b-23): "life," which leads to excessive anxiety about food; and "the body," which leads to excessive anxiety about clothing. Jesus takes up each in turn ("food": vv. 24-26; "clothing": vv. 27-28) in a highly poetic sequence featuring the kind of *a fortiori* logic that we have seen before (see esp. 11:5-13). The ravens do not sow or reap or have storehouses or barns because God cares for them. But if God cares for birds, how much more for "you"! The lilies of the field do not toil or spin, yet if God clothes in such splendor the grass of the field destined soon to be burnt, how much more will God clothe "you"! Hearers could protest that human beings have a lot more to be anxious about and a lot more responsibility than birds or grass. But Jesus is not making a moral point. He is appealing to the imagination, attempting through poetic exaggeration to inculcate a basic attitude to God. Get that right first and other things, including legitimate concerns, will fall into place.

The mainspring of it all is Jesus' passionate conviction concerning the riches available to human beings if only they will truly open up their lives to relationship with God. It is the Father's "good pleasure" ("determination" might be a better word) to "give you the kingdom" (v. 32). In the context of that divine generosity all else pales into insignificance. It makes good sense to sell one's possessions and give alms (v. 33). You are not really losing anything but investing in a supremely secure, heavenly "bank" that God has guaranteed. And if your treasure is there, your heart will be there as well (v. 34). This last statement might seem more logical the other way round. The idea seems to be that if the heart, the inner core of a person that determines attitudes and actions, is anchored upon God, then everything the person says or does reflects the sense of security flowing from this relationship. Such persons, free from obsessive self-concern, become themselves agents of the hospitality of God.

Watchfulness and Faithfulness: 12:35-48

Jesus has told the disciples, "Fear not" (v. 32). Now there is a sharp change of tone. There is something his disciples should fear: being found unwatchful and unfaithful at the coming judgment. This theme in general pervades the series of warnings that follows.

The first of three images (vv. 35-39) pictures Christian life in terms of servants waiting for their master to return from a banquet. Entirely positive, it depicts the "blessedness" of their state if they are found watching: in an extraordinary reversal their master will make them sit down to eat and serve them. The image wonderfully catches Luke's sense of God wanting simply to be "hospitable" to human beings and sending Jesus as the agent and servant of that hospitality.

The second image (vv. 39-40) reflects Jesus' ability to use images stirring strong feeling. Thieves naturally give no warning as to when they will strike. Imagine what it's like to come home and find your house broken into and all your goods plundered. So a house owner has always to be on the watch. Believers are in that situation with respect to the return of the Son of Man—here imaged as a thief!

The final image (vv. 41-48), sparked off by a question from Peter, targets those who have positions of leadership and responsibility. They are in the situation of a slave whom an absent master has set up as manager of other slaves, male and female. If they act for the benefit of those placed under them (notably, giving them their due allowance of food), they will receive a "blessing" (vv. 43-44). But those who take advantage of the master's absence to abuse their authority will be severely punished on his return.[13]

Jesus' Own Prophetic Anguish: 12:49-53

In line with this general theme of accountability, Jesus offers a strikingly tormented reflection upon his ministry and destiny. The "fire" that

---

[13] "Cut in pieces" (v. 46) should not be taken literally (physically). It seems to be a vigorous way of saying "cut off" (from authority) completely. The final remarks (vv. 47-48), based upon the rather grim image of slaves deserving and receiving a beating, once again (see also 8:18) make the point that much more will be expected of the gifted than of the less endowed.

he has come to spread upon the earth (v. 49) is, as John the Baptist had prophesied (3:16), the fire of the Holy Spirit. And, indeed, at Pentecost the gathered disciples will receive the Spirit in the visible form of "tongues as if of fire" (Acts 2:3). But the Spirit cannot be given until Jesus has faced and gone through the destiny (suffering and death) that awaits him in Jerusalem. That is the "baptism" with which he is stressed until it be "accomplished" (v. 50).[14] It is for this that he had "set his face" for Jerusalem at the beginning of the journey (9:51).

The anguish is not something for Jesus alone. It affects also the hearts of those to whom his summons is directed. Despite the proclamation of the angels at his birth—"Peace on earth" (2:14)—Jesus is not bringing peace but inner-family hostility and division (vv. 51-53). The division arises because the salvation he proclaims is not something that leaves the depths of human beings untouched. Exactly as Simeon had predicted (2:34-35), his message stirs up the "thoughts" that lurk in those depths and need conversion. Only when conversion occurs at this level can there be true and lasting messianic peace.

---

[14] The "baptism" image here (see also Mark 10:38b) hardly stems from the Christian rite or from the earlier baptizing activity of John. Being immersed in water out of control is a standard biblical image for being overwhelmed by troubles and hostility (e.g., Pss 42:7; 69:1-2; 88:7, 16-17). Jesus' usage probably reflects this.

The Prophet Continues His Way II
12:54–14:35

Jesus' anguished reflection on his ministry (12:49-53) forms a bridge to a new series of warnings addressed to the crowds in general (12:54–13:30). Then the "hospitality" theme returns: first negatively, with a reflection on the coming inhospitality awaiting him in Jerusalem (13:31-35); then, more positively, in a series of instructions given in the context of a meal to which Jesus has been invited (14:1-35). From this emerges the attractive sense of Christian life as a life "under invitation."

Further Prophetic Warnings: 12:54–13:21

The warnings begin with two images (vv. 54-59). Jesus points out how good the crowds are at reading the weather patterns (vv. 54-56). Why, then, are they so poor at reading (interpreting) the present time—that is, to see it as a space for conversion before the storm of the judgment arrives? Secondly (vv. 57-59), they know how much better it is, when accused, to settle matters with one's accuser out of court rather than before the court itself. Why not, then, settle affairs with God's emissary (Jesus), while still "on the way" (to Jerusalem)? Soon it will be too late.

Warning Events (Pilate's Atrocity, the Tower of Siloam): 13:1-9

Mention of two disasters, one caused directly by human agency (Pilate's massacre of some Galileans sacrificing in the temple[1]) and the other accidental (the collapse of a tower at Siloam with large loss of life), carry further the warning to repent. Jesus firmly refutes any suggestion that the victims were being punished for a sinfulness from which others were exempt. To interpret such disasters in this selective way is entirely wrong—though the religious instinct is always prone to do so. Without

---

[1] There is no other historical source chronicling this event, though it fits in well with the character of Pilate's administration as known from other sources. Galileans were considered the most revolt-prone of Palestine's citizens.

attempting to judge the sinfulness of others, people should see such events as a warning to take stock of their own lives lest far greater disaster befall them in the judgment. The warning concludes with a parable about a fig tree given one last year to be productive (vv. 6-9). Those who hear the parable should understand that they are in that final "year."

Healing on the Sabbath (the Crippled Woman): 13:10-17

At first sight a healing episode seems out of place in this context of warning. The main point, however, is not so much the cure as the resistance it provokes, precisely the kind of resistance to conversion that Jesus has been speaking about (the "triangular" pattern once more). The woman, bent over for eighteen years, stands up straight at Jesus' touch and begins to praise God. This beautiful moment of restoration the leader of the synagogue can see only as an offense against the Sabbath (v. 14). Jesus does not conceal his scorn. How hypocritical that religious leaders who do not hesitate to work for the benefit of their animals on the Sabbath (v. 15) will not allow him to free this human being, a member of God's people ("daughter of Abraham"), from the power of Satan[2] on the Sabbath. Is this not what the Sabbath is all about: the enhancement of life in obedience to God's will ("Was it not necessary . . . ?" [v. 16])? The compassion of Jesus for suffering humanity ("eighteen long years"), his outrage at the limited sense of God projected by the complaint, rings through the account. The rejoicing of the crowd (v. 17), in contrast to the discomfiture of the leaders, illustrates once more the divided response to his ministry (see also 7:29-30).

Two Parables—the Mustard Seed and the Yeast: 13:18-21

The two brief parables that follow—pairing off, typically for Luke, a man and a woman—seem to comment upon this divided response. Both image the kingdom of God. Luke's version of the mustard seed parable (vv. 18-19) does not focus upon the smallness of the seed (cf. Matt 13:31-32; Mark 4:30-32). It tells the story of a man who seems to act with casual abandon: he "throws" the seed into his garden.[3] What his intentions were, we do not know. He scarcely meant to provide a roosting

---

[2] The statement reflects the ancient perception that physical illnesses are attributable to demonic forces—without any suggestion of moral failing on the part of the sufferer.

[3] The NRSV translation "sowed" (as in Matt 13:31) obscures this Lukan nuance.

place for the birds of the air. But that is what happened. Wild and free, they took advantage of his casual gesture. There is something similarly "wild" about the kingdom; it reflects the exuberant generosity of God. Like the birds of the air, the lowly and disreputable take advantage of it; the respectable, like the synagogue leaders, cannot cope.

By contrast, the parable of the yeast (vv. 20-21) does seem to revolve around the sense of something very small (the yeast) that produces effects greatly beyond what one might expect. Just so the simple act of liberation that Jesus has performed in the synagogue is already a beachhead of the kingdom (see 11:20). Such small acts progressively and cumulatively shake the grip of Satan on human lives.[4]

Jerusalem Will Not Be Hospitable: 13:22-35

The gospel pauses to remind us that Jesus is on a journey, making his way to Jerusalem (13:22; see 9:51). The reminder introduces a sequence loosely connected around the theme of Jerusalem.

Seek God's Hospitality While It Is Still Available: 13:22-30

As Jesus moves on to the city of destiny, the growing sense of crisis prompts a question about the number who will be saved (v. 23). But Jesus will not respond to speculations in these terms. Instead, he turns the question back once more into a warning not to miss the opportunity while it is still available. When an entrance is narrow and many are trying to get through, it pays to struggle and get to the front right away (v. 24).[5] Or (the image alters [vv. 25-28]), to gain entry to a house, do not wait till all is barred and locked up for the night; it will be no use standing outside knocking, claiming all kinds of familiarity with the householder. The image—again taken from daily life—seems to be that of travelers arriving rather late at a large household or inn, hoping for special consideration on the grounds that the householder knows them. Jesus plays upon the feelings of his audience: imagine how you'd feel finding the lodging full up with others (the Gentiles [v. 29]) who have gotten in before you and yourself out on the street for the night in a strange city! The hospitality of God is ample and generous. But it will

---

[4] See Luke Timothy Johnson, *The Gospel of Luke*, Sacra Pagina 3 (Collegeville, MN: Liturgical Press, 1991), 214–15.

[5] Note that Luke does not have the contrast between the "wide gate" and the "narrow gate" found in Matt 7:13-14.

not be available forever. Human beings can exclude themselves from salvation by not being prepared to accept that hospitality at the time—and in the company—of God's choosing.

Jesus and Jerusalem—An Intertwined Fate: 13:31-35

A warning from some Pharisees about King Herod's murderous intent[6] prompts Jesus to reflect upon his mission and its eventual climax (vv. 31-33). No threat of death will deter him from the liberating program (casting out demons and performing cures) upon which he is presently ("today and tomorrow" [v. 32]) engaged. Nonetheless (v. 33),[7] in due course ("the third day"), he "must be on his way"[8] because it is in Jerusalem that prophets meet their fate. Speaking in the persona of divine Wisdom and anticipating his later weeping over the city (19:41-44), Jesus adds a prophetic lament (vv. 34-35). Jerusalem's tendency has always been to reject with violence the emissaries (prophets) sent to it by God—even though the divine intent was ever benign, as benign, in fact, as the action of a hen gathering her brood under her wings (v. 34). The tone is not condemnatory but tragic:[9] as a result of not accepting this benign "visitation," Jerusalem's "house" will be left desolate (v. 35a)—an allusion to the destruction of the temple by the Romans in 70 CE.[10]

---

[6] Scholars are divided as to whether the warning is well-intentioned (so Joseph A. Fitzmyer, *The Gospel according to Luke X-XXIV*, AB 28A [Garden City, NY: Doubleday, 1985], 1030) or hypocritical and hostile (so Johnson, *Gospel of Luke*, 221–22).

[7] The Greek conjunction *plēn* at the beginning of v. 33 seems to suggest some note of correction.

[8] Once again the Lukan "must" (Greek: *dei*) gives expression to the divine purpose (completely independent of human agents such as Herod) driving Jesus to Jerusalem.

[9] See Robert C. Tannehill, *The Narrative Unity of Luke-Acts: A Literary Interpretation: Volume One: The Gospel according to Luke* (Philadelphia: Fortress, 1986), 155.

[10] The time reference of the statement to the effect that Jerusalem will not see him "until the time comes when you say, 'Blessed is the one who comes in the name of the Lord'" (v. 35b) is obscure. The occasion of Jesus' entry into the city (19:37-38) is hardly in view, since only Jesus' disciples, not the citizens in general, utter the acclamation. Nor can the reference be to the final coming in judgment, since those about to be judged would hardly acclaim their judge with a blessing. The reference could be more open-ended: that the city will not "see" him, that is, see in him its messianic Savior, until it is prepared to be converted.

Invited to the Banquet: 14:1-35

A leading Pharisee invites Jesus to a meal on the Sabbath (14:1). This, once again, sets up an occasion for conflict and instruction in the context of hospitality.

Healing on the Sabbath (the Man with Dropsy): 14:1-6

First of all (14:1-6), there is present at the meal a man suffering from dropsy.[11] This Jesus cannot ignore (see 13:32). In an exchange that closely parallels the earlier episode concerning the bent woman in the synagogue (13:10-17), Jesus reclaims the Sabbath as an occasion for healing and fullness of life.

Associating with the Lowly: 14:7-14

But this disturbing guest has more to say. Jesus notices that at this banquet the guests inevitably choose the highest (the most honorable) places they can find. His comment upon this (vv. 8-10) at first sight seems to be simply a piece of practical advice: choose the lowest place because, if there has to be a rearrangement (to seat everyone according to rank), it is much better to be promoted to a higher place than required to move down to a lower one. But Luke introduces the episode as a "parable" (v. 7), and that immediately signals that something more significant than everyday advice is at stake. As in all parables, Jesus taps into the everyday life of his audience that he knows so well, playing upon the feelings of honor and shame that run so deep. At a formal public meal—a wedding banquet, for example—to have to move down and take the lowest place before the eyes of all would be a horrible experience, the loss of face immense and long-lasting.

The sense of horror involved gives bite to the situation the parable actually refers to: the great reversal that is to come (v. 11). If everything is going to be reversed when the kingdom of God is established (recall the *Magnificat* [1:51-53]; the Beatitudes and Woes [6:20-26]), those who choose now to sit with the poor and lowly are destined for promotion, while those who sit now with the rich and powerful will find themselves

---

Adopting this interpretation, Tannehill (*Narrative Unity*, 1.155-56) finds in the saying a hint that Jerusalem, despite having rejected Jesus at his first "visitation," will have a second chance.

[11] The swollen condition now medically identified as edema.

ordered down to the lowest places. The challenge is clear: if in the case of banquets like this present one you would experience such shame at finding yourself demoted before the eyes of all, just think how much more painful it will be to experience that at the end of the age, when all is decided and set forever! Once again, an episode from ordinary life (of no moral content at all) provides a springboard, not to a moral maxim but to a profound understanding of the implications of the gospel.

Speaking directly to his host, Jesus follows up with a related point (14:12-14). Better, when issuing invitations, not to invite your friends and relations; all that will get you is a similar invitation in return. Invite instead the poor, the crippled, the lame, and the blind. They may appear to have nothing to offer. But being hospitable to them now stores up for you the welcome that truly matters: the welcome into the hospitality of God that lasts forever (see 16:9).

The Parable of the Declined Invitations: 14:15-24

At this point one of the other guests makes a pious observation: "Blessed is anyone who will eat bread in the kingdom of God" (v. 15b).[12] We note the future tense "will eat"—this removes the banquet of the kingdom to the indefinite future. The parable that Jesus tells in response radically transforms the situation. The crucial point is that, while the banquet itself may still lie ahead, the *invitations* are out and the focus lies upon the responses they receive. Contrary to what one would expect in a case like this, the responses are negative. No one, it seems, wants to come to the banquet. The excuses typify the attachments Luke sees as creating problems for response to the call of the kingdom. The respondents have just bought new things (a piece of land, five yoke of oxen) or entered new situations (just married). Eager about these, they brush off the invitation (vv. 18-20). So the banquet has to be filled with the kind of people who never receive invitations to such occasions: the poor, the crippled, the blind, the lame (v. 21). Even these are not enough, and more have to be "compelled" from the "roads and lanes," that is, the truly homeless (vv. 22-24).

This wonderful parable sheds so much light on Luke's understanding of the mission of Jesus and the vision of God it implies. The "banquet" image accurately conveys what the "kingdom of God" is all about—not power and domination, like the kingdoms of this world—but gifting

---

[12] The observation recalls the exclamation of the woman in 11:27.

and honoring human beings with the superabundant hospitality of God. The banquet, the full kingdom, still lies ahead, it is true. But not in the purely future way the dinner guest suggested (v. 15a). The invitations are out, and it is Jesus' mission to issue them. Long before enjoying a celebration to which we've been invited, we can derive great enjoyment simply from the fact of having been invited. Again and again, in the days and weeks leading up to it, we savor the sense of being valued and wanted that it conveys. Just so, those who respond to the message of Jesus live now in the joy and anticipation of the banquet to which they have been invited. As people "under invitation," believers savor already the hospitality of God.

In its immediate context, however, the parable addresses an issue running all through this central section of the gospel: why the response to the summons of Jesus is so largely negative, at least among those whom one might think to be the experts in the affairs of religion. Conventional attachments are holding them back, while those who have nothing to which they can be attached (the poor, the crippled, the lame) are receiving places in the kingdom. They bring no beauty, dignity, or honor to the banquet—at least outwardly that seems to be the case. But precisely because they think they have nothing to give, they have an emptiness, a capacity that God can fill.

The Cost of Discipleship Once More: 14:25-35

Still pursued by large crowds, Jesus turns once more (14:25; cf. 9:23-27, 57-62) to warn about the cost of following him. The demands he makes at this point ("hating one's father and mother, wife and children, brothers and sisters, yes, and even life itself" [v. 26]; giving up "all possessions" [v. 33]) provide the most extreme expression of this theme in the gospel. The language of "loving/hating" reflects a Semitic idiom of expressing preference. If you prefer one thing or even one person over another, you are said to "love" the one and "hate" the other. There is no positive injunction literally to "hate" members of one's family.[13] The short parables about the builder who could not finish the tower he had begun (vv. 28-30) or the king going out to face a stronger king (vv. 31-32) seem

---

[13] "The thought therefore is not of psychological hate, but of renunciation" (I. Howard Marshall, *The Gospel of Luke: A Commentary on the Greek Text*, NIGTC [Grand Rapids, MI: Eerdmans, 1978, repr. 1987], 592 [citing O. Michel, Art. *miseō*," *TDNT* 4.592–93]).

to address situations where believers suffer persecution: discipleship means "carrying one's cross in following Jesus" (v. 27; see also 9:23). The command to give up "all one's possessions" (v. 33) is matched by the idea elsewhere in the gospel that the only truly "useful" thing to do with wealth is to use it to give alms to the poor so that one may have "treasure in heaven" (18:22). Without preparedness to undergo a life of renunciation in these various ways, a disciple is as worthless as "salt that has lost its taste" (vv. 34-35).[14] Taken in isolation, all these injunctions are stark indeed. But they need to be heard in the context of the invitation to the kingdom that has just been elaborated. In comparison with this supreme positive good, the losses entailed in the present conditions of discipleship find some proportion.

[14] The final image about salt that has lost its taste (vv. 34-35), as in the Markan (9:50) and Matthean (5:13) parallels, is obscure. Can salt lose its taste? And how could salt be "fit for the land or the dunghill" (v. 35)? For a thorough discussion of the multiple uses to which salt was put in the ancient world and the possible meaning of the image in this context, see Marshall, *Gospel of Luke*, 595–97.

Celebrating God's Acceptance
15:1-32

With the parables in chapter 15, particularly the long third one—traditionally but inaccurately known as "the Prodigal Son"—we come upon one of those passages in the gospel that have truly shaped Christian identity. Without this parable—as also perhaps without that of the Good Samaritan—Christianity would be something different. The parable has been, and continues to be, an inexhaustible source of interpretation. What I offer here is a personal interpretation along the lines of the approach taken in this book. In no sense do I claim to offer *the* interpretation.

First, it helps to note the careful construction of the sequence as a whole. The three parables (the Lost Sheep, the Lost Coin, the Lost Son and Brother) share a common theme (loss—finding—celebration) that becomes explicit, in a refrain-like way, at several points (v. 6 and v. 9; v. 7 and v. 10; v. 24 and v. 32). An opening indication of setting (vv. 1-3) provides a unifying framework for the whole: tax collectors and sinners are approaching Jesus to hear him, provoking the Pharisees and scribes to complain "this fellow welcomes sinners and eats with them" (v. 2). So Jesus tells the three parables as a defense and justification for celebrating the acceptance of God ("the year of acceptance on the part of the Lord" [4:19]). In essence, the sequence replaces a "sin/forgiveness" trajectory with a trajectory of "human beings lost/human beings found." The first trajectory is that of the scribes and Pharisees, the second that of Jesus and ultimately of God.

The Parables of the Lost Sheep and the Lost Coin: 15:4-10

The first two parables show Luke's tendency to use paired episodes, very often one featuring a man, the other a woman, to make the same basic point.[1] Both parables begin with a question: the first (more di-

---

[1] The parable of the Lost Sheep has a parallel in Matt 18:12-14, where it serves to make a rather different point: the duty incumbent upon the strong in the community to care for "the little ones" in danger of being lost.

rectly), "Which of you . . . ?"; the second, "What woman . . . ?" Both, then, invite hearers to reflect upon what would be their own response. We should note that the response might well be, "None of us!" or "Not if I were the woman!" We have to reckon with the possibility that what is being described in each case is rather foolish behavior and that this might be precisely where the provocation lies.

So it is in the case of the lost sheep (vv. 4-6). Would a responsible shepherd really leave ninety-nine sheep defenseless in the wilderness while he goes in search of one that is lost? Would he not run the risk of losing many more? The gesture of carrying the sheep home on his shoulders, as if in triumph, and summoning his friends and neighbors for a joyful celebration seems extravagant, "over the top." The friends and neighbors might join in. But they might also mutter a bit among themselves: "He must be crazy about that sheep!" And this may in fact be the point the parable makes at the end (v. 7). "Heaven," that is, God and the entire heavenly court, rejoices over one sinner who repents more than over ninety-nine who have no need of repentance. Why? Because God is crazy with love over each individual human being and rejoices exuberantly over finding one that had been lost in the death that is sin. Jesus' celebration of joyful meals with repentant sinners simply enacts on earth that exuberant heavenly joy. At stake, then, is the image Jesus' critics have of God. In making them feel the "resistance" of the friends and neighbors to the shepherd's invitation, the parable makes them confront the true depth of their own resistance to what Jesus is offering.

The same pattern recurs in the case of the woman who spends the whole day turning her house upside down to find a single coin (vv. 8-10).[2] Are the friends and neighbors summoned to rejoice with her really going to participate all that enthusiastically in her joy? Again, her behavior seems extravagant. They might well remark, "She's a bit obsessive about that coin. Surely it would have turned up one day. Why all this fuss!" But again the last sentence (v. 10) makes the point: "heaven" (here "the angels of God") reacts like that to the recovery of a single sinner who had been lost. Why not share on earth the joy of the celebration in heaven?

---

[2] The value of the coin ("drachma") is difficult to estimate; see Joseph A. Fitzmyer, *The Gospel according to Luke X-XXIV*, AB 28A (Garden City, NY: Doubleday, 1985), 1081, who also points out that there is nothing in the text to support the suggestion (J. Jeremias) that the ten coins could have represented the woman's dowry.

The Parable of the Lost Son and Brother: 15:11-32

It has always been difficult to find an accurate title for the long final parable (vv. 11-32). The traditional title, "the Prodigal Son," reflects a long-standing tendency to concentrate totally on the first part of the story, that of the younger brother (vv. 12-24), to the neglect of the second half (vv. 25-32), with its far less resolved and more challenging ending. It is tempting to dub the parable simply "the Lost Son," which brings out well the parallel pattern across all three parables: lost sheep, lost coin, lost son. It is not quite adequate, however, because it fails to bring in the older son, who is equally the focus of attention. If the father has lost a son, this son has lost a brother and his attitude to the loss is crucial. Hence I call it—perhaps a little clumsily—"the Lost Son and Brother." We have once again the "triangular" pattern (father, younger brother, older brother) so frequent in this gospel.

The situation presupposed by the parable is that of a wealthy family, with considerable household property and servants. The younger brother's request to be given the property that falls to him (v. 12) has already a callous ring about it. Strictly speaking, a share of the property should accrue to him on his father's death. His demand for it now in some sense says to the father, "You're as good as dead as far as I'm concerned." Very soon, of course, his dissolute style of living squanders the entire sum. In a few quick strokes the parable depicts the personal degradation that then follows (vv. 14-16). He is in a foreign country; his hunger forces him to become a hired laborer for one of its citizens; the work he is given to do, feeding pigs, is for a Jew the most degrading imaginable. He even envies the pigs because the food they have to eat is not available to him.

The Greek phrase "coming to himself" (v. 17) signals a measure of self-knowledge—a moment of realism, though not necessarily at this point moral conversion. The young man calculates that the hired hands on his father's farm, though only servants, have at least food enough to eat. Better to join them in their servitude than to die of hunger in this foreign place. So he prepares a set speech to win over his father: "Father, I have sinned against heaven and before you; I am no longer worthy to be called your son; treat me like one of your hired hands" (vv. 18-19). The speech introduces a distinction between "son" and "hired servant" that from now on is crucial to the narrative.

As the young man makes his return (v. 20a), the father reenters the story. That he should catch sight of his son while he is still "afar off" gives the impression that he spends his days ever on the watch for his son's return. Then he too (like the shepherd, like the woman with the coin) "goes overboard." Filled with compassion (the same Greek word, *splagchnistheis*, used to describe the reaction of the Good Samaritan on seeing the wounded traveler [10:33; also 7:13]), he runs out, falls upon his son's neck (the literal expression), and kisses him (v. 20b). We modern readers have to understand that this is totally unconventional behavior for a dignified man of affairs in the Palestinian cultural world.[3] To leave the house to meet one of lower rank, to run rather than walk sedately, to display emotion extravagantly in public: all this involves serious loss of face and dignity. And that is not all. The speech the son has prepared is cut off by the father before the part about becoming one of the hired hands. That possibility never arises. Orders are quickly given (vv. 22-23): bring out the best robe, put a ring on his finger, sandals on his feet. All symbolize complete reinstatement as son: where slaves went barefoot, members of the family wore shoes; the ring would even signal a measure of authority in the household.[4] Finally—as in the earlier parables—there is to be a communal celebration. The calf that has been fattened is to be killed and eaten. And the reason (v. 24): "for this son of mine was dead and is alive again; he was lost and is found" (v. 24).

We may note that the topic of "sin" and "repentance" has no place in the father's explanation—though that trajectory had certainly been in the young man's mind ("Father, I have sinned . . ." [v. 18, v. 21]). The father thinks only in terms of "dead" and "alive," "lost and found." And so the celebration gets under way (v. 24c).

Now the parable turns to the older brother (vv. 25-32), who, as he will later remind his father (v. 29), has been out in the field working (like a hired servant!) all day. He is surprised at the sound of the music and the dancing, sure signs of a celebration. When he summons a servant to ask what it is all about, he receives a very accurate report: "Your brother has come, and your father has killed the fatted calf, because he has got him back safe and sound" (v. 27; see also v. 23). Immediately, overcome with anger and resentment, he refuses to go in and join the party (v. 28a).

---

[3] K. E. Bailey's discussion of the parable (*Poet and Peasant: A Literary-cultural Approach to the Parables in Luke* [Grand Rapids, MI: Eerdmans, 1976], 158–212) brings out this aspect of the situation very well.

[4] In Gen 41:42 Pharaoh puts his own ring on Joseph's hand to signify the handing over of authority. See François Bovon, *A Commentary on the Gospel of Luke*, Hermeneia, vol. 2 (Minneapolis: Fortress, 2013), 428; I. Howard Marshall, *The Gospel of Luke: A Commentary on the Greek Text*, NIGTC (Grand Rapids, MI: Eerdmans, 1978, repr. 1987), 610.

Again the father forsakes his dignity and leaves the house to meet a son, this time to plead (v. 28b). Patiently he listens while the man pours out his resentment, a resentment directed in the first instance against the father himself: "For all these years I have been working like a slave for you, and I have never disobeyed your command; yet you have never given me even a young goat so that I might celebrate with my friends. But when this son of yours came back, who has devoured your property with prostitutes, you killed the fatted calf for him" (vv. 29-30). Each detail here is significant. First, the man thinks of himself as a servant (for years he has worked "like a slave") rather than a son. He thinks that such work should have earned a decent reward; he is in a "contract" relationship with his father. He disowns his brother as brother, referring to him simply as "your son"; his father, too, he bluntly addresses as "you." What he resents particularly is that his brother has "devoured" the family property, lessening the amount that will eventually fall to himself.[5] As hearers of the parable, we cannot fail to note the reflection here of Luke's sensitivity to the dehumanizing effects of preoccupation with wealth.

Once again (cf. vv. 23b-24), the father makes his explanation (vv. 31-32). He first dwells upon their own immediate relationship: "Son, you are always with me, and all that is mine is yours" (v. 31). Whatever the older brother may have felt, there was never any doubt in the father's mind that he was a son, not a servant. Nor was he working for reward in a contract kind of way; the family property was shared. Had he wanted a calf to celebrate with his friends, he had only to ask or perhaps simply to take it. Then, as regards the younger brother, comes the now-familiar refrain: "But we had to celebrate and rejoice, because this brother of yours was dead and has come to life; he was lost and has been found" (v. 32; cf. v. 23). Where the older brother sees life in terms of a contract relationship—one his brother has forfeited—for the father, the person is more important than what he has or has not done; he can never cease being a brother and a son, and as a brother and a son he has returned.

And there the story ends. We never learn whether the man was persuaded, whether he went in to join the music and the dancing or remained outside, stubbornly and bitterly nursing his anger.

And this is precisely where the parable makes its point. While almost from the start the older brother does not come across as an attractive character, his reaction is in many ways understandable, one with which not a

---

[5] The added detail "with prostitutes" gratuitously embellishes the description (v. 13) of his brother's behavior.

few in the audience might be inclined to agree.[6] The father has in several respects acted extravagantly, certainly over-tolerantly. The story invites the audience to feel the older brother's anger and maybe recognize in themselves several aspects of his resistance: the "contract" mentality, the concern over property squandered, the resentment that others are getting favored treatment instead of what they seem to deserve. It leaves the question, "Well, where are you in the end? Inside, joining in the celebration, or stuck outside, hearing the music and dancing but too angry to go in?"

In its Lukan setting, the story suggests that those who criticize Jesus place themselves in this last situation. He is celebrating the return of the lost family of God. They, for the reasons the parable suggests, make themselves unwilling and unable to join in. Ultimately, then, this last parable joins the others in putting to its audience the question about God. Can you cope with a God imaged by the father in this parable? Do you find in yourself some stirrings of the resistance of the older brother? Can you be part of a family whose hospitality is so extravagant, so uncalculating, so indulgent of human failing as this?[7]

In its original setting the parable serves, as we have noted, to ward off the criticism the scribes and Pharisees mount against Jesus' celebration of God's acceptance. Doubtless, the early church found in it, too, an analysis of Israel's problem with accepting the crucified Messiah and the inclusion of Gentiles in the people of God. The applications are endless. One perhaps that we should not omit considering is that of finding in ourselves and our communities the rather different patterns of sinfulness shown by the two brothers: the overt sinning of the younger, the resentment and resistance of the older—and to ask which of the two patterns the parable suggests to be the more difficult for God to deal with. But sinfulness is not in the end the main point. Fundamentally, like all the parables, the three stories in this chapter ask, "Do you really know God?" Or rather, "Are you comfortable with the God who acts with the foolishness of love displayed by the characters in these parables?"

---

[6] Discussing the parable in workshops and groups, I have always been struck by the number of people who say they sympathize with the older brother and resent what the younger man gets away with.

[7] Interpreting the parable in this way, I am conscious that many women readers will sense acutely the absence of the mother in this story. Nor will they perhaps be much helped by the observation sometimes made to the effect that the father acts more like a mother than a father—or at least displays attributes of both parents. For a critical feminist reading see Susan Durber, "The Female Reader of the Parables of the Lost," *Journal for the Study of the New Testament* 45 (1992): 59–78.

The Hospitality of the Poor
Two Responses to Wealth: 16:1-31

Luke's preoccupation with the challenge wealth poses for conversion comes to a head in chapter 16. At first sight the content of the chapter seems rather disparate. However, the opening parable about the Rogue Manager (vv. 1-13) and the concluding one about the Rich Man and the Beggar Lazarus (vv. 19-31) stand in counterpoise to one another in a mutually illuminating way. It is on these, rather than the block of sayings in between (vv. 14-18), that I shall focus—though even these sayings have a certain role within the overall pattern.

The Parable of the Rogue Manager: 16:1-13

Almost from the time it left the lips of Jesus the parable of the Rogue Manager (vv. 1-8a) has presented a puzzle for interpreters. The sayings appended to it (vv. 8b-13) reflect attempts at various stages of the tradition to make sense of the parable. It is nothing unusual for Jesus to have disreputable characters at the center of his parables. But this one stands in a class of his own. Moreover, his roguish activity is praised by the master (v. 8a) in such a way as to suggest that what he is doing is something to emulate.[1]

The key to understanding the parable lies in being clear about where the manager's "dishonesty" lay. The most obvious solution is to see it consisting in what he does with his master's creditors—getting them to write down reduced amounts of what they owe; in this way he is defrauding his master. But, according to the story (vv. 1-2), the master finds fault with the manager before he has recourse to this stratagem. His dishonesty, or perhaps better his incompetence, has to do with the way he has conducted his master's affairs before his dismissal and is in fact the reason for it. What he does after receiving notice—reducing the debts—is opportunistic but it need not necessarily be wrong.

---

[1] Interpreters are not agreed as to where the parable proper ends: after v. 7? after v. 8a? after v. 8b? With most commentators, I locate the ending after v. 8b—the master's praise of the manager seems essential to the shock or "bite" of the story.

What, in fact, is the steward doing?[2] It is quite likely that the parable envisages a situation where a manager enjoying considerable autonomy lets out items of his master's property for a commission or interest that includes some proportion for himself. There is nothing dishonest in this as far as the master is concerned; he gets his interest and the manager gets a cut as well. What the manager does, after receiving notice of dismissal (vv. 5-7), is to strip away the portion of the interest accruing to himself. He cancels his own cut because he reckons that it will be more advantageous, when he is out of work—and too weak to dig and too ashamed to beg (v. 3)—to have the goodwill of people who may be able to help him, welcoming him into their homes (v. 4). His master praises him for what he has done (v. 8a) because, in his own interest, he has acted "sensibly": he has not clung to his wealth but used it to win goodwill that will serve him in his coming hour of need.

The parable, then, refers to the great reversal that will take place with the coming of the kingdom. Faced with a crisis, the worldly-wise manager took vigorous action. He acted "violently" against his own immediate interest (stripping away his wealth) to preserve his long-term future. In this sense, as a "child of this world" he showed himself more shrewd than the "children of light" (v. 8b). If the worldly manager is prepared to take violent action against himself, how much more—in view of the higher stakes operative—should the hearers of Jesus ("children of light") be prepared to do so? They should be ready to give away their wealth now in the form of alms so that when the great reversal comes and the poor have their privileged places in the kingdom (6:20), these same poor will welcome them into "eternal dwellings" (v. 9), offering them the hospitality of God. As generally for Luke, the only really useful thing to do with money is to give it away now so that it will store up "treasure in heaven" (12:33).

The appended sayings (vv. 10-13) sit in some tension with the parable. They presuppose the idea of the Christian life as a stewardship in which the wealth one handles is not one's own but wealth God wishes the entire world to share. Such a responsibility is grave and requires absolute single-mindedness. You cannot wholeheartedly serve both the "wealth" of God and the everyday wealth of this world (v. 13).

---

[2] Here I follow in particular the interpretation of Joseph A. Fitzmyer, *The Gospel according to Luke X-XXIV*, AB 28A (Garden City, NY: Doubleday, 1985), 1097–98.

Controversy with Pharisees: 16:14-18

It is hard to account for the series of sayings lying between the two parables in this chapter. The sayings seem disconnected, both with the wider context and among each other. Clearly, polemic against the Pharisees is central. Characterized as "lovers of money," they are portrayed as ridiculing the attitude toward wealth they have just heard from Jesus (v. 14). In response Jesus renews an earlier charge against them (11:37-44): attentive to external observance, their main concern is to appear righteous in the eyes of others; but what God looks to and prizes is the intention of the heart (v. 15).

What seems to be at stake in the sayings that follow (vv. 16, 17, 18) is the issue of the continuing validity of the Jewish law. All along we have noted Luke's desire to emphasize both continuity and newness with respect to the law. The first statement (v. 16) seems to reflect this: the law (along with "the prophets" [the rest of Scripture]) has been in effect right up to the ministry of John the Baptist (v. 16a). Since then, the preaching of the kingdom has created a totally new situation—one where, through the ministry of Jesus, the disreputable (tax collectors and sinners, for example) are "forcing" their way in to the people of God (v. 16b).[3] But (v. 17) this does not mean that Jesus is overthrowing the law. On the contrary—this seems to be the necessary implication—he is actually fulfilling the true intention of the law at a deeper, more comprehensive level.

The ruling excluding divorce in verse 18[4]—otherwise inexplicable in this context—would then illustrate this deeper fulfillment. The law, in

---

[3] The saying (appearing in another form also in Matt 11:12) remains one of the most obscure in the gospel tradition. In its Lukan form it displays the evangelist's sense that the history of salvation falls into distinct epochs: that of the "Law and the prophets" (time of the promises); that of the preaching of the kingdom (the ministry of Jesus); that of the mission of the disciples after Pentecost (understandably, not mentioned here). The sense of the final verb *biazetai* here is obscure, since it can be understood in either a passive ("are being forced") or middle sense ("force themselves"). The latter is perhaps preferable: those who truly welcome the onset of the kingdom ("all") are prepared to do violence to their worldly attachments (on the model of the rogue steward in the preceding parable) in order to enter the kingdom. See further, Brendan Byrne, "Forceful Stewardship and Neglectful Wealth: A Contemporary Reading of Luke 16," *Pacifica* 1/1 (1988): 1–14, esp. 12–13; François Bovon, *A Commentary on the Gospel of Luke*, Hermeneia, vol. 2 (Minneapolis: Fortress, 2013), 466–67.

[4] The Lukan statement (contrast Mark 10:11-12) reflects the Palestinian situation where only the male partner could initiate a divorce.

the shape of Deuteronomy 24:1-4, allowed a man to divorce his wife and marry another woman as if she were just another item of exchangeable property. Jesus' exclusion of this practice, rigorous as it may seem, defends human dignity, especially that of the woman. As the law elsewhere teaches (Gen 2:20-24), marriage involves the union of two persons in companionship. It is totally inappropriate for one partner (the male) simply to dismiss the other as though she were any other possession. In this way, contrary to the misinterpretation of adversaries such as the Pharisees, Jesus is not overthrowing the true intention of the law.

Parable of the Rich Man and Lazarus the Beggar: 16:19-31

This is the only parable in the gospel tradition where a character (here Lazarus) is named or where a biblical figure (Abraham) intervenes. It also falls into two quite distinct parts: the story proper (vv. 19-26), then a kind of epilogue dealing with conversion (vv. 27-31).[5] In its full form the parable illustrates two of Luke's major themes: first, the coming reversal of all things—in particular, the fortunes of the rich and the poor (the parable virtually enacts the first beatitude [6:20; cf. 6:24]); second, resistance to conversion.

The parable proper (vv. 19-26) displays a carefully contrived structure. The structure places maximum emphasis upon the reversal that occurs when both characters have died.[6] Though their respective fortunes are totally reversed, the situation remains in one crucial respect absolutely the same: between the rich man and the beggar there is no exchange. The fixity that existed on earth, with the rich man completely oblivious to the plight of Lazarus outside his door, has been cemented into an eternal fixity in the life after death. Between Hades and the bosom of Abraham there is no commerce whatsoever.

There are more detailed correspondences as well. In the earthly situation the rich man is inside, Lazarus outside; in the afterlife situation Lazarus is inside ("in Abraham's bosom"), the rich man outside

---

[5] Similar stories involving reversal of fortune and retribution in the afterlife circulated in the wider milieu at the time of Jesus. It is possible that he or the early church tradition took up and adapted a preexisting folk tale of this kind. For examples of such, both from within Palestine and beyond (esp. Egypt), see Bovon, *Luke*, 2.476–78.

[6] In technical terms, the structure is chiastic in that the elements correspond in reverse order around a middle ("crossover") point (here the deaths of each character described in v. 22).

(in Hades). Where once Lazarus had an unfulfilled longing (to sate his hunger with scraps from the table), now the rich man has an unfulfilled longing (to slake his raging thirst). Where Lazarus had been licked by dogs,[7] the rich man is tormented in flames. The central statement (v. 22) indicating the deaths of both characters is the "axle" upon which the reversal turns. We can set it out as follows:

A Fixed position (contrast)	Rich Man (inside), v. 19
	Lazarus (outside), v. 20
B Unfulfilled longing (hunger)	Lazarus (outside), v. 21a
C Torment (sores; dogs licking)	Lazarus (outside), v. 21b
	Lazarus: angelic transport
D Axle: Deaths—Reversal (v. 22)	
	Rich Man: burial
C' Torment (flames)	Rich Man (outside), v. 23
B' Unfulfilled longing (thirst)	Rich Man (outside), v. 24
A' Fixed position (contrast)	Rich Man (outside), vv. 25-26
	Lazarus (inside)

At the end (vv. 25-26) the authoritative voice of Abraham brings out the central point: the fixity of the situation set up by the rich man in this life, in that he chose to ignore the beggar at his gate, encases an eternal fixity as well. The difference is that where once that fixity operated to his benefit and the disadvantage of Lazarus, now (the reversal) it is the other way round. And just as there was no "crossing" on earth between the rich man at his sumptuous table and Lazarus, so now there is fixed a "great chasm" ruling out any crossing from "here" (Abraham's bosom) to "there" (Hades). He had not been hospitable to Lazarus; now Lazarus cannot be hospitable to him.

Note that the story does not portray Lazarus as notably virtuous in any way. It is his poor and neglected condition that is the object of God's action. Nor is the rich man wicked in other respects. It is simply that his luxury so absorbed him that he did not notice—and not noticing sealed his fate.

Ultimately, then, the parable is about failure in conversion, which explains why it has a sequel (vv. 27-31) prolonging the dialogue between

---

[7] Since dogs were considered unclean, this canine attention is not benign. It adds to the indignity of Lazarus's situation and shows up the fact that he receives no human relief.

the rich man and Abraham. Unable to do anything about his own fate, the rich man wants Abraham to send Lazarus on an errand to warn his five brothers before they, too, end up in the same plight (vv. 27-28). Abraham suggests that all that they need to hear is contained already in the Scriptures ("Moses and the prophets" [v. 29]); the Scriptures, after all, contain ample warnings about the need to care for the widow, the orphan, the needy stranger at the door (Deut 10:18; 24:19, 21; 27:19; Ps 94:6; Isa 1:7; Jer 22:3; Zech 7:10; etc.). But the rich man knows that this will not be enough to change his brothers. Sadly and knowingly Abraham replies, "If they do not listen to Scripture, neither will they be convinced even if someone rises from the dead" (v. 31). At the level of the story the one who would come back from the dead would of course be Lazarus. Christian readers, however, would not fail to hear an allusion to the risen Lord. The story, then, does not simply have Jewish leaders in view (see v. 14) but also the wealthy in the Christian community with whose attitude Luke is so preoccupied.

From this aspect of conversion the two parables in Luke 16 shed light on each other. The manager, rogue though he may have been, took vigorous action when he saw a crisis coming, even though that action meant paring away at his present wealth. The rich man, on the contrary, took no action at all and was completely caught out when the crisis came. Inhospitable to Lazarus, he found himself eternally excluded from the hospitality of God. Both parables, singly or together, do not cease to grow in relevance in a world where so much of the population sits like Lazarus outside the door.[8]

---

[8] For an integrated interpretation of the entire chapter, Luke 16, along these lines see Byrne, "Forceful Stewardship" (n. 3 above).

Toward the End of the Journey
17:1–18:30

As his journey to Jerusalem enters its final stages, Jesus continues to instruct his disciples on various topics, occasionally turning aside to engage opponents as well. The content on the whole remains disparate, held together simply by the growing sense of crisis as the path to Jerusalem shortens. Jesus does not conceal that it will be a crisis for his disciples and his opponents as well as for himself.

Instructions and a Healing: 17:1-19

Life in the Community of Faith: 17:1-10

The instructions for the disciples no longer concern initial conversion but ongoing life in the community of faith. They particularly address community leaders. First (vv. 1-2) there is a severe warning about providing occasion for "little ones" to stumble.[1] Then (vv. 3-4), since there will inevitably be instances of misbehavior and injury, structures of correction ("rebuke") and reconciliation must be in place. When the offender repents, forgiveness must be ample and overflowing—even though the pattern be repeated seven times.[2]

In reaction, it would seem, to this demanding teaching, the apostles ask Jesus to increase their faith (v. 5). His response (v. 6) does not imply that the disciples have no faith but that the little faith they have ("the size of a mustard seed") is enough to work outstanding miracles if only they exploit its possibilities to the full.[3] To take the risk of faith seriously is to clothe oneself with the power of God.

---

[1] "Little ones" seems to refer simply to ordinary members of the community. Their nurturing in correct faith is a serious responsibility.

[2] Luke does not have the "seventy times seven" (18:21) of Matthew's more structured pattern of dealing with intra-community dispute.

[3] I follow here C. H. Talbert, *Reading Luke: A Literary and Theological Commentary on the Third Gospel* (New York: Crossroads, 1989), 161; see also Joseph A.

The final warning (vv. 7-10) rests on an image from the everyday practice of slavery. That Jesus should use such an image is off-putting, as is also perhaps the actual content of what is said. Does God really regard us as "worthless slaves" (v. 10) who deserve no gratitude whatsoever? Once again Jesus is making a point from an aspect of life familiar to his audience without necessarily approving or disapproving the practice itself; we ought not to press too much out of the image in a moralizing kind of way. The point is simply that community leaders should not think they have a right to rewards or perquisites simply because of their office or status. To serve others in God's name is a privilege; it requires no further reward.[4]

A Grateful Samaritan: 17:11-19

As Jesus began his journey to Jerusalem, a Samaritan village proved inhospitable (9:51-53). When the disciples wished to respond violently, Jesus held them back (9:54-55). Later, in one of his parables (10:29-37), a Samaritan illustrated neighborliness in an extraordinary degree. Now, as the end of the journey approaches, a Samaritan once again displays the appropriate response.[5] On the border between Samaria and Galilee ten lepers, keeping their distance as they were obliged to do, cry out to Jesus for mercy (vv. 12-13). All ten are made clean when they follow Jesus' instructions to go and show themselves to the priest (see Lev 13:49). For nine, that is the end of the matter. But the tenth, who happens to be a Samaritan, returns, loudly praising God. He prostrates himself before

---

Fitzmyer, *The Gospel according to Luke X-XXIV*, AB 28A (Garden City, NY: Doubleday, 1985), 1143. The Greek term translated "mulberry tree" designates a fairly large tree, known for its extensive root system. Hence the difficulty of its being uprooted. The idea of a tree "planted" in the sea is odd. Again we have a case of hyperbole on the part of Jesus.

[4] It is well to keep in mind here the rather opposite direction of a very similar image in 12:37, where the master who finds his servants watching when he returns actually does sit them down and wait upon them; see also Jesus' observation to his disciples that he is among them "as one who serves" (22:27).

[5] It may have been the note of thanksgiving that caused this episode to be linked to the preceding instruction in the tradition. Robert Tannehill (*The Narrative Unity of Luke-Acts: A Literary Interpretation: Volume One: The Gospel according to Luke* [Philadelphia: Fortress, 1986], 119) notes that the scene introduces a person whose character combines features that the audience would not normally expect to find together: "Samaritan" (negative) and "grateful recipient of salvation" (positive); see 10:29-37 ("Samaritan" and "model of neighborliness").

Jesus in gratitude and receives the assurance: "Get up and go on your way; your faith has saved you" (v. 19; cf. 7:50; 8:48; 18:42; also 19:9). All ten received physical healing. But only the one on the margins ("this foreigner," as Jesus calls him [v. 18]) fully experiences salvation. The episode well illustrates Luke's sense of the "knowledge of salvation" (1:77): beyond physical healing or rescue, salvation includes praise and gratitude to God for the healing and freedom received. It means coming to "know" God (in the deep biblical sense of "know") in a new way and being transformed and set on a fresh path of life through that knowledge.

Teaching on the Kingdom and the End Time: 17:20-37

The Kingdom of God: 17:20-21

The phrase "kingdom of God" traditionally referred to God's undisputed and undisturbed rule over a faithful people. A query from the Pharisees (v. 20a) about when this blessed state would arrive elicits from Jesus significant teaching concerning the kingdom. He takes the Pharisees' question to imply that one can calculate the coming of the kingdom by observing historical signs and portents. For Jesus this completely mistakes the nature of the kingdom. The kingdom is principally about reclaiming human beings from the grip of Satan for a life-giving relationship with God—something that is already in train in his own preaching and healing (see 11:20). Thus (v. 21) the "kingdom of God" is "among you" or "in your midst"[6] in the sense of something "you" would see if only you would view with converted hearts the messianic activity going on all around.[7] The "when" question implies blindness to all this.

The Day of the Son of Man: 17:22-37

While the kingdom of God may be present in this sense, there is a great deal that must happen before the final, definitive establishment of

---

[6] The Greek phrase *entos hymōn* is open to various translations: (1) "within you" (in the sense of "in your heart" as an invisible, inward power; (2) "among you" or "in your midst"; (3) "within your grasp," "at your disposal (if only you would take advantage of it)." The first, while traditionally favored, introduces a sense of the kingdom never otherwise attested in Luke-Acts; the third would fit the context well but linguistic evidence for it is sparse. It seems best to adopt the second meaning; see Fitzmyer, *Luke X–XXIV*, 1161–62; François Bovon, *A Commentary on the Gospel of Luke*, Hermeneia, vol. 2 (Minneapolis: Fortress, 2013), 515–17.

[7] In this sense the statement recalls Jesus' response earlier on to the messengers from John the Baptist (7:22).

God's rule in the world. The long instruction directed to the disciples that follows provides a balance to the statement about the presence of the kingdom.[8] To think that one is already in the final age when, externally, the conditions of the present, unredeemed time prevail, is a sure recipe for discouragement and falling away. It is essential that believers have a correct grasp of the "program" of the end.

The title "Son of Man" refers to a heavenly figure who will function as judge of the world and vindicator of the persecuted faithful before the final establishment of God's reign in the universe.[9] Early Christian tradition applied this role to the risen and exalted Jesus and keenly awaited his return as Son of Man to complete his messianic work.[10] The instruction warns believers against repeating the error the Pharisees made about the kingdom (v. 20), thinking that the arrival of the Son of Man is something that can be foreseen or calculated. His arrival will be as sudden as lightning (v. 24). The crucial thing is not to be so absorbed in possessions and everyday affairs (vv. 27, 28) as to be left out—like the people in the biblical instances quoted (the days of Noah; the destruction of Sodom [vv. 26-32]). The biblical examples end with Lot's wife (v. 32): she was lost because she looked back wistfully to the possessions she was leaving behind.[11] An attempt to "save one's life"—illustrated by people on the rooftops going down to secure their possessions—will result in losing it (v. 33; see the parallel in 9:24).[12]

---

[8] This is the first of two instructions on the end of the age given by Luke. It is based on the "Q" source Luke shares with Matthew. The second instruction, in 21:8-36, derives from Mark 13:5-37. In contrast to Luke, Matthew combines material from both sources to construct a single, lengthy discourse, 24:4–25:46.

[9] The origin of the expectation of a "Son of Man" figure in this sense is disputed. It is most likely, however, that behind all such expectation lies the vision of "one like a son of Man" in Dan 7:13-14, a collective symbol for the persecuted faithful who are soon to be vindicated when God confers sovereignty and kingship upon them. Later speculation personified the collective symbol into an individual redeemer figure from heaven. Christian application of the title to Jesus seems to have involved fusion between this "heavenly redeemer" idea and the more this-worldly expectation of a Messiah, Son of David, also applied to him. See further, Byrne, *A Costly Freedom: A Theological Reading of Mark's Gospel* (Collegeville, MN: Liturgical Press, 2008), 11–13.

[10] Whether Jesus in his historical life identified himself as Son of Man in this sense is disputed.

[11] See Luke Timothy Johnson, *The Gospel of Luke*, Sacra Pagina 3 (Collegeville, MN: Liturgical Press, 1991), 267.

[12] The context gives a rather different meaning to this saying of Jesus than the meaning in the parallel instance in 9:24.

The final illustrations (vv. 34-35)—two (men) in one bed; two women grinding corn, with one being "taken," one "left"—reflect the social conditions of village life in Palestine in Jesus' day, where members of a family slept together on a single large bed and where women rose early to grind corn. The point of one being "taken" (presumably for salvation) while the other is "left" (for destruction)[13] reflects in both cases the discriminatory judgment that the coming of the Son of Man will bring; it will cut right across bonds of family unity and collaboration.[14] In short, no measures that human beings can take will guarantee salvation on the day of the Son of Man. The only way to cope with the uncertainty of the time of his arrival is to give undivided attention to the relationship with God. Those who do so will have no problem with the arrival, however sudden, of the Son of Man.

At the close of the instruction (v. 37), the "when" question having been dealt with, the disciples try a new tack: "Where, . . . ?" To this equally inappropriate question—since the kingdom of God is not confined to a place—Jesus gives a grim response: if you want to find a corpse, look for hovering vultures. The appearance of the Son of Man will be equally obvious.

How to Pray in the Time of Waiting: 18:1-17

The next three episodes all have to do with the appropriate way for disciples to pray during this time of waiting for the full arrival of the kingdom.

The Parable of the Unjust Judge and the Widow: 18:1-8

In its Lukan setting (v. 1; vv. 6-8),[15] this parable addresses the temptation to give up hope and lose heart in the midst of the evils of the time. It appears to commend praying to God with the kind of persistence displayed by the widow in her dealings with the judge. But matters are not quite so simple. The parable hardly means to suggest God needs to

---

[13] The sense in each case could be precisely the opposite: "taken" for judgment; "left" (alive) for salvation.

[14] See Bovon, *Luke*, 2.523.

[15] It is not altogether clear where the original parable ended, that is, whether it included v. 6. Without this concluding comment the point of the parable is hardly clear. But the fact that "the Lord" must refer to Jesus suggests that the story proper has already come to an end.

be worn down like the judge. Basically it commends an attitude of trust in God that would motivate such persistence.

At the center of the action stands an unsavory character (see also 16:1-8a): a judge who fears neither God nor fellow human beings and so takes no action in defense of a widow who had appealed to him. Lacking the support of a husband and possibly adult sons (see 7:11-17), widows were particularly dependent on the smooth and fair working of the institutions of justice. Hence the plight of this woman, whose entreaties the judge so long ignores. He stirs himself on her behalf only when he suspects that her verbal entreaties are about to give way to actual physical violence.[16] Like the rogue manager (16:1-8a), he moves against his own previous inclination because he realizes that a stage has been reached where to take no action may incur serious loss.[17] The point of the parable, brought out by the comments in verses 6-7, rests, once again (see especially 11:5-13), on an *a fortiori* logic. If the unjust judge at long last—albeit through base and self-interested motives—moves to grant justice to the woman, how much more certainly and readily will the God of all goodness move to grant justice to chosen ones who make entreaty day and night.

It is understandable that the final comment (v. 8b) has to do with faith. Faith in God, displayed in prayer that is both trusting and calm as well as constant and persistent, is the right attitude for the time before the full realization of the kingdom. The parable also offers a sharp challenge in a world where so much injustice prevails and where the poor, like the widow, continue to cry out for justice day and night. Those whose actions or inertia allow the world to remain for the majority an unjust and inhospitable place must reckon with the truth that God is a God of justice. How long can such a God allow the situation to go on without redress?

The Parable of the Pharisee and the Tax Collector: 18:9-14

This parable continues the theme of prayer but is addressed not to the disciples in general but to those who "trusted in their own righteousness and regarded others with contempt" (v. 9). "Righteousness" is

---

[16] Literally, the Greek reads "lest she come and give me a black eye" (*hypopiazein*). The expression comes from the boxing arena. While figurative meanings ("besmirch the reputation," "wear out completely") are attested for this word (see Fitzmyer, *Luke X-XXIV*, 1179), the more literal sense seems preferable here. We have already been told (v. 2) that the judge had no regard for his reputation.

[17] The story is comical and may allude to some known incident where a desperate widow threw a few punches to get action in her case.

"Bible-speak" with little meaning for people today. Basically it denotes living in accordance with the requirements of the covenant. "Being justified" is the verdict of acceptance one has or hopes to have in the eyes of God on the basis of such "righteous" behavior. In a strongly religious society, the issue as to who is righteous and who is not will always be central. In the milieu of Jesus, the gospels particularly associate such concern with the Pharisees—though we must be careful not to conclude that the kind of judgmental behavior represented by the Pharisee in this parable was typical of Pharisees in general, let alone of Judaism as a religion. It affects all religions, Christianity included.

The Pharisee prays, it is true. But, whereas in prayer the focus should be above all upon God, this man's concentration is upon himself[18] and—worse still—upon the failings of his fellow human beings (vv. 11-12). Before beginning to enumerate his positive virtues—in themselves quite admirable (fasting, giving up a tenth of one's income)—he moves to detach himself from the sinful mass of humankind ("thieves, rogues, adulterers"), of which a representative is so conveniently at hand in the person of the tax collector at the back. The Pharisee illustrates the attitude of those who can only bolster their own self-image by putting down other people. Life is a competition in virtue, and God assesses and bestows prizes on the winners. Prayer is keeping God informed about how successfully one is doing compared with the shortcomings of others.

In contrast, the tax collector stands at the very back, scarcely lifting his eyes to heaven, praying simply that God be merciful to him, a sinner (v. 13). In what sense does he own himself to be a sinner? Is it because of personal moral failure, for which he now repents? We should not immediately jump to this conclusion. Could it simply be that he finds himself trapped in an occupation that makes him a sinner in his own eyes and those of his world—an occupation that, with a family to support and no other possibilities of employment, he cannot simply abandon? All this the parable leaves open. In any case, as Jesus points out (v. 14a), God's view reverses both verdicts. The one who came to God's house in his own eyes a sinner went home with God's favor ("justified"); the one so sure of his virtue went home without it.

The parable perfectly illustrates Luke's theme of reversal (v. 14b). God will one day move to align the human situation with the nature of God

---

[18] This seems to be the meaning of the curious Greek phrase describing his prayer, which literally reads, "He prayed these things with respect to himself" (*pros heauton*).

as God truly is—not as persons like the Pharisee perceive God to be. That reversal will take place in the full realization of the kingdom (6:20-26 [the Beatitudes and Woes]). The task of Jesus is to summon human beings to align themselves with that new perspective so that when the reversal comes they will be in the right position to benefit from it. The parable, then, offers more than a simple instruction on prayer. It belongs to the preaching of the kingdom.

It could also offer comfort to many people today who find themselves or their loved ones (for example, their children) caught in situations judged objectively sinful on more traditional thinking—whether in the area of sexuality or marital involvement or professional occupation. In a complex world, responsibilities often run in several directions, excluding simple application of rules and norms to the pattern of individual lives. The parable suggests that God may be able to cope with "disorder" in terms of objective morality or church discipline far better than those who guard the tradition sometimes imagine.

Prayer, as the Pharisee failed to see, consists not in our telling God how things are but in allowing God to communicate to us the divine vision of life and reality. Two people came up to God's house to pray. Only one really found the hospitality that was there. As so often in Luke's gospel (the "triangle" once more), we are left with the challenge: Which one are you going to be?

Blessing of the Children: 18:15-17[19]

This episode continues several themes set running by the two parables. The disciples have still to learn that those on the margins have privileged access to the kingdom. They do wrong, then, when, like "minders," they shoo away people who bring along their infants for Jesus to touch. It is to "such as these" that the kingdom of God belongs (v. 16).[20]

Jesus makes a further point (v. 17): whoever does not receive the kingdom of God as a little child will never enter it. The saying does not idealize little children in a way oblivious to the self-centeredness and cruelty

---

[19] At this point (18:15) Luke's gospel resumes the sequence of Mark (Mark 10:13-16), thereby concluding its "Great Insertion" (9:51–18:14) into Mark's much shorter journey narrative.

[20] By writing "infants" (*brephē*) rather than "little children" (*paidia*), as in Mark 10:13 and Matt 19:13, Luke accentuates the sense of the kingdom as reaching out to embrace all, without distinction or necessary predisposition, since a newborn infant is incapable of any disposition at all.

that all children from time to time display. The point—and the link with the preceding parable—is that a child has no capacity to earn or pay for what it needs. Receiving everything as pure gift, it has nothing to give in response, save affection and love. Such is the case with the kingdom. It is God's unmerited, unearnable gift, calling simply for a response of grateful love. Jesus' welcome of the children and their receptivity to him is the perfect paradigm of the "welcome" extended to all in the hospitality of God.

The Difficulty and Reward of Following Jesus: 18:18-30

The Rich Ruler: 18:18-23

As Jesus' long journey approaches its goal, the gospel provides yet another reminder of what following him involves (see 9:57-62). A person of influence ("a certain ruler") seeks guidance on what he should do to inherit eternal life (v. 18). Jesus' two-stage response—pointing first to the commandments (v. 20), then inviting the man to sell all and follow him (v. 22)—illustrates the leap beyond conventional religion that discipleship involves. By selling all he owns[21] and distributing the money to the poor, the man will replace the security his wealth has provided up till now with credit in a heavenly "bank" ("treasure in heaven"; see 12:33-34). With this new security, he will be set on the path to eternal life in the company of Jesus ("Come, follow me").

This man wants eternal life but, on these terms, too much is being asked. He does not respond with anger or rejection of Jesus, nor in Luke's account are we told that he goes away. We learn simply that he "becomes sad" (v. 23). In his heart he knows what he wants—relationship with God in the company of Jesus. But attachment to wealth gets in the way. He is going to miss out on the joy of the kingdom.

Reflection upon Detachment: 18:24-30

The episode prompts Jesus to offer a reflection notorious for its seeming exaggeration: "With what difficulty those with possessions enter the kingdom of God! It is easier for a camel to pass through the eye of a needle . . . " (vv. 24-25)![22] When hearers protest that this makes salvation

---

[21] Characteristically Luke adds "all," a qualification lacking in Mark and Matthew.

[22] A further instance of Jesus' poetic exaggeration (see p. 78, n. 4 above). There is no evidence that Jesus was alluding to some small gate ("Needle Gate"?) existing in Jerusalem at the time.

impossible (v. 26), he replies that God can achieve what is not possible for human beings.

This prompts Peter, speaking on behalf of the other disciples, to point out that they have in fact done what Jesus invited the rich ruler to do: left their homes and followed him (v. 28; see 5:11). Jesus replies in more general terms. Everyone who has left house (therefore wealth) and family ties (wife, brothers, parents, children) for the sake of the kingdom of God will receive "very much more"[23] in this age and in the age to come "eternal life." They will receive, then, what the ruler asked for: eternal life. But even before that, in this age they will experience the joy of the kingdom (see 10:20-24). This foretaste of the kingdom in the company of Jesus is "very much more" than any joy emanating from marriage or family life or possessions.

While the Christian tradition, particularly in more recent times, has placed a high value upon marriage and family life, it is no secret that the New Testament displays ambiguity in this area. The Synoptic Gospels consistently portray Jesus requiring his followers to surrender family ties in order to devote themselves wholeheartedly to the kingdom. Only with the Deutero-Pauline and post-Pauline Letters are family values reaffirmed (see Eph 5:21–6:4; Col 3:18-21; Titus 1:6; 2:1-8; 1 Pet 3:1-7). The Catholic tradition has dealt with this ambiguity by encouraging a separate class of believers (monks, nuns, members of religious congregations) to live out the ideal of celibacy, while the majority pursue family life; for more than a millennium Latin Christianity has also required celibacy of its clergy. This arrangement is clearly now in the melting pot—partly, though by no means totally, because of the renewed realization (Vatican II) that the New Testament calls all believers to perfection and that every Christian life should in some way reflect the freedom and renunciation of the kingdom. Whatever shape (or shapes) this call will take in the future, being a follower of Jesus will always require placing the relationship with God above all other ties and commitments.

---

[23] "Very much more" in Luke corresponds to the more familiar "hundredfold" in Mark (10:30) and Matthew (19:29).

Hospitality in Jericho

18:31–19:27

Jesus' long journey is now fast approaching its goal: the "visitation" of Jerusalem. As the last stop before Jerusalem, he visits the city of Jericho. Here he finds and gives hospitality in a remarkable exchange—a stark contrast to what he will receive from the leaders in Jerusalem.

The Scripture to Be Accomplished: 18:31-34

While still on the road, Jesus takes the select band of the apostles aside to make clear once more all that awaits him in Jerusalem (v. 31). This third warning about the passion (see 9:22; 9:43-45) is very explicit: Jesus is going to be handed over to the Gentiles, mocked, insulted, spat upon, flogged, killed, and on the third day rise again—all to "accomplish" what has been "written about the Son of Man by the prophets" (v. 31b). For the present, it all escapes the apostles' understanding.[1] Full understanding will come only when the gap between reality (the suffering and death of Jesus) and expectation (their conventional messianic hopes) is overcome by the risen Lord explaining how all this does, in fact, "accomplish" the Scriptures (24:25-32, 44-47).[2]

A Blind Person Finds Healing: 18:35-43

It is ironical, in view of the "blindness" with regard to his fate that the apostles display, that the last cure Jesus works in the gospel is to restore sight to a blind person.[3] As Jesus approaches Jericho,[4] a blind beggar,

---

[1] The passive construction ("was hidden from them") suggests divine agency in the lack of understanding; see also 24:16.

[2] While stressing the apostles' failure in understanding, Luke omits at this point the major episode in Mark (10:35-45) that graphically illustrates it: the request of the sons of Zebedee; see also Matt 20:20-28.

[3] Not counting, that is, Jesus' healing of the severed ear of the high priest's servant on the occasion of his arrest (22:50).

[4] In Mark and Matthew the healing takes place as Jesus *leaves* Jericho. Luke transposes the time in order to allow for a highly significant episode to take place *in* Jericho: his stay with Zacchaeus (19:1-10).

correctly hailing him by his messianic title, "Son of David," cries out for help. The disciples, once again playing the role of "minders" (see also 18:15), try to silence the man. But the beggar, another of those marginalized ones who truly know their need for salvation, has the faith to break through barriers to obtain what he wants. As Jesus observes (v. 42), the man's faith brings him salvation. His sight restored, he follows Jesus, glorifying God, while all the people praise God for what they have seen (v. 43). The healing brought about through the faith of an individual has once again become a communal experience of salvation (see 7:16).[5]

Zacchaeus Exchanges Hospitality with Jesus: 19:1-10

As Jesus passes through Jericho, a man called Zacchaeus wants to see him but suffers exclusion on two grounds (vv. 2-3). First, he is too short of stature to see over the crowd. Secondly, he is a tax collector, a member of a class compromised in the eyes of most Jews because it made a living collecting revenue for the occupying power, Rome. The physical problem symbolizes the exclusion he suffers on the socioreligious level. No one in the crowd is going to stand aside for him.

The tax collector overcomes the physical problem by climbing a tree (v. 4), something a child or young person would be more likely to do than a dignified person of affairs. That is, he does something extravagant—thereby joining a long list of characters in the gospel who perform extravagant gestures in pursuit of or in response to salvation.

The gesture breaks through the barrier and gives Zacchaeus access to Jesus. The visitor to Jericho that the whole town has come out to see stops below his tree and declares, "Zacchaeus, make haste and come down; for I must stay at your house today" (v. 5). As readers of the gospel, we recognize in that "must" (Greek: *dei*) the divine purpose that drives the mission of Jesus and shapes its direction.

Zacchaeus, as we might expect, welcomes Jesus joyfully (v. 6). But "they" all begin to murmur: "He has gone to be the guest of one who is a sinner" (v. 7). The negative reaction from the nameless "they" signals the presence of a third party in need of conversion—the Lukan "triangle" once more.

In contrast to the similar situation in the house of Simon the Pharisee (7:36-50), Jesus does not on this occasion tell a parable. Emboldened by

---

[5] Only Luke's version (cf. Mark 10:52; Matt 20:34) makes mention of the wider praise of God among the people.

the presence of his guest, Zacchaeus makes a striking declaration about his professional conduct (v. 8). Most translations (the NRSV among them) put this double declaration in the future tense: "Look, half of my possessions, Lord, I will give to the poor; and if I have defrauded anyone of anything, I will pay back four times as much." This implies that the tax collector has undergone a conversion and is declaring an intention to abandon his controversial trade and the exploitation it involves. But in the original text the two Greek verbs stating his intent are quite unambiguously in the present tense. Zacchaeus does not say "I will give," but "I give . . . " On this understanding he would not be declaring his intentions for the future but describing—and defending—his current practice.[6] *He* has not undergone a conversion; he didn't have to. As far as conversion is concerned, it is those who have misjudged him, labeled him "a sinner" (v. 7), who primarily come to mind.

Jesus, at any rate, accepts the tax collector as he is and goes on to make one of the great declarations of the gospel: "Today salvation has come to this house" (v. 9a). The statement raises echoes of the great "Today" sounded at Nazareth (4:21), when Jesus declared that he was fulfilling "Today" the prophecy of Isaiah 61:1-2 concerning the Messiah. (We will hear it again when he assures another outcast, the thief dying next to him on a cross: "Today you will be with me in paradise" [23:43].) In Zacchaeus's case Jesus adds an explanation: "because this one too is a son of Abraham" (v. 9b), a biblical way of saying, "He's one of us; he's at home in the people of God; he's included within the community of salvation" (see "daughter of Abraham" in 13:16).

---

[6] This interpretation, long suppressed in the Christian interpretive tradition, has been forcefully revived by Joseph Fitzmyer (*The Gospel according to Luke X-XXIV*, AB 28A [Garden City, NY: Doubleday, 1985], 1220–21), who, aside from the tense of the verbs, points out that Jesus makes no reference to Zacchaeus's faith, repentance, or conversion and pronounces not forgiveness but vindication (contrast 7:37-48; also 5:20-21, 27-32). For an equally vigorous defense of the traditional interpretation (taking the verbs as futuristic presents in light of the requirements of the context) see two short articles by Dennis Hamm, "Luke 19:8 Once Again: Does Zacchaeus Defend or Resolve?," *Journal of Biblical Literature* 107 (1988): 431–37; Zacchaeus Revisited Once More: A Story of Vindication or Conversion?" *Biblica* 72 (1991): 248–52; also François Bovon, *A Commentary on the Gospel of Luke*, Hermeneia, vol. 2 (Minneapolis: Fortress, 2013), 598–99. While adopting here the position revived by Fitzmyer, I readily concede that the evidence, one way or the other, is finely balanced.

The total statement ("Today salvation . . .") implies that what has happened to Zacchaeus provides an illustration—a definition in action, so to speak—of "salvation" as Luke understands it. "Salvation" is not something purely for the future—though a future, transcendent aspect is not lacking. Salvation begins here and now ("Today") as Jesus—and subsequently the church in his name—seeks out, finds, and incorporates within the community the excluded and the lost, rich tax collectors like Zacchaeus among them. The Son of Man has not come to judge and condemn but to seek out and save the lost (v. 10). That is the whole point of his saving mission.

If we are right to translate Zacchaeus's statement in the present tense, rather than personal conversion, what changes for him is his position with respect to the community. Jesus brings him in from the margins to the center. If any party has to undergo conversion in this episode it is the third party in the "triangle," the murmuring, criticizing "they." Did they remove the label "sinner" from Zacchaeus? Did they accept his inclusion? We do not know. As in the case of Simon the Pharisee (7:36-50) and the older brother (15:25-32), their final attitude remains up in the air. The gospel leaves a challenge to the reader. The one everyone thought was outside or ought to be outside is inside. Can you be "at home" in this inclusive community that the Son of Man has sought out and saved?[7]

The episode with Zacchaeus, along with that of the woman who anointed Jesus in the house of Simon (7:36-50), offers a perfect paradigm of Luke's sense of the hospitality of God. Zacchaeus, one of the marginalized despite his wealth, provides hospitality to Jesus and finds in return the hospitality of God: a welcome into the community of salvation, his dignity and decency defended. At the same time, the exchange of hospitality that occurs between himself and Jesus enlarges the sphere of God's hospitality. It challenges the community to become more effectively a beachhead of the kingdom, where lost human beings can find welcome and new life in the grasp of a hospitable God.

Jerusalem—But Not Yet the Full Kingdom
(The Parable of the Pounds): 19:11-27

As the very last episode before Jesus enters Jerusalem, the gospel has Jesus tell a parable remarkable for the complexity of its construction and

---

[7] I am always put in mind here of the practice of the L'Arche communities (founded by Jean Vanier): always to give central place in the community to the mentally or physically challenged persons for whom they care.

the violence of the world it portrays (esp. the ending, v. 27)—hardly Luke at his most approachable. On one level the story deals with the interaction between a man of high station who goes abroad for a time and servants to whom he entrusts sums of money. Overlaying this relatively simple story[8] and to some extent transforming it is a similar story about a man of noble birth who goes to a distant land to have himself appointed king; on his return as ruler, he deals vindictively and bloodily with a group of citizens who had sought to frustrate his ambition. The chief character in the parable, then, deals independently with two quite separate groups.[9]

An introduction (v. 11) explains the purpose of this complex parable. Jesus tells it to counter expectations, arising out of his closeness to Jerusalem, that the kingdom of God was about to appear (see also Acts 1:6). Some believe that the messianic king's entrance into the city will trigger the full arrival of the kingdom, with all that implies for Israel as God's people. Such persons have failed to hear Jesus' reiterated warnings to the effect that what awaits him in Jerusalem is rejection and suffering, rather than recognition as king (9:22; 9:43-45; 18:31-34). He is indeed the Messiah and he will enter Jerusalem as its king but the full establishment of the kingdom must await two things: first, his rejection and death and then a long indefinite period before his triumphant return as Son of Man to judge the world. The double focus of the parable addresses separately these two developments that have to occur before the full arrival of the kingdom.

The "throne claimant" thread of the story (visible in details such as the phrase "to claim royal power" [v. 12], the delegation of citizens [v. 14], the bloody reckoning [v. 27]) addresses the rejection Jesus will suffer from the leading authorities of the city; Jerusalem will "not want to have this man (Jesus) as its king" (see v. 14). Like all Jesus' parables, this one draws upon a familiar aspect of contemporary life without endorsing or challenging it from a moral point of view.[10] The king's brutal revenge

---

[8] Corresponding to Matthew's parable of the Talents (25:14-30).

[9] What seems to have drawn both strands together in the tradition behind the gospels is the common motif of a leading person who goes away for a time and makes a reckoning on his return.

[10] After the death of King Herod the Great, his son Archelaus traveled to Rome to obtain the title "king," which his father had enjoyed. A delegation of Jews and Samaritans followed him to oppose the bid; see Fitzmyer, *Luke X-XXIV*, 1235.

is not commended. Even less should it be seen as a paradigm for the action of God. It is simply the sort of thing that happened in the world of Jesus and his audience (see 13:1-5). In the action of the parable the bloody punishment the resisters in the end receive (v. 27) is prophetic of the fate that will befall Jerusalem in 70 CE—an event that Luke regards in a tragic rather than a punitive light.[11]

The major story line, where the ruler interacts with servants whom he has charged with differing sums of money, addresses once again the situation faced by the early communities who have to live in the gap (unforeseen in conventional eschatology) between the messianic enthronement of Jesus (his resurrection and ascension) and his triumphant return as Son of Man in power. The third servant loses all (the protest of the bystanders [v. 25] drives home the point) because he failed to grasp that what this time required was an imaginative and vigorous "trading" with the money entrusted to him. Once again, we should not allegorize the parable so as to identify the harsh master (vv. 21-22) with the God proclaimed by Jesus. The parable makes the simple point that the time before the arrival of the Son of Man is a time of opportunity for creative service, for which the particularly gifted will be required to give a strict account (see 12:35-48).

The complex story addresses the program of salvation as Luke sees it to be unfolding. Instead of entering immediately into possession of his messianic kingdom, Jesus will suffer rejection and an entire, unforeseen epoch (that of the church) will elapse before the full establishment of God's reign. The parable, then, has a distinct focus upon the post-Easter situation. But in the drama of the gospel it also serves to set a direction for understanding the events now to unfold in Jerusalem.

[11] See Robert C. Tannehill, *The Narrative Unity of Luke-Acts: A Literary Interpretation: Volume One: The Gospel according to Luke* (Philadelphia: Fortress, 1986), 161, 258–60.

Jesus in Jerusalem

19:28–21:4

The drama of Luke's gospel reaches its climax as Jesus arrives in Jerusalem to begin the "visitation" of the city (19:44). He enters David's city as its messianic King but immediately runs into conflict with those who currently hold power. Controversies with representatives of various interests fill the time leading up to his arrest and trial. Each incident serves to clarify further his unique status and the nature of the salvation he brings. The sequence falls into two main sections: first, Jesus' entry into the city and the temple (19:28-48); then, a series of contests with various parties whose authority and hold over the people he threatens (20:1–21:4). For the most part Luke follows Mark closely in this part of the gospel. There are, however, distinctive Lukan emphases, upon which I shall dwell.

Jesus Enters Jerusalem and Occupies the Temple: 19:28-48

Jesus Enters Jerusalem: 19:28-40

In the first instance, Luke portrays Jesus as a pilgrim: leading his disciples, he "goes up" to Jerusalem in the traditional way (v. 28). We recall an earlier pilgrimage made with his parents (2:41-50), which, to their astonishment, ended up with precocious behavior on his part in the temple. Now that pattern will be repeated in a far more dramatic way as Jesus claims the city and the temple as its King.

Jesus both asserts and radically redefines the kingly claim. He does so by the mode of entry that, with prophetic foresight, he deliberately sets up (vv. 29-34). Those who would rule with force and power do not enter cities on donkeys. Jesus' decision to ride on a colt removes any such threat.[1] He does allow his disciples to treat him as king—notably

---

[1] Unlike Matthew (21:4-5)—and also John (12:14-15)—Luke makes no direct allusion to the prophecy of Zechariah (9:9), which seems to underlie this ges-

through the gesture of spreading their cloaks before him (vv. 35-36). But the acclamation that surrounds him is a collective praise of God. And the grounds for the praise are "all the deeds of power" that the disciples had seen him perform—not worldly power, that is, but a sustained ministry of healing and liberation (v. 37). He is a king who "comes in the name of the Lord," bringing the peace announced by angels at his birth (v. 38; 2:14).

The enthusiasm of the disciples disturbs the Pharisees[2]—a first hint of the city's rejection (v. 39). But Jesus responds in prophetic tones: if the people were silent, the very stones would cry out (v. 40). So long awaiting its messianic king, the ancient city of bricks and mortar could not hold back from acclaiming his arrival when at last he came.

Jesus Weeps over Jerusalem: 19:41-44

In contrast to the enthusiasm of the disciples, as Jesus catches sight of the city he weeps over it. Luke on the whole plays down the emotions of Jesus. To present him weeping over the city at this point is a powerful statement. Jesus weeps because he knows that the city, whose name (on a popular but not strictly accurate etymology) means "city of peace," is not going to recognize "the things that make for [its] peace" (v. 42). That is, it is not going to see in him the peace-bringing "visitation" from God (v. 44) for which the holy ones of Israel had longed (1:68-79). The visitor from God will not find Jerusalem hospitable to himself or to the message that would make it the "city of peace." Instead, because it has not known the time of its visitation from God, it will suffer violence and destruction. The stones that would have "cried out" (v. 40) will not be left "one upon another" (v. 44).

These prophetic words (vv. 41-44) reveal Luke's perspective on the eventual fate of Jerusalem. The rejection Jesus will suffer in Jerusalem—not on the part of the entire populace but from those who have responsibility and power—will lead directly to the destruction of 70 CE when the Romans will set up ramparts, surround the city, and "crush it to the

---

ture of entering upon a colt. But it is hard to interpret the gesture in any way other than as an attempt to deflect the royal entry in a direction of lowliness and approachability.

[2] This is the last time we read of this group in the gospel. Though they have become increasingly hostile to Jesus, they give way now, as opponents, to the chief priests, scribes, and rulers of the people.

ground" exactly as Jesus describes (vv. 43-44a).[3] The destruction is not so much a divine punishment as a consequence of the fateful choice that Jerusalem makes. The rejection now of the King of peace and the subsequent choice of the way of insurrection and violence (soon to be prefigured at Jesus' trial in the choice of the rebel Barabbas [23:18-25]) will lead inevitably to destruction. The gospel invites readers not to gloat over Jerusalem nor to judge it but to weep with Jesus over the tragedy of the fateful choice it has made.[4]

Jesus Cleanses the Temple: 19:45-48

It was in the temple that the entire action of the gospel had begun (1:8-23), and once in his infancy (2:21-40) and again at the beginning of his adult life (2:41-51) Jesus had appeared in the temple, referring to it on the second of these occasions as "my Father's house" (2:49). Now, clad with prophetic authority and citing the words of Isaiah ("My house shall be a house of prayer; but you have made it a den of robbers" [v. 46]),[5] he drives all trade out of the temple, purifying it for the worship of God alone. The swift action fulfills the messianic prophecy of Malachi: "The Lord whom you seek will suddenly come to his temple" (3:1).[6] It also provokes a divided response (vv. 47-48): fascination on the part of the people, intense hostility on the part of the leaders; from now on they look for a way to kill Jesus. The drama of the passion has begun.

---

[3] The details in vv. 43-44a describe very accurately what actually took place in the siege of Jerusalem especially as told by the Jewish historian Josephus. Luke's account almost certainly reflects knowledge of what had taken place only a few years before he wrote.

[4] Acts portrays Jerusalem's rejection of Jesus as a tragic act of "ignorance" foreseen in the saving plan of God (see esp. 3:17-18). While the citizens of Jerusalem are given a second chance, the fate of the city itself has been sealed.

[5] The first part of the quotation comes from Isa 56:7, the phrase "den of robbers" from Jer 7:11. After the first phrase "house of prayer" Luke, along with Matthew (21:13), omits the phrase "for all the nations" in the Isaiah quotation (also preserved in Mark 11:17). At the time Luke wrote the temple had been destroyed. It could no longer function as a house of prayer for the nations.

[6] See Joseph A. Fitzmyer, *The Gospel according to Luke X-XXIV*, AB 28A (Garden City, NY: Doubleday, 1985), 1246; Luke Timothy Johnson, *The Gospel of Luke*, Sacra Pagina 3 (Collegeville, MN: Liturgical Press, 1991), 301–2.

The Struggle for Authority in Jerusalem: 20:1–21:4[7]

"By What Authority?": 20:1-8

The struggle begins with a double question from the leaders questioning Jesus' authority (v. 2). As readers of the gospel we know that Jesus received authoritative commissioning from the Father immediately following his baptism by John (3:21-22). Instead of pointing to this directly, Jesus throws back at his opponents a counter question concerning the origin of John's baptism (vv. 3-4). This silences them, since there is no answer they can give that will not erode their hold over the people (vv. 5-8). Round one to Jesus.

Parable of the Wicked Tenants: 20:9-19

Jesus then goes over to the offensive with the parable of the Wicked Tenants.[8] The parable (vv. 9-16a), along with the additional comment based upon Ps 118:22 (vv. 16b-19), reflects in an anticipatory way upon the "career" of Jesus in relation to God's people, Israel. Those currently exercising leadership in Jerusalem are like tenants of a vineyard for whom the time has come to deliver to the owner the share of its produce that accrues to him. Jesus represents the last of a series of emissaries whom the tenants have rebuffed and mistreated. Instead of respecting at least this final and most exalted "visitor" ("my beloved [and only] Son" [v. 13]; see 3:22; 9:35), they see his coming as their chance to eliminate the heir and seize the vineyard for themselves. So they expel him from the vineyard and kill him. But that, of course, is not where the matter rests. The owner will come and destroy the tenants and give the vineyard to others.

Following the shocked reaction of the hearers (v. 16b), Jesus continues with the saying about the "cornerstone" (v. 17). The text from Psalm 118:22 has proved prophetic for the situation where a rejected figure

---

[7] Luke adheres closely to Mark 11:27–12:4, omitting only the question concerning the great commandment (Mark 12:28-34), which Luke has dealt with in his own way in 10:25-28.

[8] The parable may go back in some form to the historical Jesus. But, as it now appears in all three Synoptic accounts, it bears unmistakable traces of reworking in the early Christian tradition to make it allude more explicitly to the fate of Jesus (note esp., in the Lukan version, "my beloved Son" [v. 13; see 3:22]). The "planted vineyard" alludes to Isa 5:2, making it clear that the vineyard in question is Israel.

(Jesus) has become foundational for a new community ("building"), while those who rejected him have themselves suffered destruction (v. 18; see 2:34 [Simeon's second oracle]).

From a Lukan perspective, then, the parable and its elaboration link the rejection that Jesus was to experience with the ultimate fate of Jerusalem (70 CE) and the passing of authority in Israel—a broadened Israel that includes Gentile believers—to the apostles and their successors. Encapsulating the entire vision of Luke in a single parabolic narrative, it sets that rejection—the bitterest problem that the early Christians had to confront—within the wider design of God.

At the same time, the parable is open to an anti-Jewish, if not anti-Semitic, reading suggestive of the "displacement" of the Jewish people by the Christian church. Such a reading, apart from its dangerous insensitivity to the suffering Jewish people have endured from Christians through the ages, misreads in a simplistic way Luke's sense of the tragedy of Israel. It also neglects the constant stress in Luke-Acts that human rejection does not thwart God's saving design but in fact allows it to expand in unforeseen ways.

Taxes to Caesar?: 20:20-26

The question about the legitimacy of paying taxes to the Roman emperor continues the struggle between Jesus and the leaders for the allegiance of the people. Once again (see vv. 3-4), Jesus wins the contest by deflecting the issue back upon his opponents. By making *them* produce the coin and say the word "Caesar's," he draws from them the implication that, yes, the coinage shows that tax should be paid to Caesar (vv. 24-25a).[9] At the same time, by asserting God's claim as the climax of his response (v. 25b; see also Acts 5:29), he insists that Caesar's rights and God's rights are not to be played off against each other. Members of God's people, as responsible citizens of the civic realm—a favorite Lukan theme—must constantly discern how they are to discharge civic obligations within the overall claim of God. Jesus' pronouncement is open-ended. In the matter of relations between church and state it bequeaths a task rather than detailed ethical prescription.

---

[9] The accusation later made at Jesus' trial that he forbade the payment of taxes to Caesar (23:2) is, then, false.

Concerning the Resurrection: 20:27-39

Another leading group, the Sadducees, bring a challenge. It arises, naturally, out of a characteristic tenet of their sect: the refusal to believe in any kind of resurrection from the dead. The quibble (vv. 28-33) that they have conjured up from the legal prescription requiring a man to raise up offspring for a brother who has died (Deut 25:5-6; see Gen 38:8) seeks to make belief in life after death ridiculous. It rests upon a crass assumption that life after death would simply be a repetition or extension of life in the present time, with the same conditions applying. This flaw in their argument enables Jesus to respond with a majestic two-stage clarification. First (vv. 34-36), in the case of the risen life, we are dealing with a totally new situation: since no one dies anymore (being "like the angels and children of God"[10]), there is no longer any need for procreation—hence no need for marriage, the institution designed to supply it.[11]

More significantly (vv. 37-38), the quibble trivializes both the nature of God and human relationship with God. The same Moses who wrote the prescription cited by the Sadducees also spoke, in a far more central passage, of God as the "God of Abraham, Isaac and Jacob" (Exod 3:6). The description implies the continuing personal existence of those with whom God remains in relationship—including, necessarily, the three patriarchal figures listed. The relationship God seeks to forge with human beings here and now is one that transcends death; otherwise it would not be truly personal.

David's Son: 20:41-44

When the scribes commend Jesus for his victory in the scriptural contest with the Sadducees (v. 39), Jesus directs a scriptural question at them. The question arises out of an exegesis of Psalm 110, a psalm traditionally interpreted as referring to the expected Messiah and attributed, as were all the psalms, to King David. In verse 1a of the psalm ("The LORD says to my lord, 'Sit at my right hand'") "David," recording the address of God ("the Lord"), seems to refer to the Messiah as "my lord."

---

[10] The phrase "children of God" seems here to be more or less synonymous with "angels." It connotes the idea of immortality, since angels, as spiritual beings, are immune to death. The language is polemical: Sadducees did not believe in the existence of angels or any spiritual reality whatsoever.

[11] We should not seek to find here a complete theology of marriage. Jesus is responding to the Sadducees on their own terms.

Since normally sons or descendants were inferior to parents or ancestors, this is odd. It implies a mysterious "superiority" of the Messiah over David, the paradigm of Israelite kingship. Jesus provides no answer to the question. He simply leaves the implication hanging in the air. Without disputing that the Messiah would be of David's line, his intention is to broaden the whole notion of messiahship so that it could encapsulate his own mysterious and exalted being (recall the "two-stage" description of his status at the annunciation of his birth [1:32-34]). The controversy foreshadows the centrality of the messianic issue in the narratives of Jesus' passion and risen life. Will his suffering and death quash lingering hopes that he might be the Messiah? Or will they, in light of a new understanding of Scripture, actually confirm that he enjoys that status but in a new and exalted way outstripping previous hopes and expectations (24:26-27, 45-47)?

The Widow's Gift to the Temple Treasury: 21:1-4

The widow's gift to the temple treasury has traditionally been interpreted as providing an example of the total dedication of one's being to God. Her offering of all she has to live on would represent a final instance in Luke's gospel of the poor and marginalized demonstrating a devotion to God that shows up the failings of others. This interpretation is certainly valid. But following immediately upon Jesus' complaint about the scribes "devouring the property of widows" (20:47), the action may present something that Jesus deplores rather than commends. What he would be deploring would not be the widow's act in itself or her motivation but the whole religious system administered by the scribes. This pressured people like her to contribute not what they could afford but what they needed to stay alive.[12] Like the understanding of the Sabbath challenged by Jesus in his Sabbath healings (13:10-17; 14:1-6), religion here works to suppress life rather than enhance it. Jesus draws attention to the injustice, to expose it and deplore it in the name of a correct vision of God and what God wants for human beings.

---

[12] For interpretation along these lines, see Fitzmyer, *Luke X-XXIV*, 1320–21 (following an earlier study of A. G. Wright: "The Widow's Mites: Praise or Lament?—A Matter of Context," *Catholic Biblical Quarterly* 44 [1982]: 256–65). For a reassertion of the more traditional interpretation, see François Bovon, *A Commentary on the Gospel of Luke*, Hermeneia, vol. 3 (Minneapolis: Fortress, 2012), 95–96.

Hope and Endurance

The Discourse on the Future: 21:5-38

In all three Synoptic Gospels Jesus pronounces a long discourse on the future during his last days in Jerusalem. Luke has provided some fore-taste of this in the instruction on the day of the Son of Man (17:20-37).[1] Now we have a longer sequence. It follows Mark 13:5-37 fairly closely but certain embellishments and alterations reflect Luke's particular situation and concerns. Here we encounter by far the most difficult part of the gospel for the contemporary reader. It will help to make some clarifications at the outset.

Introduction

First, to clarify what I understand by two key terms: "eschatology" and "apocalyptic."[2] "Eschatology" refers to teaching or speculation about what is going to happen in the future—more specifically, what will take place in that "final" future when the whole universe will undergo radical transformation at the hands of God. It is a "content-term" in the sense that it refers to what something (a teaching, for example) is *about* (namely, the "end"). "Apocalyptic," an adjective, is a "how-term": it describes a cast of thinking or mode of literary expression in which or through which some content is expressed.[3] Typical of apocalyptic discourse (and, in fact, what provides its name [Greek: *apokalypsis* = "revelation"]) is the presentation of its content as something received by "revelation" (through

---

[1] The material in 17:20-37 derives from "Q." Luke keeps this separate from the Synoptic Apocalypse proper derived from Mark 13, which he now presents in the setting Mark gave it. Matthew (24:1-36) inserts the "Q" material into the Markan framework so as to construct a single, composite discourse.

[2] I am indebted here to Joseph A. Fitzmyer, *The Gospel according to Luke X-XXIV*, AB 28A (Garden City, NY: Doubleday, 1985), 1323–24.

[3] The corresponding noun is "apocalypticism"—though, to avoid this ungainly word, many New Testament scholars, in imitation of the German, use the word "apocalyptic" as a noun as well as an adjective.

angelic intervention or through a vision or "tour" of the heavenly realm granted to a seer).

Also characteristic of apocalyptic discourse is vivid imagery depicting upheavals and calamities on a cosmic scale, and the conflict between good and evil in a starkly dualist mode. The purpose of apocalyptic discourse is to give encouragement to the faithful by revealing the divine plan and program whereby the present evil order will soon be overthrown and victory and vindication will be theirs in the final triumph of God. Thus the discourse that Jesus speaks here (like the shorter one in 17:20-37) is "eschatological" in that it treats of events that will happen at or before the final transformation. It is "apocalyptic" to some extent in its imagery but more so in its purpose, which is to give encouragement and promote vigilance in view of what is to happen in the future.

Though the gospel locates the discourse in the time before Jesus' death, it really looks out beyond his death and resurrection to the time of the church. In a sense it deals with what might be called the "passion of the disciples" (though that is more true of the discourse in its Markan rather than its Lukan form). It addresses the problem raised for the early church by the modification of what they had originally been led to expect.

Jesus proclaimed the imminent arrival of the kingdom of God. The titles "Messiah" and "Son of Man," each in their own way, refer to some agency on his part with respect to the kingdom. As his public life draws to a close, however, he signals increasing awareness that the arrival of the kingdom will be deferred beyond events totally unforeseen in conventional Jewish messianic expectation: the suffering and death of the Messiah—that is, of Jesus himself. Even his resurrection from the dead and heavenly exaltation (ascension) would not mean the full arrival of the kingdom (cf. Acts 1:6; 3:20-21). In the long space of time before the kingdom was finally in place, the post-Easter community of believers, empowered with his Spirit and sent on mission to the ends of the earth, had to take up Jesus' proclamation of the kingdom. This would mean enduring the hostility and suffering that had been part of his own messianic struggle with evil.

The eschatological discourse addresses this situation by showing that Jesus had accurately foreseen the trials the community would have to suffer. He placed those trials in the context of a sequence of events leading up to the overthrow of evil and the final triumph of God at the time of his own return as Son of Man. The discourse also had to dampen down false hopes and expectations arising out of events that might reasonably have been seen as signs that the final days were at hand—leading to intense disillusionment and loss of faith when these expectations were not fulfilled. Within the community such misleading events could be the appearance of persons claiming to be the returned Messiah Jesus (those who come in his name saying, "I am he!" [v. 8]). On a wider scale, events such as wars, famines, earthquakes, and other calamities could be taken as indications that the final cosmic upheaval was underway (vv. 9-11). Above all, the catastrophe represented by the fall of Jerusalem and destruction of the temple (70 CE) was surely an occasion, appropriate as no other, for the arrival of the Son of Man.

This means that the discourse contains what is, in effect, a double message: (1) yes, the Son of Man will come soon—so be confident in your sufferings, vigilant and watchful in your pattern of life; (2) but no, don't be dismayed if he has not yet arrived and if he delays a little longer; all these things (the calamities) must take place, but "the end" will not follow immediately (v. 9). It is this "double message" ("yes—but not just yet") that makes the discourse seem to send conflicting signals. Taking account of the situation it addressed should help us see that the signals are not so much conflicting as complementary.

We also have to appreciate that, while the trigger for the discourse is a question about the temple—when its destruction, as foretold by Jesus (v. 6), will take place (v. 7)—the issue concerning the temple immediately gives way to concern for the city of Jerusalem as a whole, the historical destruction of which in 70 CE is clearly in view (vv. 20, 24b). But this event, in its turn, becomes a symbol of what will take place for the world at the culminating eschatological event, the arrival of the Son of Man. So we have an unfolding development: from the temple, to the city of Jerusalem, to the coming of the Son of Man (final arrival of the kingdom). Interwoven with these three, both preceding the destruction of the temple and continuing on afterwards, is the suffering of the community, a major concern of the discourse.

There is also the fact that, while the discourse primarily addresses the situation of the community in Luke's day—that is, the time after the fall of Jerusalem—the drama of the gospel sets it within the life of Jesus and so portrays all these trials in the future. What the discourse essentially communicates to the later community is a sense of assurance: all that has taken place—dismaying, disillusioning, contrary to expectation though it may be—fits within a pattern accurately foreseen and foretold by Jesus. All leads to the eventual triumph of the kingdom, which the church in continuity with Jesus proclaims, while continuing also to proclaim the "day of acceptance" that prevails in the meantime.

That "day" has extended vastly beyond anything the early believers, including Luke, ever expected or foresaw. The "not yet" aspect of the message of the discourse has become very elastic indeed as we stand in the early decades of a third Christian millennium. We also interpret the eschatological events in a very different way.[4] But the seeds of that nonliteral interpretation were already there in the "flexibility" built into the discourse by its "yes—but not yet" pattern. We retain the doctrine of the "Second Coming" in our affirmations of faith, not because we literally believe—as fundamentalists do—that Jesus will one day appear as Son of Man on the clouds of heaven, but because we believe that the biblical assertions to that effect affirm the eventual triumph of God's sovereignty in the universe and that all is provisional till that occurs. Wars and famines and earthquakes continue; those who work for justice and a more humane life for all members of the community are often overthrown, cast into prison, and condemned. Grounds for dismay, disillusionment, loss of faith are ever present. Hence the centrality of this difficult discourse to the total message of the gospel. The situation it addresses, the warning, the encouragement, the hope it seeks to communicate are addressed to us as much as to the early generations of believers.

The Discourse Proper: 21:5-36

What I have said by way of introduction to the discourse should make understanding its individual sections easier. I shall not, then, move through it in detail but offer a swift review of its various parts.

Functioning as prelude or trigger to the discourse (21:5-7) is an admiring remark on the beauty of the temple (v. 5). Reacting to the remark, Jesus predicts the total destruction of the temple (v. 6). This leads, in turn, to the disciples' question (v. 7) concerning when this would occur and what would be the sign of its occurrence. These two connected questions—"When?" and "With what sign(s)?"—control the discourse that follows.

The discourse proper (vv. 5-36) begins with a section (vv. 5-11) concerned with the "but not yet" aspect of the message. It lists things that must take place before the fall of the temple: appearance of figures claiming to be the returning Messiah (v. 8), political and natural calamities (vv. 9-11a), portents in heaven (v. 11b). But even these latter events are not immediate precursors of "the end" (fall of the temple).

---

[4] See my earlier remarks on interpreting the prophetic teaching of Jesus, pp. 123–24.

Somewhat out of proper time sequence the next section (vv. 12-19) lists two kinds of challenges that the community will have to confront even before the events just mentioned. First (vv. 12-15) are challenges coming from outside: persecution, imprisonment, arraignment before kings and governors (v. 12). These will provide opportunity for testimony (*eis martyrion* [v. 13]).[5] In such situations, the disciples should not prepare a defense beforehand because Jesus himself will put words in their mouths that none of the adversaries will be able to refute (v. 14).[6]

Secondly (vv. 15-19) and more poignantly, there will challenges on a personal level: betrayal from within one's family or circle of friends (v. 15), leading in some cases to being put to death (v. 16); being the object of universal hatred through loyalty to Jesus (lit., "on account of my name" [v. 17]). The concluding reassurances ("not a hair of your head will perish" [v. 18] and "by your endurance you will gain your lives" [v. 19]) stand in palpable tension with the situations described—especially the actual loss of life mentioned in verse 16. Luke lets such reassurance stand to make the point that, no matter how dire the situations believers find themselves in, their lives are precious to God (recall 12:7). The God who raised Jesus following his testimony unto death will also ensure that they too will share his risen life.

The discourse then returns (vv. 20-24) to a full description of the fall of Jerusalem, with advice and warning as to what action the disciples should take.[7] "These are the days of vengeance" (v. 22), the days that will occur as a consequence of Jerusalem's rejection of God's peaceful visitation in the person of Jesus. Concerning these days Jesus had wept

---

[5] The Greek phrase is rather cryptic. It is usually understood in the sense of providing witness to outsiders (such as might make a salutary impression at least on some). But *martyrion* more usually has the sense, not of the *activity* of bearing witness, but of the *evidence* provided. In this sense what would be in view is evidence that would tell in favor of the disciples and against their opponents in the heavenly court at the Last Judgment. See I. Howard Marshall, *The Gospel of Luke: A Commentary on the Greek Text*, NIGTC (Grand Rapids, MI: Eerdmans, 1978, repr. 1987), 767–68.

[6] This repeats a similar instruction in 12:11-12, where, however, the assistance is attributed to the Holy Spirit. The risen Jesus, through the agency of the Holy Spirit, functions as the attorney for believers in such situations of trial.

[7] The descriptions in vv. 20-24 cohere remarkably with what is known of the siege and capture of Jerusalem from other sources, notably the Jewish historian Josephus—and also from the imagery so graphically depicted on the Arch of Titus in Rome.

over the city on first sight of it (19:41-44; cf. 13:34-35); also concerning them he will warn the daughters of Jerusalem on his way to the cross (23:27-31).

The perspective then turns away from historical events toward the strictly eschatological event of the coming of the Son of Man (vv. 25-38). Cataclysmic events signaling his imminent arrival (vv. 25-27) will terrify the inhabitants of the world, but for the faithful they should be a sign to "raise [their] heads" because their "redemption" (*apolytrōsis*) is at hand (v. 28). Early in the gospel the infancy stories had portrayed faithful souls who longed for the "redemption" (*lytrōsis*) of Israel (2:38; cf. 1:68; 24:21). Now Jesus points to "redemption" (primarily rescue from evil) on a worldwide scale. Just as the appearance of leaves on the fig tree points to the arrival of summer, so the faithful should regard the events just described as signs pointing to the imminent arrival of the kingdom (vv. 29-31). Though the signs may involve the destruction of "heaven and earth" as presently known, Jesus' words will not pass away but find fulfillment (vv. 32-33).[8]

The discourse ends with an admonition containing typical Lukan warnings against absorption in the pleasures and worries of this life (vv. 34-36; cf. 8:14; 12:13-31; 14:15-24). The faithful are to be alert at all times, praying to escape all that will take place and be able to stand confidently before the Son of Man.

Summary: 21:37-38

Rounding off this entire section of the gospel is a summary description of Jesus' last days in Jerusalem (see 19:47-48). By day he teaches in the temple, by night he retires to the Mount of Olives—a location where, for the time being at least, he is safe from those who are plotting his destruction. They are the leaders in the city. The populace at large, we are reminded (v. 36), are still eager to hear his word. Thus Luke continues to reinforce the crucial distinction between the attitude of the leaders (hostile, murderous) and that of the people (favorable, eager).

---

[8] The precise reference of Jesus' statement, "Truly, I tell you, this generation will not pass away until all these things have been accomplished" (v. 32), is obscure. At the time when the gospel was written, two or more generations after the death of Jesus, the "end" had still not come. For Luke the reference of the statement was probably sufficiently vague to justify its retention. It enhances the sense of urgency in the discourse.

Jesus' Journey to God
The Passion Narrative I: 22:1-53

We have accompanied Jesus on his long journey "going up" to Jerusalem. But the journey is not complete with his arrival in the city nor with the ministry he has exercised there teaching in the temple (21:37-38). The final stage of the journey occurs in what was described at the transfiguration as his "exodus" (9:31): his death in Jerusalem and "being taken up" (9:51) to sit at the right hand of God (22:69).

The Passion Narrative: Introduction

Nowhere else is the gospel tradition so united in sequence and historical detail as in the story of Jesus' suffering and death. Together, the four passion narratives have created in the imagination of most Christians a kind of composite account of the events of Jesus' last meal, arrest, trials, and crucifixion. In this case it is more than ordinarily difficult to attend simply to what one account is saying without "interference" from the other three. I propose, however, that we do try to attend to the Lukan account. No one evangelist exhausts the full reality of the passion. Each brings a distinct perspective highlighting particular aspects of the total truth. What each communicates may not be the total story—but it is an inspired approach to the total story.

We must remember, too, that no more and no less than the other three evangelists is Luke attempting to describe "the facts" in a fully objective sense. Certainly, most scholars believe that the passion narratives form the earliest strata of ordered traditions concerning Jesus. But from the start a very strong impress of interpretation accompanied what memory there was of the historical details. Interpretation was necessary to make some sense of the catastrophic fact that the one whom the disciples believed to be God's chosen Messiah suffered so appalling and degrading a death at the hands of the authorities.

Central in the process of finding meaning was the task of searching the Scriptures (the Old Testament) to see if Scripture contained any indication that this would be how things would go. According to a very early creedal fragment cited by Paul, "Christ died for our sins *according to the Scriptures* . . . and was raised on the third day *according to the Scriptures*" (1 Cor 15:3b-5). A concern to unpack that expression "according to the Scriptures" has strongly marked all passion narratives—a concern that Luke in particular extends into the account of Christ's risen life. The disciples come to full faith when, beyond simply recognizing him as the risen Lord, they understand from his instruction that the suffering and death of the Messiah was something that "had" to happen according to the plan of God announced in the Scriptures (24:25-27, 32, 44-46).

Luke scales down many details of the broader passion tradition to make his own account focus more simply and cleanly on the nature of the messiahship Jesus represents—specifically, in what sense he is "Savior." Those who plot his destruction—the chief priests, the scribes, and elders of the people—seek to portray him as a messianic pretender in the conventional sense: that is, as a king of David's line who would bring about the political and social restoration of Israel. If the Roman authorities can be led to see him as "King of the Jews" in this sense, his removal at their hands is guaranteed. Jesus never denies that he is the Messiah, but neither will he simply accept that he is Messiah in this sense. Nor will the Romans be convinced that this charge against him is proven. At stake here, as throughout the gospel, beginning with Gabriel's explanation to Mary (1:32-35), is messiahship of a different kind, a more transcendent vision of salvation.

So the Lukan passion account presents the condemnation of Jesus on a false charge of sedition as a travesty of justice. Again and again his innocence is recognized by the Roman authority: four times by Pilate (23:4, 14, 22), who also mentions that Herod found no guilt in him (23:15); once by the centurion who had supervised the crucifixion (23:47). If, as his followers could not deny, he had been executed by the Roman state on the grounds of sedition, this was because reluctantly and against his own better judgment, the governor gave way to intolerable pressure brought by Jesus' adversaries. Jesus is the martyr victim of a power struggle in Jerusalem, not so much between himself and Pilate as between the kind of authority he represents as "visitor" from God and that of those who currently hold leadership in Israel. Jesus is the messianic king, yes—but a king who would bring peace to Jerusalem, not strife and rebellion against Rome. In the account of Jesus' passion no less than elsewhere in his total project (Luke-Acts), Luke strives to promote a sense of Christian identity that can live at peace within the hegemony of Rome.

The main antagonists of Jesus in the Lukan passion are the chief priests, the scribes, and the elders of the people. From the outset of his arrival in Jerusalem, as we have been reminded several times (19:47-48; 20:19, 20, 26; 22:2), they have consistently sought to destroy him but have been frustrated by the hold he has upon the people. Beneath this struggle a deeper contest is engaged. The authorities are simply the tools of Satan; this is their "hour" and the "power of darkness" (22:53). When Judas, one of the Twelve, breaks the deadlock and offers them a covert way to lay hands on Jesus, it is because "Satan has entered into him" (22:3). Correspondingly, Jesus is open throughout his passion to the presence of the Father, whose salvific will, preannounced in the Scriptures, guides all that is taking place (22:37). From time to time the evangelist lifts the veil between the earthly and the heavenly realm to show Jesus in communion with the Father.

In agreement with this, Luke stresses the freedom and control of Jesus. He does not die with a cry of abandonment on his lips (cf. Matt 27:46; Mark 15:34); he gently yields his spirit to the Father (23:46). He heals the ear of one of those come to arrest him (22:51), pleads forgiveness for his executioners (23:34), speaks words of consolation and assurance to a thief dying beside him. This is a very different perspective from that of Mark—and, to some extent, that of Matthew. We might say that in this respect Luke's account is well on the way toward the passion account of the Fourth Gospel. To ask which tradition is closer to the original facts is natural but not in the end useful. What Luke brings out are certain aspects of the meaning of Jesus' death: that he died in the freedom of love, a human love enacting the divine love that drove his entire mission; that his death brought forgiveness; that attending it were all the qualities—healing, assurance, peace—that had been features of his ministry as a whole.

I do not propose to treat all episodes of Luke's long passion narrative in the same detail. Rather, I shall concentrate on those that are particularly distinctive of this gospel and most reflective of the theme I am pursuing.

The narrative itself breaks down into four major sections plus a number of preliminary, bridging, and aftermath scenes. We can set it out as follows:

Conspiracy, betrayal, Passover preparation: 22:1-13
Passover meal: 22:14-38

Personal struggle and arrest on the Mount of Olives: 22:39-53
Hearing before the Jewish Council: 22:54-71

Roman trial: 23:1-25

Way of the cross: 23:26-32
Crucifixion and death: 23:33-49

Aftermath: 23:50-56

Passover Meal (Last Supper): 22:1-38

Conspiracy, Betrayal, Passover Preparation: 22:1-13

The Lukan passion narrative begins with a report on the continuing, yet up till now frustrated, desire of the chief priests and scribes to bring about Jesus' death (22:1-2). Judas Iscariot, one of the Twelve but now an agent of Satan (v. 3), breaks the deadlock by offering to betray Jesus when opportunity presents (vv. 5-6).[1] The rejection of Jesus now reaches even into the innermost circle of his companions. The suspense created by Judas's action becomes foreboding as we are told of the arrival of "the day of Unleavened Bread, on which the Passover lamb had to be sacrificed" (v. 7). Unmistakable is the hint that a sacrifice of another order may also take place this Passover.

In contrast to the accounts in Mark and Matthew, Luke's gospel has Jesus take the initiative with regard to making preparations for the Passover meal (vv. 8-13). This reinforces the sense that when he takes his place with the apostles at table (v. 14), he does so very much as host. At this Passover he is to offer them the hospitality of God in a climactic way and institute something (the Eucharist) that will sacramentally continue that hospitality in the life of the church.

The Eucharist: 22:14-20

The action of the supper begins with Jesus giving expression to his longstanding desire to celebrate this Passover with his apostles before he suffers. He will not eat it (again) until it is "fulfilled" in the kingdom of God (vv. 15-16). Immediately afterwards he takes a cup, gives thanks, and shares it with them, adding again, "I tell you that from now on I will not drink of the fruit of the vine until the kingdom of God comes" (vv. 17-18). Mark and Matthew also have this remark about the kingdom but place it after the words over the bread and the cup (Mark 14:25; Matt 26:29). The allusion to the kingdom in Luke is distinctive not only because it occurs twice (vv. 16, 18) but also by the fact of its placement before the words over the bread and the (second) cup that make up the

---

[1] Luke omits the episode of the anointing at Bethany, which in Mark (14:3-9) and Matthew (26:6-13) falls between the account of the conspiracy and the betrayal. Luke had, of course, described a similar episode in the house of Simon the Pharisee in 7:36-50. The omission improves the flow of the narrative by allowing the betrayal (22:3-6) to follow immediately upon the conspiracy (22:1-2) and so become part of it.

institution narrative proper.[2] The effect in Luke is to set the Eucharist far more explicitly within the context of the kingdom.

Throughout his public life Jesus had announced the imminence of the kingdom. Now he openly acknowledges something that had been implicit for some time: before he would celebrate the Passover in the kingdom—the Passover that would "fulfill" all preceding Passovers (v. 16)—there would be a "gap," a time of absence created by his death. The blessings over the bread and the cup that the disciples are commanded to repeat "in remembrance" of him (v. 19) will be the mode in which he will be present in the community during this space of time before the final establishment of the kingdom.[3] The eucharistic rite will enable the church to carry on in his name the celebration of the hospitality of God that has been the center of his mission. It will do so in anticipation and pledge of the everlasting hospitality of the kingdom.[4]

We can set it out diagrammatically as follows:

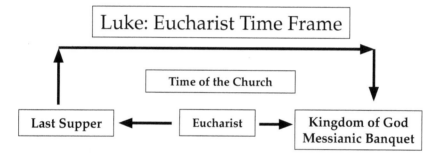

[2] Significant manuscripts of the Western tradition omit everything in vv. 19-20 after the phrase "This is my body," thus eliminating the qualification of "body" ("which is given for you"), the command, "Do this in memory of me," and the blessing of a second cup following the blessing over the bread (v. 20). Along with many scholars, especially since the early papyrus P[75] came to light, I accept as original the "longer" form of the Lukan text. For a critical review of the issue, see François Bovon, *A Commentary on the Gospel of Luke*, Hermeneia, vol. 3 (Minneapolis: Fortress, 2012), 154–56.

[3] This presumably explains why in the fleeting moment of eucharistic celebration that the risen Jesus will provide for the two disciples at Emmaus (24:30-31) there is no sense of disappointment on their part at so instantly losing the presence of the Savior they had just regained. From now on the Eucharist will be the mode of his presence among them.

[4] When discussing Luke's version of the Lord's Prayer above (p. 119, n. 12), I mentioned the alternative translation of the third petition: "Give us today our bread for tomorrow" (11:3). This could have a eucharistic resonance: the Eucharist is "bread for today" because it is celebrated now, in this "space" between the

The bread over which Jesus gives thanks, which he breaks and gives to them, is "my body, which is given for you" (v. 19). The (second) cup "poured out for you" is "the new covenant in my blood" (v. 20). The qualifications over the bread and the cup (in close alignment with the form of the eucharistic tradition recorded by Paul in 1 Cor 11:23-25) express the meaning of the death that Jesus is about to undergo. His body will be broken in death so that others may find life and freedom. His blood will be poured out in death so that others may enter the new covenant of life promised by Jeremiah (31:31-33). Believers of subsequent generations who participate in this rite will recognize when they see the broken bread and poured out wine that they are the beneficiaries of the blessings stated here. They will experience the hospitality of God in full knowledge of its cost, cost not only to Jesus who gave himself up for them but also cost to the Father who sent the "beloved Son" in visitation of Israel and the world (3:22; 9:35; see also John 3:16; Rom 8:32).[5]

The Discourse at the Supper: 22:21-38

The second distinctive feature of the Supper as described by Luke is that, following the institution of the Eucharist, Jesus gives a series of warnings and instructions. These create a kind of supper discourse reminiscent of the long narrative of the supper in the Fourth Gospel (John 13–17).

The first warning concerns the betrayal (vv. 21-23).[6] Jesus does not unmask the traitor at this point. His words simply show that, though the power of darkness is proceeding, all is foreseen and held in some way within the plan of God.

Then, provoked by the disciples disputing among themselves as to which of them is the greatest, Jesus gives a brief instruction on how they are to exercise authority (vv. 24-27). Where pagan rulers lord it over others and rejoice to have honorific titles bestowed upon themselves

---

death of Jesus and the time of the full kingdom; it is "bread for tomorrow" in that its present hospitality is a foretaste and pledge of the hospitality of the kingdom.

[5] The qualifications expressed over the bread and the cup would seem to imply that a sense of Jesus' death as expiatory is not absent in Luke, despite the widespread view that such is the case; it is clearly present also in Acts 20:28 (Paul's speech to the elders of Ephesus). See further, I. Howard Marshall, *The Gospel of Luke: A Commentary on the Greek Text*, NIGTC (Grand Rapids, MI: Eerdmans, 1978, repr. 1987), 800.

[6] Mark and Matthew place this before the institution of the Eucharist.

(literally, to be called "benefactors"), in the community of the kingdom service is to be the hallmark of authority. This follows the pattern of Jesus himself: he presides at the table as host, yet is among them "as one who serves" (v. 28).[7] What should give them the freedom to exercise authority in this way is a sense of the wonderful dignity and destiny that awaits them as companions of Jesus (vv. 28-30). Inasmuch as they have stood by Jesus in his trials, he will confer a kingdom (= royal dignity) upon them, as the Father has conferred a kingdom upon him (vv. 28-29). This means that they will eat and drink at his (royal) table in his kingdom (v. 30).[8] Why should they squabble about precedence now, when one day they will themselves judge the twelve tribes of Israel?[9]

For the present, however, a great trial looms. Addressing Peter ("Simon, Simon,"), Jesus indicates that the chief adversary Satan (see already 22:23) has demanded of God the right to "sift" the community (lit., "you" [plural]) like wheat (v. 31). The image would seem to refer to the test and "shaking" that the now imminent events of Jesus' passion and death will present for the faith and loyalty of the disciples.[10] Over against the influence of Satan, however, will be the power of Jesus' prayer (v. 32a). This will ensure that Peter's faith, though sorely tested (in the triple denial), will not ultimately fail (v. 32b). Then, when he has "turned" (v. 32c)—a biblical expression for conversion—he will be in a position to "strengthen" his brothers and sisters (v. 32d).

The command "strengthen" suggests a distinctive role for Peter vis-à-vis the other disciples—corresponding in its way to the sense of "primacy" present in Matthew 16:17-19 and John 21:15-19. In the immediate context, however, Peter protests his willingness to follow Jesus to prison and death (v. 33), evoking from Jesus the prophecy of his triple denial before cockcrow that very day (v. 34). The accuracy of Jesus' prediction,

---

[7] Here we have a Lukan echo of the statement that concludes the episode of the sons of Zebedee (James and John) in Mark and Matthew: "For the Son of Man came not to be served but to serve, and to give his life as a ransom for many" (Mark 10:45//Matt 20:28). The Fourth Gospel depicts Jesus enacting such a role at the Supper by washing the feet of his disciples (John 13:1-17).

[8] The image is that of a king's chief associates sitting in privileged places closest to him at a solemn banquet (see Luke Timothy Johnson, *The Gospel of Luke*, Sacra Pagina 3 [Collegeville, MN: Liturgical Press, 1991], 345).

[9] "Judge" here has the biblical sense of "exercise authority" rather than that of deciding the fate of accused persons at a legal procedure.

[10] For a range of possible meanings of the image see Marshall, *Gospel of Luke*, 820–21.

when validated a few hours later (22:61-62), will show Peter's failure foreseen and encapsulated within the unfolding divine plan. The one who has deeply explored not only his own weakness and failure, but also the power of the Lord's assistance in that weakness, is best equipped to strengthen the faith of others and to exercise authority as "one who serves" (v. 28). This is the particular note attaching to Luke's presentation of the leadership of Peter (see also the account of Peter's call in 5:1-11)—a leadership that, as the command "strengthen" suggests, is to continue beyond the immediate circumstances of Jesus' passion and resurrection into the ongoing life of the church.

The discourse ends with a warning about the time presently upon the disciples (22:35-38). Whereas before Jesus has sent them out "vulnerably," without purse, bag, or sandals (9:1-6; 10:1-12), now is the time for those things and even a sword. The moment has come for the scriptural predictions concerning the suffering of the Messiah (Isa 53:12) to find fulfillment. The disciples will understand this after the resurrection. For the present—to Jesus' exasperation ("It is enough!" [v. 38b])—they take it all literally, indicating that they have a sword. One of them will soon wield it in the garden (22:50).

The Mount of Olives: 22:39-53

Following the Passover meal, Jesus goes out to the Mount of Olives "as was his custom" (v. 39). The last phrase is chilling. It reminds us that Judas the betrayer knows where to find him (see 21:37). The traitor is now in a position to set in motion the process of Jesus' arrest.

Jesus' Personal Struggle: 22:40-46

The tradition that Jesus shrank from the suffering and death that lay before him is widespread in the New Testament, appearing in John 12:27 ("Father, save me from this hour") and Hebrews 5:7-8, as well as the Synoptic Gospels. The fact that it is so widely recorded is all the more impressive in view of the increasing tendency in the early tradition to play down strong expressions of the humanity of Jesus. Clearly we are dealing with something firmly rooted and highly valued in the early tradition. Its testimony to the cost involved for Jesus is by the same token a testimony to the extremity of his love.

The Lukan gospel has given us the traditional term "agony" (v. 44) by which this scene is known. But what Luke describes is not a per-

son in "agony" in the normal English sense of the word. In contrast to
Mark (14:32-42) and Matthew (26:36-46), Luke does not dwell upon the
emotional distress of Jesus or have him turn for support three times to
three select disciples. Luke portrays Jesus in prayer, wrestling with the
thought of what lies before him. He longs that "this cup" (his suffering
and death) should be removed but prays that the Father's will, not his,
be done (v. 42). As if in response to his prayer he receives support from
heaven in the shape of an angel[11] and enters so deeply into the struggle
that his sweat becomes as drops of blood.[12] What Luke depicts is a mighty
contest (the true meaning of the Greek word *agōn*), a struggle to the death
as in a gladiatorial combat.

The unnamed adversary is, of course, Satan, who once again tries
to deflect Jesus from his path. In the temptation story (4:1-13) the devil
had urged Jesus, since he was the Messiah, to take a self-serving, easy,
and spectacular road to messianic power. Jesus rebuffed the suggestion, electing to follow the pattern set out by God, treading the ordinary
human road of suffering and death. It was for this that he had "set his
face" at the start of his journey to Jerusalem (9:51). Now, the prospect
of imminent suffering provides the "opportune time" (4:13) for Satan
to renew the attack.

Luke makes much of the contrast between Jesus and the disciples.
The episode is "framed" at beginning and end by a warning to "pray so
that they might not enter into temptation" (v. 40b; v. 46b; see the final
petition of the Lord's Prayer [11:4c]). Where Jesus watches and prays,
the disciples, despite this warning, fall asleep because of grief (v. 45).[13]
They model an inappropriate response to the time of trial, just as Jesus

---

[11] I am hereby accepting the originality of vv. 43-44, the ones referring to the
angel and Jesus' sweat like blood. On this see Joseph A. Fitzmyer, *The Gospel
according to Luke X-XXIV*, AB 28A (Garden City, NY: Doubleday, 1985), 1443–44
(who in the end judges the verses not to be original); Johnson, *Gospel of Luke*,
351 (who accepts them).

[12] The text nowhere suggests that Jesus sweated blood. The mention of blood
is part of an unusual image: the sweat was so profuse as to give the appearance
that what was coming from Jesus' body was a more copious effusion, namely,
blood stemming from a wound.

[13] The indication of grief as cause of the inclination to sleep is Luke's way of
exculpating the disciples to some extent, as well as lending further atmosphere
to the drama. The ancient world in general held yielding to strong emotions
such as grief to be a sign of weakness, leading to impaired judgment. The opposite emotion, joy, causes a similar problem in 24:41.

models what is truly right. Behind physical trials and opposition is a malign spiritual power. The only way to emerge victorious is through intense union with God. Otherwise they will "enter into temptation" in the sense of yielding to the easy way out.

The scene is the climax of the many occasions when Luke has shown Jesus at prayer. Prayer has been the great vehicle and channel of his communion with the Father. Like the disciples, readers of the gospel, in good times and in bad, are invited to become Jesus' apprentices in this respect, so that in their lives God's will may be done and they may not be led into temptation by the powers arrayed against them. It is precisely when they do not feel the strength of those powers that they are most in danger. The long hours saints spend at prayer flow from their keen sense of this warning.

The Arrest: 22:47-53

As if to illustrate the warning, a crowd led by Judas comes to place Jesus under arrest. He yields to physical force, but the inner victory is already his. His comments—first to Judas (v. 48),[14] then to the arresting crowd (vv. 52-53)—show his control of the situation. This is their hour and the power of darkness (v. 53). But it is also the time when a deeper purpose is being fulfilled. The disciple who lashes out with the sword (v. 50) is resisting physical violence with violence in a way that does not overcome it. Jesus masters the violence when, in a last gesture of healing, he touches the ear of his injured adversary and heals him (v. 51).

---

[14] In contrast to Mark (14:45) and Matthew (26:49), Luke leaves open whether Jesus allowed Judas to kiss him.

Jesus' Journey to God

The Passion Narrative II: 22:54–23:56

Jesus Before the Council: 22:54-71

Jesus is now physically in the hands of his enemies. Taken to the house of the high priest (v. 54), he is held there a prisoner for the remainder of the night. In the Lukan account anything in the nature of a public trial or hearing has to wait until the meeting of the full council in the morning.

During the Night–Denial and Mockery: 22:54-65

In the meantime, during the night, Jesus suffers two injuries. First, Peter has followed the arresting group into the high priest's house and taken a seat among the servants. Here, challenged by the servants, he denies his master three times, precisely as Jesus had predicted (vv. 56-60; see v. 34).[1] In what is perhaps the most poignant moment in the entire gospel, Jesus turns and looks at him as the cock crows (v. 61). If there is remonstrance in this look of Jesus, there is also healing—certainly not judgment or condemnation. Peter goes out and weeps bitterly (v. 62), the beginning of a conversion of heart that will give him the capacity to strengthen his brothers and sisters (v. 32).

The second injury Jesus suffers is more physical. Like so many others held without proper legal procedures down to this day, he suffers mockery and physical abuse from his captors (vv. 63-65).

Hearing before the Council: 22:66-71

The morning arraignment of Jesus before the council is hardly a trial in any proper sense. There is no formal accusation or a hearing of witnesses. Moreover, in contrast to the multiple charges leveled against Jesus

---

[1] Mark and Matthew give the impression that the denial took place more or less simultaneously with Jesus' trial before the council, which they locate at night. The Lukan narrative, which postpones the trial till the morning, moves straight to the denial (23:54-62) after describing Jesus' arrest and detention.

in the other Synoptic accounts (Mark 14:55-59; Matt 26:59-61), there is a single focus upon the messianic issue. In this regard the members of the council put two questions to Jesus. First, is he the Messiah (v. 67)? A straight admission to being the Messiah, understood in the political sense in which they will certainly take it, would provide a pretext for handing him over to the Roman authorities. So on this Jesus refuses to be drawn (vv. 67b-68). But he adds, "From now on the Son of Man will be seated at the right hand of the power of God" (v. 69), a mysterious allusion to the heavenly exaltation that will follow his "exodus" (9:31) to the Father. The interrogators, apparently hearing in this some measure of the response they want, press the messianic question in alternative form: "Are you, then, the Son of God?" (v. 70a).[2] As the entire gospel has made clear, Jesus is the Son of God. But he will not accept the title in the (purely political) sense of their understanding. Hence his throw-back response: "You say that I am" (v. 70b). Despite Jesus' clear refusal to compromise himself in this way, his adversaries now feel that they have the admission they want. They do not need witnesses (v. 71a). They have heard enough from his own lips to haul him before the governor on a charge of sedition.

Luke's depiction of Jesus' arraignment before the council is remarkably "untheological." There is no suggestion at the end, as in Mark (14:63) or Matthew (26:65), that Jesus has blasphemed—that is, taken upon himself in some way the honor due to God. Having arrested him with swords and clubs "as if he were a bandit" (v. 52), they have simply tried to wring from him messianic claims that they can portray to Pilate as seditious. In this way Luke communicates the sense that the case against Jesus on the part of the Jerusalem authorities is purely political and false

---

[2] On the lips of those who interrogate Jesus the phrase "Son of God" does not necessarily represent a more exalted form of the messianic title. The wider evidence of the gospels (where "Son of God" is voiced also by demons), as well as circumstantial evidence from biblical and postbiblical Jewish literature, suggest that the title could function simply as an equivalent to "Messiah." Luke certainly finds more in the title when applied to Jesus, as illustrated by the progression in Gabriel's description of the status of the child to be born to Mary (1:32, 35). I am not sure, however, that Joseph Fitzmyer is right (*The Gospel according to Luke X-XXIV*, AB 28A [Garden City, NY: Doubleday, 1985], 1462) in seeing that progression operative in the present case (22:70) where the title occurs on the lips of Jesus' interrogators; see further, Brendan Byrne, "Jesus as Messiah in the Gospel of Luke: Discerning a Pattern of Correction," *Catholic Biblical Quarterly* 65 (2003): 80–95, esp. 90–91.

at that. They do not countenance for a moment that he might really be the Messiah—a Messiah who would bring "peace" to Jerusalem and to Israel in a way that would have political ramifications, yes, but would outstrip the purely political, being centered totally upon God. As readers of the gospel, we know the truth of this. But as the passion proceeds we see how the major players—the Jewish leaders, Pilate, Herod—completely bypass this reality because the issue for them is whether Jesus is (or can be made out to be) guilty of the purely political charge.

The Roman Trial: 23:1-25

The Accusation: 23:1-5

In accordance with their view of the outcome of the hearing, when the leaders bring Jesus before the Roman governor, they accuse him on three accounts, all political in nature: he has been "perverting our nation, forbidding us to pay taxes to the emperor, and saying that he himself is the Messiah, a king" (v. 2). The second and third charges are simply explicit instances of the first, which is generic. The reader of the gospel knows that both are false. Jesus has not forbidden the payment of taxes to the emperor (20:20-26). Nor in the hearing just conducted did he admit to being the Messiah in the "kingly" sense of their understanding; indeed, he had sought on an earlier occasion (the question about David's son [20:41-44]) to push messiahship in a more transcendent direction. So, when Pilate asks him (v. 3), "Are you the king of the Jews?" (putting the messianic question in political form), Jesus again gives a deflecting response ("You say so"), refusing to be drawn. This leads Pilate to make the first of several declarations on his part that he believes Jesus to be innocent of the charges laid (v. 4).

Pilate's Resistance Overcome: 23:6-25

When the stratagem of remitting Jesus to Herod fails (vv. 6-12),[3] Pilate a second time declares that he finds Jesus innocent and proposes

---

[3] The episode, recorded only by Luke, fulfills the messianic prophecy contained in Ps 2:2: "The kings of the earth set themselves, and the rulers take counsel together, against the LORD and his anointed [Christ]," a text that is explicitly cited, with mention of both Herod and Pilate, in the prayer of the community in Acts 4:25-28. A Roman governor (Festus) also brings Paul before another Herod (Agrippa II) in Acts 25:13-27. Luke is inclined to feature such

to release him after a flogging (vv. 13-16; see also v. 23). This leads the crowd to cry out that he do away with Jesus and release another prisoner, Barabbas, instead (v. 18). All four gospels mention Barabbas in connection with the condemnation of Jesus. But Luke underlines this episode in a particular way. He twice notes that Barabbas had been put in prison for an insurrection (*stasis*) that had taken place in the city and for murder (vv. 19, 25; see also Acts 3:14-15). The mention of *stasis* would inevitably remind readers of the gospel in Luke's day of the failed Jewish revolt that led to the fall of Jerusalem in 70 CE.[4] There is a terrible irony, then, in the choice for Barabbas. Rejecting, on a trumped up charge of sedition, the messianic King who would truly bring it peace (19:41-44), Jerusalem, in the person of its leaders, opts instead for one who represents violence, murder, and sedition. The choice is symbolic—a premonition of the fate lying in wait for the city that has not known or wished to know the true moment of its "visitation" (19:44).[5]

In the face of increasingly insistent cries that Jesus be crucified, Pilate makes a third and last attempt to protest Jesus' innocence (23:22). But to no avail. Against his own better judgment—and Roman justice—he gives in to the demands of the crowd, handing Jesus over to them to be crucified. Jerusalem's rejection of its "visitor" has reached its peak.[6]

The Crucifixion and Death of Jesus: 23:26-56

Way of the Cross: 23:26-32

The journey to the place of execution is an extended scene in Luke's account. As in Mark (15:21) and Matthew (27:32), a passerby, Simon of

---

parallels in his narrative; see further François Bovon, *A Commentary on the Gospel of Luke*, Hermeneia, vol. 3 (Minneapolis: Fortress, 2012), 261–66.

[4] The Jewish historian Josephus consistently attributes the revolt and its failure to *stasis*, a term encompassing both rebellion (against Rome) and strife between the various factions involved; see further, Brendan Byrne, "The Choice for Barabbas in Luke's Passion Narrative," *Vaiharai* (*The Dawn*, Tamilnadu, India) 4, nos. 2–4 (1999): 128–38.

[5] See Robert C. Tannehill, *The Narrative Unity of Luke-Acts: A Literary Interpretation: Volume One: The Gospel according to Luke* (Philadelphia: Fortress, 1986), 164–65.

[6] The extended mockery of Jesus on the part of the soldiers recorded in Mark 15:16-20 and Matt 27:27-31 does not follow at this point. In the Lukan account Jesus has already been mocked by Herod and his court (23:11), while the soldiers take part in the general mockery of Jesus upon the cross (23:36-37).

Cyrene, is pressed into carrying Jesus' cross. But Luke makes Simon a model of discipleship: like the "one who would be a follower" of Jesus (9:23), he carries the cross "after Jesus" (v. 26).

Next, among the great number of people who follow the procession are women who "beat their breasts and wail for him" (v. 27). These women represent the people of Jerusalem who have not followed the leaders in bringing about Jesus' condemnation. Tragically, however, they will be powerless to avert the fate that is to befall the city as a consequence. So Jesus turns their expressions of sympathy back upon themselves (vv. 28-31). In the biblical tradition fertility is a blessing, barrenness a curse. To say "blessed are the barren . . . " is to make a prophecy of doom in the strongest sense, reinforced by the quotation from Hosea 10:8 ("Mountains, fall on us; hills, cover us"). If this is what can occur when the city is at peace ("in the green wood"), think of what horrors may break out when it is at war and under siege ("when it is dry")![7] On this account Jesus himself had wept over the city, because it "did not know the time of its visitation" (19:41-44).

Crucifixion: 23:33-34

Jesus' "exodus" (9:31) to the Father reaches its climax in the scene of his crucifixion and death at the place of the Skull. Luke depicts it as a solemn tableau, with many participants—though the focus remains always upon the central figure, Jesus. The drama falls into four moments:

1. The crucifixion (vv. 33-34)
2. The response of the onlookers before Jesus dies (vv. 35-43)
3. The moment of Jesus' death (vv. 44-46)
4. Response of the onlookers after Jesus' death (vv. 47-49)

Like the other three evangelists, Luke recounts the horrible process of crucifixion with the simple phrase, "they crucified him there" (v. 33); for the original audience of the gospel there was no need to elaborate on the procedure. The fact that he was crucified with two criminals, one on his right and one on his left, and that lots were cast for his clothing (Ps 22:19), fulfills the scriptural prophecy that "he was counted among

---

[7] See Luke Timothy Johnson, *The Gospel of Luke*, Sacra Pagina 3 (Collegeville, MN: Liturgical Press, 1991), 373. The historian Josephus catalogs in considerable detail the horrors suffered in Jerusalem in the final stages of the siege in 70 CE.

the lawless" (v. 33b; see 22:37; Isa 53:12). The additional detail that he prayed, "Father, forgive them; for they do not know what they are doing" (v. 34a),[8] accords well with Luke's tendency to depict Jesus at prayer. It is also a fitting climax to the constant dispensing of forgiveness throughout his ministry.

Responses—Mockery and Faith: 23:35-43

The gospel then describes the responses of others present at the scene. Repeating a distinction prevalent throughout Jesus' time in Jerusalem, it notes (v. 35a) that "the people" simply stand by watching while the leaders become the first of three parties that mock Jesus while he hangs upon the cross. In all three cases the mockery focuses upon the pretended messianic claims of Jesus and the capacity to "save" that, were he truly the Messiah, he might have been expected to show. So they scoff: "He saved others; let him save himself if he is the Messiah of God, his chosen one!" (v. 35b). Next the soldiers mock him (vv. 36-37). They hail him as "King of the Jews," the title that featured in his Roman trial (v. 3) and now stands in the inscription attached to his cross (v. 38).

The mockery reaches its climax from a third direction, that of the criminals crucified with Jesus. The criminal on Jesus' left taunts him about "salvation" in terms that echo the taunt of the elders: "Are you not the Messiah? Save yourself and us!" (v. 39). The man desperately needs "salvation" in the shape of rescue from his terrible death. But seeing Jesus, the pretended Messiah, reduced to the same impotence as himself, all he can do is join in the bitter taunts of the others.

The man on Jesus' right, however, turns everything around. His words (vv. 40-42) record a total process of conversion. He rebukes his mocking fellow for lacking a salutary fear of God. He owns his wrongdoing and admits the justness of the penalty they have incurred. (The reader might well wonder what crime could "justly deserve" so monstrous a death as crucifixion.) He recognizes the total innocence of Jesus. Having distanced Jesus from himself and his fellow criminal in this respect, he then truly and genuinely turns to him for salvation (v. 42).

---

[8] This detail is not secure in the textual tradition. It could be a non-original reflection of the similar prayer attributed to Stephen in Acts 7:60. For a strong case in favor of originality see Tannehill, *Narrative Unity*, 272, n. 126; against: Fitzmyer, *Luke X-XXIV*, 1503. Bovon, *Luke*, 3.307, plausibly explains the omission of the prayer in some manuscripts as due to an anti-Jewish impulse in certain strains of the early tradition.

The terms in which he does so are very significant. The word "save" has been debased in the preceding threefold mockery. At this point it can only refer to rescue from the present plight upon the cross. But that is not the path "salvation" is taking now, neither for Jesus nor for the man himself. So he does not specify the kind of salvation he seeks. Addressing Jesus simply by his personal name, he begs: "Jesus, remember me when you come into your kingdom." The plea acknowledges that Jesus is King but recognizes as well that his kingdom is not simply identifiable with the messianic kingdom of conventional expectation; it is one to which Jesus is going even as he dies upon the cross. The man does not seek a high place in this kingdom; he simply asks that Jesus keep him in mind when allocating places in it.

The majestic response of Jesus transforms the whole perspective. Not in the distant future, not even tomorrow or the day after, but "today you will be with me in Paradise" (v. 43). Here again we hear the great Lukan "today" (see 4:21; 19:9), transferring salvation from the remote future to the present on the basis of a renewed relationship with God. The man had asked to be included in the kingdom—something we know from the prelude to the institution of the Eucharist to be postponed to an indefinite future (22:16, 18). Jesus assures him that he will have a foretaste of salvation in his own company in Paradise "today."[9] The essence of salvation is not to be saved from physical death but to be "with Jesus," to accompany him on the "exodus" to the Father now underway. The man's conversion of heart and faith in Jesus has readied him for this journey. This climactic moment in the gospel provides a "point of insertion" for all readers prepared to take a similar path.

---

[9] "Paradise," a rare term in the New Testament, raises overtones of the garden in which Adam and Eve dwelt preparatory to their fall (Gen 2:8-15). Its use here raises the possibility that Luke is depicting Jesus in Adamic terms, as the new founder of the human race (see 3:38). In this sense the term would signal that in dying Jesus does not in any sense "depart" from the human sphere but, as in Paul's view (Rom 5:12-21; 1 Cor 15:20-22, 45; 2 Cor 4:4-6), inaugurates a new possibility of being human. "Paradise" may also reflect the sense that the full kingdom remains outstanding and will remain so for some time. The man cannot yet be in the kingdom, as he asks. But he can be "with Jesus" in an intermediate state of blessedness denoted by the term.

Death of Jesus: 23:44-46

The moment for Jesus to complete that journey has now arrived. The fading (or "eclipse") of the sun, creating "darkness over the whole land," lends an apocalyptic aura to the scene (vv. 44-45a). Outwardly at least, this is the "hour" of Jesus' adversaries and "the power of darkness" (22:53). But the rending of the veil of the temple (v. 45b) signals that the way to the presence of the Father is totally open. So Jesus makes this *transitus*, commending his spirit to the Father with a loud voice and gently breathing his last (v. 46). He dies, then, peacefully and in control, in prayer and communion with the Father as throughout his entire life. This is not a literal description of a person dying from crucifixion. The narrative tells the story in a way that brings out the deeper meaning of the whole: that the death of this person, while brought about by human machination, is an act of divine liberation comparable to, and indeed surpassing in its saving power, the exodus of old.

Inaugurating his ministry at Nazareth years before, Jesus experienced rejection from his townsfolk. They had sought to kill him by throwing him down from a hill. On that occasion he had slipped through their clutches and gone on his way (4:28-30). Now, though actually brought to his death following rejection on a much wider scale, he "passes through" death to rise and "be taken up" (9:51) to glory at the right hand of God.

Responses Following the Death of Jesus: 23:47-49

Concerned as ever with human response, Luke describes in some detail the reaction of those who have witnessed the death of Jesus. First, the Roman centurion who had supervised the execution undergoes a conversion, prompted, it would seem, by the manner of Jesus' death (v. 47). He praises God and declares Jesus innocent—the sixth and final declaration to that effect in the passion narrative.[10] The Lukan form of the centurion's confession may seem somewhat lame compared to the parallel ("Truly this man was God's Son") in Mark (15:39) and Matthew (27:54). But the issue all along in the Lukan account has been whether Jesus is the troublesome messianic pretender ("King of the Jews") the chief priests and scribes allege him to be. Now a further representative of Rome acknowledges the falsity of that accusation. Before long the

---

[10] Pilate made this declaration three times on his own account (23:4, 14, 22) and once on behalf of Herod (23:15); the criminal crucified on Jesus' right gave voice to the same view (23:41).

gospel will go to the Gentile world and speak powerfully to pagans, such as he, who have undergone conversion and become worshipers of God ("God-fearers"; see Acts 10:1-2; 13:12, 43; 16:14; 17:4, 17; 18:7).

We see, too, a beginning of conversion in the crowds who had witnessed Jesus' death. They return to their homes, "beating their breasts" (v. 48). They have not only seen a miscarriage of justice. They have experienced something of the power and presence of God.

Finally, also watching but at a distance are his "acquaintances" and the women who had followed him from Galilee (v. 49). Luke had listed these women earlier in the gospel (8:1-3). He does not name them now, as do Mark and Matthew, but their presence and that of the "acquaintances" (male disciples) means that Jesus has not died wholly in the company of strangers. They, too, form a "point of insertion" into the scene for readers of later generations, an invitation to follow Jesus right up to this moment of his passing to the Father.

The Aftermath: 23:50-56

The Burial: 23:50-53

Jesus may have died among criminals. But he does not receive a criminal's burial (normally, interment in a common, unmarked grave). He receives a respectful burial from a surprising source,[11] a member of the same council that had handed him over to Pilate but who personally had not gone along with their plan and action. Luke describes Joseph of Arimathea as "a good and righteous man" who was waiting expectantly for the kingdom of God (v. 51b); his attention to Jesus' burial shows concern for the law, which required the burial of the bodies of executed criminals before sunset (Deut 21:22-23). Joseph recalls the faithful and observant figures in the infancy stories who wait for the redemption of Israel (Zechariah, Elizabeth, Simeon, Anna). In his caring for Jesus' body and placing it in his own tomb, this faithful Israelite makes a final gesture of hospitality to Jesus. Along with the sorrowing daughters of Jerusalem (v. 27) and the repentant crowds (v. 48), Joseph's act does much to relieve the sense of rejection.

The Women: 23:54-56

The women disciples who had followed Jesus from Galilee (8:1-3) see the tomb and note how Joseph has laid Jesus' body in it. In due course

---

[11] Only in Matthew (27:57) is Joseph of Arimathea stated to be a disciple.

they will become key witnesses. For the present, the onset of the Sabbath prevents attention to the body of Jesus. All they can do is prepare spices and ointments and rest "according to the commandment" (v. 56b)—a Sabbath rest recalling the divine "rest" on the seventh day of creation (Gen 2:2-3). The story of Jesus' death ends with a faint but unmistakable hint that a mighty creative act is about to occur.

Hospitality Continues
The Community of the Risen Lord: 24:1-53

Throughout this book I have drawn attention to Luke's fascination with the way in which people come to "knowledge of salvation." In many respects this comes to a head in the account of the resurrection. It is not simply a matter of describing appearances of the risen Lord. The narrative shows how the disciples have to put a great deal together: the traumatic events of Jesus' arrest and execution; the scriptural prophecies concerning the Messiah; what Jesus during his historical life had said about his fate; what they experience and learn from him as risen Lord. Only when all this comes together in their understanding can the disciples become true witnesses of the resurrection, ready to be transformed by the Spirit into effective ministers of the word.

The central issue remains the "messianic" one. How could Jesus who suffered so terrible a humiliation be Messiah and Savior of Israel? It is not enough for the disciples to recognize that he is alive, raised from the dead. All that has happened—suffering, death, and resurrection—must be seen as held within a plan of God that greatly outstrips their previous expectation.

Also beginning here (though it has had a prelude in the visitation [1:39-56]) is a Lukan feature that is to become particularly prominent in Acts. As I remarked in the introduction, Luke likes to build up a story by first describing experiences of individuals or groups separately, and then bringing them together to share their stories. In the sharing and combination, individual experience becomes community experience, creating a new sense of identity. The process of understanding occurs, then, not only within individuals but within communities as well.

Luke's account of the resurrection falls into four main scenes:

1. The women and Peter at the empty tomb of Jesus (24:1-12)
2. The encounter with Jesus on the way to Emmaus (24:13-35)
3. The appearance to the disciples in Jerusalem (24:36-49)
4. The ascension of Jesus (24:50-53)

The Empty Tomb: 24:1-11

As in the other gospels, Luke's account of the resurrection begins where the story of the passion left off: at the tomb of Jesus on the first day of the week. The women come to the tomb bringing the spices they had prepared to anoint the body of Jesus, a task held over during the Sabbath rest (vv. 1-3). They find the stone rolled away from the tomb and no sign of the body. At this stage they are simply perplexed (v. 4a).

Suddenly they undergo a visitation from the heavenly world (v. 4b). Two men in dazzling clothes appear and rebuke them for looking for the living among the dead. Jesus is not here but has risen. Did they not remember that, while still in Galilee, he told them that the Son of Man must be handed over to sinners, be crucified, and on the third day rise (vv. 5-7)? The angels, then, are inviting the women to put together what they have experienced—the suffering, the death, and now the empty tomb—with the predictions Jesus had made. We are told that they did make the connection ("They remembered his words" [v. 8]) and went off to share their discovery with the Eleven and all the rest (v. 9).

The sharing of the story is not at this stage successful. The apostles consider the women's report an "idle tale" and do not believe them (v. 11; see vv. 22-24). In the journey of faith the community—at least the male community—has still a long way to go. Peter, it is true,[1] runs to the tomb to check out the women's story, sees the linen cloths lying by themselves but returns home simply amazed (v. 12). Faith in the resurrection requires a lot more than the discovery of an empty tomb.

Encounter with Jesus on the Way to Emmaus: 24:13-35

The account of Jesus' appearance to the two disciples on the way to Emmaus is the masterpiece of Luke the storyteller. Rich in suspense, irony, and play upon emotion, it offers a paradigm of Christian life and mission. It also displays a careful structure:

1. Introduction and setting of the scene (vv. 13-16)

2. Dialogue with Jesus on the way (vv. 17-27)

---

[1] This tradition about Peter recorded in v. 12 is not entirely secure on textual grounds, being wanting in the Western ms. tradition. It could be an import from the very similar tradition concerning Peter at the tomb (along with "the disciple whom Jesus loved") in John 20:6-7. But it does fit the general picture of Peter developed in the gospel.

a) Jesus' opening question (v. 17)

b) The "facts" told without faith (vv. 18-24)

c) Scriptural interpretation of the "facts" (vv. 25-27)

3. Hospitality in Emmaus (vv. 28-32)

a) The invitation ("Stay with us"; vv. 28-29)

b) Breaking of bread and recognition (vv. 30-31)

c) Reflection ("hearts burning within us"; v. 32)

4. Sharing the story (vv. 33-35).

The opening verses (vv. 13-16) set the scene. Two male disciples[2] are on a journey, away from Jerusalem, to a village called Emmaus.[3] As they walk, they are discussing "all these things that had happened" there—happened, that is, to Jesus and to the group of men and women who had put their faith in him and in his cause.

Dialogue with Jesus on the Way: 24:17-27

Jesus becomes their companion on the journey (v. 15), but they do not recognize him. The Greek text is rather precise about this nonrecognition. It says, "their eyes were being held," a hint that the nonrecognition was somehow due to the action of God. Their recognition of the risen

---

[2] Later (v. 18) we are told the name of one of them: Cleophas; the other remains unidentified. That this other is also a male disciple is implied in the contrast with "some women" in v. 22. These two disciples belong to that wider male group of disciples who stubbornly refused to take the women's report seriously (see v. 11). Jesus will rebuke them (v. 25) partly on this account. If the unnamed disciple were a woman, the contrast between the response of the women and that of the men would be lost. I think Luke wants to bring out this contrast—in favor of the women. Barbara Reid misses the point when she finds that "Luke's presentation encourages his readers to disregard her [a woman's] words as sheer nonsense" (*Choosing the Better Part? Women in the Gospel of Luke* [Collegeville, MN: Liturgical Press, 1996], 202). In the person of Jesus the gospel faults the male disciples for dismissing the women's report. The latter emerge from the Lukan resurrection account with more credibility than the men.

[3] The identification of this destination has intrigued interpreters since ancient times. Definitive identification remains elusive. However, a site about 10 km from Jerusalem known as Bir El-Hammam appears to be the leading candidate. For a thorough critical discussion of suggested sites, see François Bovon, *A Commentary on the Gospel of Luke*, Hermeneia, vol. 3 (Minneapolis: Fortress, 2012), 371.

Lord must take place within a wider context of understanding. Like the women at the tomb (vv. 7-8), they will have to be "reminded."

Jesus also puts his opening question in an interesting way. Literally in the Greek it reads, "What are these words that you throw back and forth at one another as you walk along?" (v. 17a). They are attempting to share and make sense of a story. But it is an unhappy story, without hope.[4] At Jesus' query, they stand still, "their faces downcast" (v. 17b).

The unhappy tone of the conversation is clear in Cleophas's sharp and cynical response: "Are you the only visitor to Jerusalem who does not know the things that have happened there in these days?" (v. 18). Readers of the gospel cannot miss the irony in these words—the irony of accusing Jesus of being the "only *visitor* to Jerusalem who does not know what has happened there." We know that he is the divine "visitor" to Jerusalem who has stood at the very center of what has been going on.

Jesus invites the pair to tell their story (v. 19a) and hears them out. One of the wonderful things about this episode is the way in which it shows respect for human experience. Jesus does not interrupt to correct their version of events. He lets them tell their story to the end.

The disciples summarize Jesus' career and the messianic hopes it had raised, hopes so cruelly dashed by recent events, now three days old (vv. 19b-21).[5] Though he had appeared to them "a prophet mighty in deed and word before God and all the people," their "chief priests and rulers delivered him up to be condemned to death and crucified him."[6] Wistfully ("we were hoping") they tell of the messianic hope they had held in his regard: that he was "the one to redeem Israel" (v. 21).[7] The phrase reveals the conventional nature of this expectation—for a great leader who would liberate their people from the subjection under which they currently labored. While not necessarily lacking a spiritual dimension, this hope had no place for a Messiah who would suffer and die, above all on a cross.

---

[4] "With great skill the evangelist recounts the devastating effect of a story deprived of its kerygmatic dimension" (Bovon, *Luke*, 3.373).

[5] There is further irony in the reference to "the third day": the disciples have failed to "remember" Jesus' predictions that after his suffering and death he would rise on the third day (9:22; 18:33).

[6] Once again, we see here Luke's attribution of responsibility for the arrest and execution of Jesus to the leaders, not the people as a whole.

[7] The Greek verb "redeem" (*lytrousthai*) recalls the "redemption (*lytrōsis*) of Israel" that those whom the prophet Anna addressed were looking for (2:38; see also 1:58 [Zechariah in the *Benedictus*]).

Almost as an afterthought, the disciples mention the report of the women who had gone to the tomb (vv. 22-24). They had found that Jesus' body was missing; they had had a vision of angels who told them that he was alive (see vv. 1-9); of Jesus himself there was no sign (v. 25). Remarkable though this report may be and completely accurate with respect to the facts, it has not served to kindle faith or put the disciples in mind of what Jesus had predicted.

From the moment he first drew from his disciples the recognition that he was the Christ (9:18-21), Jesus had begun to make known the direction his messianic career would take. Ever more explicitly he warned them of the reception that awaited him in the Messiah's city, Jerusalem (9:22 [also 9:28-36]; 9:43-45; 18:31-34; 22:35-38). But all this had escaped their understanding. Messianic status simply did not fit with suffering, humiliation, and death. Hence the total disillusionment and shattering of hope when it all came to pass.

Jesus hears out the two disciples' story to the end. Even when they are finished, he does not immediately reveal himself. Instead, after reproving them (v. 25a) for their "reluctance" to believe (especially with respect to the women's report), he begins to tell another story—or rather he puts their story (which, of course, is principally *his* story) within the context of the wider story told in the Scriptures: "Beginning with Moses[8] and all the prophets he interpreted to them in all the scriptures the things concerning himself" (v. 27). According to the combined witness of Scripture (what "all the prophets have declared" [v. 25]) the Messiah would not immediately be a glorious king, bringing freedom and prosperity to Israel; on the contrary, it was "necessary" that the Messiah should suffer and so enter into his glory (v. 26). In this light, suffering and death did not destroy messianic credentials but confirm them within the wider plan of God.

The long scriptural catechesis gradually closes the gap between expectation and reality. Later, in a moment of reflection, the two disciples will make an illuminating comment on the process: "Did not our hearts burn within us while he talked to us on the road, while he opened to us the scriptures?" (v. 32). The "burning" they felt in their hearts can only refer to the rekindling of hope as Jesus' exposition brought together the two things that had previously seemed so much at odds. In this they begin to experience that "knowledge of salvation" that will make them

---

[8] That is the Pentateuch (the "Law"), the authorship of which was conventionally attributed to Moses.

viable eyewitnesses and ministers of the word. So much pastoral practice of their successors down the ages will have the same aim: to expound Scripture in such a way as to help people find integration between their previous hopes and the reality of their lives.

Hospitality at Emmaus: 24:28-31

In typically Lukan fashion, the final scene of the drama takes place in the context of a meal. There are, again, many delightful ironies. Jesus is still the traveler. He does not seek hospitality but rather is intent on going on his way (v. 28). The disciples "constrain" him (the Greek expression is strong: they would not take no for an answer [like Paul's host Lydia in Acts 16:15]). They are determined to give this visitor hospitality: "Stay with us, for it is towards evening and the day is far spent" (v. 29a). "So," comments the evangelist (v. 29b), "he went in to stay with them," to be their guest. He had imposed the "must" of hospitality upon Zacchaeus ("I must stay at your house today" [19:5]). Now, it is they who impose hospitality upon him.

But once more the guest becomes host. In a way clearly meant to re-call the institution of the Eucharist at the final supper (22:19-20; also the multiplication of the loaves and fishes [9:16]), Jesus breaks bread, blesses it, and gives it to them (v. 30). He, who is receiving their hospitality, provides for them the "hospitality of God."

The moment of recognition that follows ("their eyes were opened, and they recognized him" [v. 31]) is also the moment of Jesus' vanishing. Curiously, the sudden disappearance of the Lord they have just regained does not seem to dismay the disciples. Humanly speaking, one might expect that to be the case. But the narrative makes here an important point. The community of faith that is to grow out of these experiences will not have the physical presence or sight of Jesus. But that does not mean they will not have him as companion upon the journey. In the exposition of the Scriptures and in the eucharistic celebration (word and sacrament) he will be present to them throughout the remainder of the "day," the day of the church, whose preaching in his name and in his Spirit will extend the "day" of salvation (see 4:16-21) to the end of time. The "day" may be "far spent," but it is not over. Wherever the word is proclaimed and the Eucharist celebrated the community celebrates and makes available in Jesus' name the hospitality of God.

Now we can better appreciate the way Luke described the institution of the Eucharist at the Last Supper (22:15-20). Before the words of institution proper Jesus twice states that he will not celebrate the Passover again until its fulfillment in the kingdom of God (vv. 16, 18). The eucharistic meal, which he then goes on to institute (vv. 19-20), is for "the time in between," the "day" that extends between his death and the full realization of the kingdom. During this time—which has become a very long time indeed—the church goes on its pilgrim way, instructed, nourished, companioned by its Lord. At the same time, the church learns from him who walked with the two disciples, how to walk with the disillusioned and suffering of the world, hearing out their story, accepting their broken hopes. Like Jesus, it tries to set that story in the context of a wider scriptural story telling of a salvation brought by One who walked with humanity in its suffering and entered the glory that was rightfully his only after treading that path.

Sharing the Story: 24:32-35

Following the reflection about their hearts burning within them (v. 32), the disciples hasten back to Jerusalem to tell their story (v. 33). They find that the Eleven and the other disciples have a story of their own: "The Lord has risen indeed, and he has appeared to Simon" (v. 34).[9] Only when they have heard that, do the Emmaus disciples tell "what had happened on the road, and how he had been made known to them in the breaking of the bread" (v. 35). The community comes to full knowledge and faith when individuals and groups bring together and share their previously separate stories.

The Encounter with Jesus in Jerusalem: 24:36-53

A Meal with the Risen Lord: 24:36-49

Jesus' final meeting with the disciples takes place, typically, at a meal. The scene, as Luke describes it, falls into two fairly distinct phases. In the first (vv. 36-42), Jesus appears to the disciples while they are still sharing the reports about the two earlier appearances (to the disciples on

---

[9] Curiously, beyond this bald report, Luke does not provide a narrative account of the appearance to Simon Peter—though earlier (v. 12 [if the text is original]) he had told of a visit by Peter to the tomb. On the possibility that Luke's account of Simon's original call (5:1-11) contains elements of an appearance tradition "retrojected" back into the historical life of Jesus, see above, p. 67, n. 7. Paul, of course, names Peter ("Cephas") as the first of those to whom the risen Lord appeared in the list of witnesses to the resurrection in 1 Cor 15:5-8.

the road and to Simon). Strangely, in view of those reports and despite his assurance of "Peace," they are startled and terrified. They think they are seeing a ghost (v. 37). At considerable length the narrative describes Jesus' attempt to erode their disbelief by making clear the full physical reality of his presence. He urges them to see and touch him and eats a piece of fish before their eyes (vv. 38-42). Luke dramatizes here—perhaps in an overly realistic way—what Paul had insisted upon, writing to the Corinthians (1 Cor 15:35-49): you cannot believe in the resurrection without believing that it involved—both for Jesus and for believers after him—full bodily existence.

But simply recognizing the risen Lord is not enough. As the scene moves to a second stage (vv. 43-49), Jesus repeats for those present the scriptural catechesis concerning the Messiah that he had already given to the two disciples on the road. True faith comes about when people grasp that all that has happened to Jesus—his suffering, his death, and now his resurrection—fulfills all that had been written about the Messiah (lit., "me") in "the law of Moses, the prophets, and the psalms" (v. 44). Opening their minds to understand the Scriptures (v. 45; cf. 32) communicates the "assurance" (*asphaleia*) of salvation that is the true purpose of the gospel as a whole (see 1:4 [prologue]).

While repeating the pattern of the Emmaus episode in this way, the present scene takes a significant step beyond it. What the Scriptures had foretold was not simply that the Messiah was to suffer and to rise from the dead on the third day (v. 46a) but also that "repentance for the forgiveness [*aphesis*] of sins" should be proclaimed in his name to all nations beginning from Jerusalem (v. 47). Of this the disciples are to be "witnesses" (v. 48). Here the events concerning Jesus are placed within a wider divine plan reaching out beyond Israel to bring salvation to the entire world. A hint of this universalism was already present in the infancy stories—especially when Simeon described the child in his arms as "a light for revelation to the Gentiles" as well as "the glory to [God's] people Israel" (2:32). Universalism was implicit in the way Jesus' ministry had constantly reached out and found acceptance on the margins. Now it becomes explicit in the mission that the disciples will take up in Jesus' name, extending the "day" of Jesus into the "day" of the church.

The disciples are witnesses not only in the sense that they have seen the wonders of Jesus' public ministry and the climactic events of the last few days. They are more fully so because they have been instructed by him to see how his story fits together and fulfills the Scriptures. The message that they will carry to all nations will be the culmination and outworking of this divine plan.

One thing and one thing only is lacking. Just as the Spirit had empowered Jesus at the beginning of his mission (3:21-22; cf. 4:18), so the "witnesses" must remain in Jerusalem until they are similarly "clothed with power from on high," until Jesus sends upon them "what [his] Father has promised" (v. 49). Long before, the prophet Joel had recorded the divine promise to "pour out the Spirit upon all flesh" (3:1-5). John the Baptist had prophesied that, whereas he baptized with water, the "more powerful" One who is coming (Jesus) would baptize with the Holy Spirit and with fire (3:16). As the early chapters of Acts will describe, these promises will be made good when the disciples receive the gift of the Spirit at Pentecost (Acts 2:1-21). Then they will be not only "eyewitnesses" but also "ministers of the word" (Luke 1:2).[10] In continuity with the mission of Jesus, they will be empowered to proclaim "release" (*aphesis*) from sin and saving reconciliation with God (see 4:18-19).

Jesus Ascends to the Father: 24:50-53

The Gospel of Luke has consistently portrayed Jesus as a prophet. Specifically, it has frequently suggested that Jesus both follows and surpasses paths traced out by the great prophets Moses and Elijah. This feature comes to a climax at the close of Jesus' personal ministry. He completes the "exodus" of his suffering, death, and resurrection by being carried up into heaven. The parallels with the ascension of Elijah (2 Kgs 2:1-18) are unmistakable. Jesus has blessed his disciples (v. 50)[11]—the gesture of a dying or departing patriarch. He has arranged for them to receive a measure of his Spirit—just as Elijah promised a share in his spirit to his disciple and successor Elisha (2 Kgs 2:9). Jesus' personal ministry on earth comes to an end as he ascends to messianic glory at God's right hand.[12] But his power and presence will continue on the earth when in due course the Spirit

---

[10] See Richard J. Dillon, *From Eye-Witnesses to Ministers of the Word: Tradition and Composition in Luke 24*, Analecta Biblica 82 (Rome: Biblical Institute Press, 1978).

[11] The blessing imparted by Jesus here at the close of the gospel responds, in inclusive fashion, to the impotence of the priest Zechariah to bless the people after his experience in the sanctuary at the very beginning of the gospel (1:21-23).

[12] Three disciples had had an anticipatory glimpse of Jesus in this state at the transfiguration (9:28-36). The martyr Stephen, as he dies, will see Jesus rising from his seat at the Father's right hand to welcome him into heaven (Acts 7:55-56). Luke's account of Jesus' ascension gives narrative form to the motif of Christ's postresurrection exaltation that is central to New Testament Christology: see, e.g., Phil 2:9-11; Eph 4:8-10; etc.

empowers his disciples to take up his mission. This is what the otherwise fantastic episode of the ascension signals to readers steeped in the biblical tradition. Here least of all are we dealing with a narrative purporting to depict a historical event.[13]

Contrary to what we might expect, the disciples are not dismayed or bereft by the departure of Jesus. They "worship" the One they now recognize to be God's Son as well as Messiah.[14] They return to Jerusalem with great joy, remaining continually in the temple blessing God (vv. 52-53). So the gospel ends physically where it began—in the temple at Jerusalem (1:8-9)—and on the same note that rang through the infancy stories, a note of rejoicing and the praise of God.

The leading figures in the infancy stories rejoiced because they had seen in the events surrounding Jesus' birth a fulfillment of the promises of salvation made to Israel long ago. Then, throughout the gospel, we have seen individuals coming to a "knowledge of salvation" as they recognize the fulfillment of promise in the surprising events they are experiencing. Now the disciples have undergone that experience and respond accordingly in praise and joy. But just as in the infancy stories the fulfillment was partial and incomplete, so now at the closure of Jesus' personal history, we stand not at the end but at the "middle of the time."[15] Like the figures of old, the rejoicing disciples remain under a promise. It will be complete when the entire world has had a chance to know and live within the hospitality of God.

---

[13] Luke gives a second and fuller account of Jesus' ascension and leave-taking from the disciples at the beginning of the Acts of the Apostles (1:1-11). The duplication provides a kind of "overlap" between the two volumes of his work that reinforces the sense of continuity to which Luke is so devoted. There is some discrepancy in the two accounts, however, in the sense that in the Gospel of Luke all the events associated with the risen life of Jesus, including his ascension, take place on the same day (Easter Sunday), whereas in Acts Jesus ascends forty days later (v. 3). It is this "forty days" that has given rise to the separate location of the feast of the Ascension in the Christian liturgical tradition.

[14] After his resurrection, "Jesus has crossed the barrier that separates human beings from God" (Bovon, *Luke*, 3.412).

[15] The phrase "middle of the time" echoes the (German) title of the classic work on Luke's theology by Hans Conzelmann, *The Theology of St. Luke*, trans. G. Buswell from the German, *Die Mitte der Zeit* (Tübingen: Mohr, 1954; New York: Harper and Row, 1960).

Conclusion

It might help, by way of conclusion, to summarize in quasi-thesis form the leading ideas that have emerged in the course of this journey through Luke's gospel. Most of them have to do with the central idea of "salvation" in Luke.

1. Presupposed in the gospel as the condition of the human race prior to the saving mission of Christ and needing to be addressed by that mission is that human beings exist in a situation of alienation from God and from their own true humanity. They are the "lost family of God," needing to be sought out, found, and drawn back into the hospitable home of the Father.

2. While sharing this general human "lostness," Israel holds in the Scriptures the divine promises of salvation, specifically the sending of one "anointed" with the Spirit ("Messiah") to liberate people from all that alienates them from God and bring in a "day" of acceptance and freedom.

3. The promised salvation is keenly awaited by key figures in Israel (Zechariah and Elizabeth, Mary, Simeon, Anna). In the births of John the Baptist and Jesus they recognize and celebrate its dawning.

4. The adult Jesus presents himself as the Prophet "anointed by the Spirit" (Isa 61:1) to bring the promised salvation, inaugurating in his ministry a "day" of acceptance and reconciliation with God.

5. This "day" will not be confined to Israel. Following the rejection of the Anointed Prophet by the leaders of his people—culminating in his death, resurrection, and ascension—the "day" of salvation will continue as his disciples, empowered (at Pentecost) by the same Spirit, carry the message to the nations of the world.

6. The primary aim of Luke's gospel is to communicate to believers from those nations of the world a firm sense of identity ("assurance"): that the scriptural promises of salvation held by Israel are equally focused upon them, giving them a rightful place within the one "great story" of salvation. They belong to a people chosen, set

free, and brought into intimate communion with God through Jesus Christ, awaiting the fullness of salvation in the kingdom of God.

7. "Salvation" in Luke's gospel has many aspects: reconciliation with God, physical healing, freedom from dehumanizing constraints and controls, being brought from the margins of society to a central and honored place within the community (hospitality), rescue from persecution and from the troubles associated with the end of the age, eternal life in the finally established kingdom of God.

8. While "salvation" in the total sense will not be complete until the full establishment of the kingdom, one can have its essentials already in the "knowledge of salvation" communicated by Jesus. This "knowledge" consists primarily in a deep sense of being welcomed into the community of salvation, with the sure hope that the God who in Christ has been faithful to the promises made in Scripture can be trusted to bring the full process of salvation to completion.

9. It is the Spirit that communicates this sense of God and the assurance that goes with it. Hence to possess the Spirit is already to have the essentials of salvation.

10. Salvation comes most effectively and copiously to those who truly know their need for it—most especially, then, to those on the margins, who have no other resource save God. These in particular display the kind of faith prepared to break through barriers to access God's saving power.

11. For those who are not marginalized, coming to salvation usually requires a conversion at depth that often meets resistance: the enlargement or shattering of treasured assumptions about the way God operates, a willingness to confront the narrowness of previous assessments and valuations. In this connection, Luke's gospel is concerned with the conversion of communities as well as the conversion of individuals.

12. Knowledge of salvation frequently involves the overcoming—through a deeper appreciation of God's saving plan—of the gap between what one had previously hoped for or anticipated and the reality that has occurred. Bound up with this is a sense that God can bring life out of death: that rejection and failure do not have the last word but can actually serve to further God's saving design.

13. Joy, wonder, praise, celebration—sometimes in extravagant measure—are signs of the experience of salvation in human lives and communities.

14. The poor and dispossessed, as the primary objects of God's concern, generosity, and faithfulness (in the coming great reversal), are in the most advantageous position ("Blessed"). To align oneself with them, to make friends with them, is to embrace the only security that is of lasting value.

15. By contrast, to rely on wealth for security and so to be absorbed in other affairs as to neglect God's invitation to fullness of life is to expose oneself to the risk of losing all.

16. While Jesus is not a savior in a purely political sense and while renewed relationship with God lies at the heart of the experience of salvation, the dignity and destiny this relationship implies for human beings, together with the divine partiality for the cause of the presently poor and dispossessed, means that the onset of salvation necessarily challenges and seeks to overturn political, social, and economic structures that are dehumanizing and inhospitable to the majority of humankind.

17. Those who make up the community of the kingdom are not a sect completely separate from the rest of the world, its structures and institutions. They must live in it and value what is best in it, holding out to it the hospitality that they have themselves received from God.

18. At the same time, to live as God's people in a world as yet unreconciled to God will mean conflict and struggle with forces (including spiritual powers) hostile to life and to God. The effective armaments in this struggle are prayer and constant watchfulness, following the pattern set by Jesus.

19. Jesus overcame the evil of the world not by insisting on his dignity as Son of God but by choosing the way of service and treading the common human path of suffering and death. Likewise his disciples will only effectively confront and overcome evil by their readiness to take up their cross daily and carry it after Jesus.

20. As people "under invitation" to the banquet of life, believers celebrate in the Eucharist the hospitality of God they enjoy here and now, a foretaste and pledge of the final hospitality of the kingdom.

21. Beyond the present time of acceptance, in the indefinite future, lies the judgment, when God's view of things will be finally revealed and vindicated. The appropriate attitude to adopt toward the judgment is to align one's life now with God's view as revealed by Jesus and made known in new times and circumstances by the Spirit.

Bibliography

Commentaries on Luke's Gospel

Bovon, François. *A Commentary on the Gospel of Luke*. Hermeneia. 3 vols. Minneapolis: Fortress, 2002, 2012, 2013.

Culpepper, R. Alan. "The Gospel of Luke: Introduction, Commentary, and Reflections." In *New Interpreter's Bible* IX, 1–490. Nashville: Abingdon, 1995.

Fitzmyer, Joseph A. *The Gospel according to Luke I-IX*. AB 28. Garden City, NY: Doubleday, 1981.

———. *The Gospel according to Luke X-XXIV*. AB 28A. Garden City, NY: Doubleday, 1985.

Johnson, Luke Timothy. *The Gospel of Luke*. Sacra Pagina 3. Collegeville, MN: Liturgical Press, 1991.

Karris, Robert J. "The Gospel According to Luke." In *New Jerome Biblical Commentary*, edited by Raymond E. Brown, Joseph A. Fitzmyer, Roland E. Murphy, § 43, 675–721. Englewood Cliffs, NJ: Prentice-Hall, 1990.

Marshall, I. Howard. *The Gospel of Luke: A Commentary on the Greek Text*. Grand Rapids, MI: Eerdmans, 1978; repr. 1983.

Talbert, Charles H. *Reading Luke: A Literary and Theological Commentary on the Third Gospel*. New York: Crossroad, 1989.

Studies on Luke's Gospel

Bailey, Kenneth E. *Poet and Peasant: A Literary-cultural Approach to the Parables in Luke*. Grand Rapids, MI: Eerdmans, 1976.

Bovon, François. *Luke the Theologian: Thirty-three Years of Research (1950–1983)*. Allison Park, PA: Pickwick Publications, 1987.

Byrne, Brendan. "The Beatitudes and Poverty of Spirit in the Ignatian Exercises." *The Way* 47/1–2 (January/April 2008): 29–46.

———. "The Choice for Barabbas in Luke's Passion Narrative." *Vaiharai* (*The Dawn*, Tamilnadu, India) 4, nos. 2–4 (1999): 128–38.

———. "Forceful Stewardship and Neglectful Wealth: A Contemporary Reading of Luke 16." *Pacifica* 1/1 (1988): 1–14.

———. "Jesus as Messiah in the Gospel of Luke: Discerning a Pattern of Correction." *Catholic Biblical Quarterly* 65 (2003): 80–95.

Coleridge, Mark. *The Birth of the Lukan Narrative: Narrative as Christology in Luke 1–2*. Sheffield, UK: JSOT Press, 1993.

Conzelmann, Hans. *The Theology of St. Luke*. Translated by G. Buswell from the German (*Die Mitte der Zeit*). Tübingen: Mohr, 1954; New York: Harper and Row, 1960.

Dillon, Richard J. *From Eye-Witnesses to Ministers of the Word: Tradition and Composition in Luke 24*. Analecta Biblica 82. Rome: Biblical Institute Press, 1978.

Durber, Susan. "The Female Reader of the Parables of the Lost." *Journal for the Study of the New Testament* 45 (1992): 59–78.

Hamm, Dennis. "Luke 19:8 Once Again: Does Zacchaeus Defend or Resolve?" *Journal of Biblical Literature* 107 (1988): 431–37.

———. "Zacchaeus Revisited Once More: A Story of Vindication or Conversion?" *Biblica* 72 (1991): 248–52.

Moessner, David P. *Lord of the Banquet: The Literary and Theological Significance of the Lukan Travel Narrative*. Minneapolis: Fortress, 1989.

Neyrey, Jerome. *The Passion according to Luke: A Redaction Study of Luke's Soteriology*. Mahwah, NJ: Paulist, 1985.

Powell, Mark Allan. *What Are They Saying About Luke?* Mahwah, NJ: Paulist, 1989.

Reid, Barbara E. *Choosing the Better Part? Women in the Gospel of Luke*. Collegeville, MN: Liturgical Press, 1996.

Ringe, Sharon H. *Jesus, Liberation, and the Biblical Jubilee*. Philadelphia: Fortress, 1985.

Sloan, Robert B., Jr. *The Favorable Year of the Lord: A Study of Jubilary Theology in the Gospel of Luke*. Austin, TX: Schola, 1977.

Tannehill, Robert C. *The Narrative Unity of Luke-Acts: A Literary Interpretation: Volume One: The Gospel according to Luke*. Philadelphia: Fortress, 1986.

Wright, A. G. "The Widow's Mites: Praise or Lament?—A Matter of Context." *Catholic Biblical Quarterly* 44 (1982): 256–65.

Other Studies

Brown, Raymond E. *The Birth of the Messiah*. Revised ed. Garden City, NY: Doubleday, 1993.

Byrne, Brendan. *A Costly Freedom: A Theological Reading of Mark's Gospel*. Collegeville, MN: Liturgical Press, 2008.

———. *Romans*. Sacra Pagina 6. Collegeville, MN: Liturgical Press, 1996.

Crossan, John Dominic. *The Dark Interval: Towards a Theology of Story*. Niles, IL: Argus Communications, 1975.

Dodd, C. H. *The Interpretation of the Fourth Gospel*. Cambridge, UK: Cambridge University Press, 1953.

Donahue, John R. *The Gospel in Parable*. Philadelphia: Fortress, 1988.

García Martinez, F. *The Dead Sea Scrolls Translated: The Qumran Texts in English*. 2nd ed. Grand Rapids, MI: Eerdmans, 1996.

Gutiérrez, Gustavo. *A Theology of Liberation: History, Politics, and Salvation*. Rev. ed. Maryknoll, NY: Orbis, 1988.

Johnson, Elizabeth A. *Truly Our Sister: A Theology of Mary in the Communion of Saints*. New York/London: Continuum, 2004.

Koenig, John. *New Testament Hospitality: Partnership with Strangers as Promise and Mission*. Philadelphia: Fortress, 1985.

Meier, John P. *A Marginal Jew: Rethinking the Historical Jesus*. Vol. 2: *Mentor, Message, and Miracles*. New York: Doubleday, 1994.

————. *A Marginal Jew: Rethinking the Historical Jesus*. Vol. 4: *Law and Love*. New Haven, CT: Yale University Press, 2009.

Pontifical Biblical Commission (Rome). *The Interpretation of the Bible in the Church*. Rome: Libreria Editrice Vaticana; Boston: St. Paul Books and Media, 1993.

Throckmorton, Burton H., Jr. *Gospel Parallels: A Comparison of the Synoptic Gospels*. 5th ed. Nashville: Nelson, 1992.

Scripture Index

Modern Author Index

Subject Index

Note: **Bold** type indicates principal areas of definition and discussion